Government regulation of toxic substances varies dramatically between the United States and Canada. In *Risk, Science, and Politics* Kathryn Harrison and George Hoberg analyse these differences and evaluate the strengths and weaknesses of two very different regulatory styles.

Paying particular attention to how politicians and bureaucrats in the two countries deal with the scientific uncertainty that pervades environmental decision making, Harrison and Hoberg present case studies of seven controversial substances suspected of causing cancer in humans: the pesticides Alar and alachlor, urea-formaldehyde foam insulation, radon gas, dioxin, saccharin, and asbestos. They weigh the effectiveness of each country's approach according to five criteria: stringency and timeliness of the regulatory decision, balancing of risks and benefits by decision makers, opportunities for public participation, and the interpretation of science in regulatory decision making.

The Canadian approach is exemplified by closed decision making, case-by-case review that relies heavily on expert judgement, and limited public debate about the scientific basis of regulatory decisions. In contrast, regulatory science in the United States is characterized by publication of lengthy rationales for regulatory decisions, reliance on standardized procedures for risk assessment, and controversy surrounding the interpretation of scientific evidence. Harrison and Hoberg's detailed comparisons will help readers understand the complexities and subtleties involved in regulation of toxic substances.

KATHRYN HARRISON is assistant professor of political science, University of British Columbia.
GEORGE HOBERG is associate professor of political science, University of British Columbia.

Risk, Science, and Politics

Regulating Toxic Substances
in Canada and the United States

KATHRYN HARRISON
and
GEORGE HOBERG

McGill-Queen's University Press
Montreal & Kingston • London • Buffalo

McGill-Queen's University Press 1994
ISBN 0-7735-1236-5 (cloth)
ISBN 0-7735-1251-9 (paper)

Legal deposit fourth quarter 1994
Bibliothèque nationale du Québec

Printed in Canada on acid-free paper

This book has been published with the help of a grant from the Social Science Federation of Canada, using funds provided by the Social Sciences and Humanities Research Council of Canada. Publication has also been supported by the Canada Council through its block grant program.

Canadian Cataloguing in Publication Data
Harrison, Kathryn, 1958–
    Risk, science, and politics: regulating toxic substances in Canada and the United States

    Includes bibliographical references and index.
    ISBN 0-7735-1236-5 (bound) –
    ISBN 0-7735-1251-9 (pbk.)

    1. Environmental policy – Canada. 2. Environmental policy – United States. 3. Hazardous substances – Law and legislation – Canada. 4. Hazardous substances – Law and legislation – United States. I. Hoberg, George, 1958–   . II. Title.

K3672.5.H37 1994   363.7′00971   C94-900515-0

Typeset in New Baskerville 10/12
by Caractéra production graphique, Quebec City

To our Parents
Anne and Robert Harrison
and
George and Shirley Hoberg

Contents

Preface

This book has its origins in a bi-national relationship. We met while in graduate school at the Massachusetts Institute of Technology – an American in political science, and a Canadian in chemical engineering in the process of transferring to political science. We both had professional interests in the regulation of risks to health, safety, and the environment, and immersed ourselves in the byzantine system of regulation in the U.S., both in our academic work and in work for the Congressional Office of Technology Assessment in Washington, DC. In 1987 we moved to British Columbia, where we were immediately struck by the differences in Canadian and U.S. risk regulation. We decided to undertake a more systematic comparison, and the idea for this book emerged.

At the University of British Columbia we were fortunate to have excellent graduate students who took keen interest in case studies for the project. Gregory Hein, now a doctoral student at the University of Toronto, co-authored the chapter on asbestos, perhaps the most complex in the book. Colleen Rohde, now the director of legislative services (municipal clerk) of the district of North Vancouver, co-authored the chapter on saccharin. Anjan Chaklader, now a graduate student at the University of Rochester, provided valuable assistance with the formaldehyde chapter. We apologize to each of them for what must have seemed an interminable delay in producing the complete project.

Along the way we have accumulated a number of debts. The Social Sciences and Humanities Research Council of Canada provided one of us with a research grant to undertake parts of this study and the other with a doctoral fellowship. The research grant permitted the employment of invaluable research assistants: Jeff Waatainen, Randy Hansen, and Shannon Leggett.

A number of individuals have been kind enough to review parts of the manuscript or provide valuable advice, including Douglas Arnold, Steven Bayard, Alan Cairns, David Cohen, H.B.S. Conacher, J. Stefan Dupré, Michael Gough, John Harrison, Dale Hattis, James Henderson, Clyde Hertzman, Daniel Krewski, William Leiss, Ron Newhook, Len Ritter, and Andrew Ulsamer. Many government officials also provided information in interviews on a confidential basis. None of these people are responsible for any errors of fact or interpretation that we have made.

Some of this material has been published elsewhere. Parts of chapter 3 are based on Kathryn Harrison, "Between Science and Politics: Assessing the Risks of Dioxins in Canada and the United States," *Policy Sciences* 24 (1991):367–88. Parts of the section on alachlor in chapter 4 are based on George Hoberg, "Risk, Science, and Politics: Alachlor Regulation in Canada and the United States," *Canadian Journal of Political Science* 23 (June 1990):257–77. Finally, parts of chapters 3 and 8 are based on Kathryn Harrison and George Hoberg, "Setting the Environmental Agenda in Canada and the United States: The Cases of Dioxin and Radon," *Canadian Journal of Political Science* 24 (March 1991):3–27.

Abbreviations

ADI	acceptable daily intake
ADt	air-dried tonnes
AHERA	Asbestos Hazard Emergency Response Act (U.S.)
AIA	Asbestos Information Association (U.S.)
AOX	adsorbable organic halogens
CANUF	Canadian Association of Urea-Formaldehyde Manufacturers
CAPCO	Canadian Association of Pesticide Control Officials
CBC	Canadian Broadcasting Corporation
CBS	Columbia Broadcasting System
CEPA	Canadian Environmental Protection Act
CGSB	Canadian General Standards Board
CHIP	Canadian Home Insulation Program
CIIT	Chemical Industry Institute of Toxicology
CMHC	Canada Mortgage and Housing Corporation
CPSC	Consumer Product Safety Commission (U.S.)
CSN	Confédération des syndicats nationaux (labour union, Quebec)
CSST	Commission de la santé et de la sécurité du travail (Province of Quebec)
DDC	District Court of the District of Columbia
DFO	Department of Fisheries and Oceans (Canada)
D.L.R.	Dominion Law Review
EDB	ethylene dibromide

EDF   Environmental Defense Fund (environmental group, U.S.)

EPA   Environmental Protection Agency (U.S.)

ERC   Environmental Reporter Cases

f/cc   fibres per cubic centimetre

FDA   Food and Drug Administration (U.S.)

FIFRA   Federal Insecticide, Fungicide, and Rodenticide Act (U.S.)

FR   Federal Register

FTA   Free Trade Agreement (Canada/U.S.)

GAO   General Accounting Office (U.S.)

GATT   General Agreement on Trade and Tariffs

GRAS   generally recognized as safe

HUD   Housing and Urban Development (U.S. Department of)

IARC   International Agency for Research on Cancer

ILO   International Labour Organization

mg/kg/day   milligram per kilogram of body weight per day

MP   member of Parliament

MTD   maximum tolerated dose

NAFTA   North American Free Trade Agreement

NAS   National Academy of Sciences (U.S.)

NCAMP   National Coalition against the Misuse of Pesticides (U.S.)

NDP   New Democratic Party

NOAEL   no observed adverse effects level

NRC   National Research Council (U.S.)

NRDC   Natural Resources Defense Council (U.S.)

OMB   (White House) Office of Management and Budget (U.S.)

OSHA   Occupational Safety and Health Administration (U.S.)

o-TS   ortho-toluenesulforamide

PB-PK models   physiologically based pharmacokinetic models

PCDD   polychlorinated dibenzodioxins

PCDF   polychlorinated dibenzofurans

pCi/l   picocuries per litre

PCPA   Pest Control Products Act (Canada)

pg/kg/day   picograms per kilogram of body weight per day

ppm   parts per million

ppq   parts per quadrillion

ppt   parts per trillion

R.S.C.   Revised Statutes of Canada

R.S.Q.   Revised Statutes of Quebec

SAB   (EPA) Science Advisory Board (U.S.)

TCDD 2,3,7,8-tetrachlorodibenzo-p-dioxin (dioxin) or
2,3,7,8-TCDD
TSCA Toxic Substances Control Act (U.S.)
UDMH unsymmetrical demethylhydrazine
UFFI urea-formaldehyde foam insulation
U.S. United States Reports (of Supreme Court decisions)
U.S.C. United States Code
U.S.C.A. United States Code Annotated
U.S.C.S. United States Code Service
VSD virtually safe dose
WARF Wisconsin Alumni Research Federation
WL working levels
WLM working level months

Risk, Science, and Politics

1 Policy Making amid Scientific Uncertainty

THE CHALLENGE OF REGULATING TOXIC SUBSTANCES

The emergence of environmental concern in recent decades has presented modern industrialized countries with a common challenge: how to protect their citizens from the risks of hazardous substances while simultaneously reaping the benefits of the activities that produce the hazards. Uncertainty, particularly with respect to the magnitude of risks posed by many substances, complicates the problem of balancing the risks and benefits of toxic substances. Scientists often cannot answer policy makers' questions about the risks. Faced with the possibility of lives at risk, however, policy makers seldom have the luxury of waiting for scientific consensus.

The demand for policy making amid uncertainty complicates already difficult choices. Rather than "simply" choosing between the health benefits and the economic costs of control measures, policy makers must consider the possibility that their factual premises are not correct. They must balance the possibility of incorrectly assuming that a substance is harmless, with potentially tragic consequences, against the possibility of falsely assuming that a substance is harmful, at substantial unnecessary cost to business, consumers, and workers.[1]

Two neighbouring countries, Canada and the United States, have approached the policy dilemma of toxic substances within subtly different social contexts and more sharply divergent political institutions and processes. In many ways the two countries have distinctive "regulatory styles."[2] The principal purpose of this study is to evaluate the consequences of those regulatory styles for the regulation of toxic substances. The case studies in this volume compare the decisions the two countries made and the manner in which they made them. In comparing Canada and the u.s. our intent is not to arrive at facile conclusions about which country is doing a "better job" of regulating toxic substances. Rather, we believe that comparative studies can offer a better understanding of the strengths and weaknesses of both regulatory systems. Each country has much to learn from its own and the other's experience.

We have chosen cancer risk assessment as an illustration of governmental decision making about uncertain environmental health risks for a number of reasons. Cancer is a dreaded disease that is the cause of death for roughly 25 percent of Canadians.[3] The public in both countries is concerned, if not preoccupied, with chemical carcinogens. Although there is an unresolved debate over the significance of synthetic carcinogens relative to natural carcinogens and lifestyle factors, such as diet and smoking,[4] it is nevertheless true that, given high mortality rates associated with many types of cancer, each additional case of the disease can be tragic.

In undertaking this study, we were struck by the differences between the u.s. and Canadian government positions in a number of highly publicized cases of regulation of potential carcinogens, including saccharin, asbestos, and urea-formaldehyde foam insulation (uffi). Often based on the same scientific evidence, one government (though not always the same one) would conclude that a substance posed unreasonable risks and respond by adopting control measures, while the other would reach the opposite conclusion. Why? In light of scientific uncertainty, did the two governments reach different conclusions about the *magnitude* of the risks, or did they weigh the risks and benefits differently, leading to different conclusions about the *acceptability* of the risks? To date such risk management controversies have received much more scholarly attention in the United States than in Canada. This book subjects the Canadian experience with regulation of toxic substances to closer scrutiny while also attempting to explore the reasons for u.s./Canada differences.

Finally, government decisions concerning potential carcinogens provide a fascinating example of the interplay of science and values in policy making. In particular, scientific uncertainty about whether there can be a "safe" level of exposure to carcinogens has important policy implications. In recent years many policy makers have abandoned the notion of absolute safety in favour of a probabilistic conception of risk. Rather than offer a qualitative assessment that a substance is either "safe" or "unsafe," they describe risks quantitatively in terms of exposed individuals' statistical chances of contracting cancer. From a probabilistic perspective, it follows that even minute quantities of a carcinogen in the environment may present an unacceptable risk of cancer if human exposure is sufficiently widespread. The implications of this shifting paradigm are particularly profound in light of continuing improvements in our ability to detect trace levels of environmental contaminants. In contrasting the Canadian and u.s. experiences, this volume also uses the case of governmental regulation of carcinogens to explore the role of science in policy making in the two countries.

While our focus here is thus limited to carcinogens, the dilemmas for policy makers are similar to those found in other areas of health, safety, and environmental regulation. Other health concerns such as reproductive risks, or environmental concerns such as ozone depletion, global warming, or species preservation, also pose policy makers with the vexing regulatory dilemma of how to choose among policy options in the face of extensive scientific uncertainties.

In this introductory chapter we first explore the difficulties in drawing boundaries between science and policy considerations. We then introduce some of the differences between the processes by which the u.s. and Canada make regulatory decisions. The final section of this chapter provides a brief overview of the case studies and describes the evaluative criteria used in each.

SCIENCE AND TRANS-SCIENCE

In the early 1970s Alvin Weinberg observed that policy makers were increasingly being called upon to make policy decisions based on uncertain science.[5] Concerns about the impacts of modern technology on the environment compel decision makers to act despite uncertain advice because the possible consequences of waiting (e.g., global warming, adverse health effects, and depletion of the ozone layer) are perceived to be too pressing. Since Weinberg's seminal paper, a considerable literature has grown on the role of science in environmental and health policy making. The enterprise between politics and conventional science, combining elements of both in an often uneasy relationship, has been variously called trans-science, science policy, regulatory science, and mandated science.[6] Following Jasanoff's example we have adopted the terms regulatory science and research science to distinguish between policy-relevant science and more traditional laboratory science.

Salter has observed that regulatory science must combine the "truth-seeking" features of science with the "justice-seeking" features of the legal process, resulting in an enterprise with characteristic institutions, participants, and procedures.[7] A common theme in the literature on regulatory science is that policy decisions based on uncertain scientific advice inevitably contain political or value judgments, either implicitly or explicitly. Those who make policy decisions, whether politicians, bureaucrats, or scientists, must invoke their own or others' values in choosing among a number of scientifically plausible alternatives. Thus scientific and policy choices become enmeshed.

Although scientific uncertainty underlies virtually all regulatory science debates, political conflict often exacerbates and sustains disagreements about scientific questions. Conflicting personal views and political stakes in the outcome lead different participants in the policy debate to advocate different scientific positions.[8] Lynn has showed that scientists working in industry, government, and academia tend to adopt different positions in a number of scientific controversies associated with the regulation of carcinogens.[9] Those employed by industry tend to adopt more risk-tolerant scientific assumptions than scientists working in government or academia. Graham and his coauthors observed that, contrary to the common assumption that additional scientific research will reduce uncertainty and thus political conflict, new research findings can actually stimulate conflict by clarifying the winners and losers in the political debate.[10]

The field of risk assessment developed in response to demands on regulators to make decisions about the safety of substances or activities in the absence of conclusive evidence. Risk assessment has been defined as "the characterization of the potential adverse health effects of human exposure to environmental hazards."[11] The practice of risk assessment involves applying scientific evidence and knowledge to questions beyond the normal scope of science, a trans-scientific activity to use Weinberg's term. The process of assessing and managing risk can been conceptualized by an idealized five-step model.[12]

1 Hazard Identification: An attempt is made to answer the question of whether or not the substance causes cancer.
2 Risk Characterization: The magnitude and distribution of human health risks are estimated based on assessments of the carcinogenic potency of the substance under review and the extent and nature of human exposure.
3 Identification and Comparison of Control Alternatives: Costs, technical and administrative feasibility, and distributive consequences of alternative control strategies are reviewed.
4 Choice of Risk Management Strategy: An acceptable level of risk and the means to achieve it are chosen based on intuitive or political

rationales or more formal decision criteria including risk-benefit analysis, cost effectiveness, "best available technology," or health protectiveness without regard to cost or feasibility.

5 Implementation, Review, and Adjustment of Control Strategy: Implementation of the control strategy is monitored to assess its effectiveness and to change the strategy if performance is not satisfactory.

The case studies in this volume focus primarily on the first four stages of risk assessment and management. In light of our interest in the role of science in policy making, the chapters focus in particular on the hazard identification, risk characterization, and risk management steps. The important task of comparing policy implementation in Canada and the U.S. remains for future work. We do, however, analyze one key component of that implementation stage: risk communication. The process by which regulators communicate information about risks to the public and attempt to justify their actions to the public is a fundamental element of the regulatory process.[13]

William Lowrance first proposed a rationalist distinction between risk assessment and risk management.[14] The essence of the distinction is that risk assessment seeks the answer to a question of fact – what is the risk? – while risk management seeks to answer a question of values – what should we do about it? Both U.S. and Canadian regulatory authorities purport to distinguish between risk assessment and risk management.[15]

Inasmuch as the assessment of risk clearly relies on science and the choice of risk management strategies clearly depends on values and politics, there has been a tendency to depict the risk assessment/risk management distinction as a separation between science and politics.[16] A more realistic appraisal recognizes that political considerations and values invariably enter into the risk assessment step, just as scientific understanding of risks constrains the risk management step.[17] Although risk assessment poses a question of fact, policy makers typically cannot answer it factually. In light of scientific uncertainty, they cannot avoid making value-laden choices among alternative scientifically plausible assumptions.

In practice risk assessment and risk management decisions are not always sequential, as the idealized model suggests. Even in the absence of scientific uncertainty, subjective values are engaged in deciding which questions of fact the risk assessment will address.[18] For instance normative conclusions about the reasonable limits of manufacturers' culpability could lead policy makers attempting to assess the risks posed by hazardous products, such as pesticides, to consciously ignore certain worst case scenarios, such as the extreme exposure that could result from blatantly disregarding safety precautions. Moreover, risk assessors could unconsciously adopt other assumptions based on their own conclusions about the feasibility of different risk management strategies. Finally, decision making may be influenced by selfish interests and political power, quite apart from the purely rational and ethical criteria implied by the rational model.

While we acknowledge the incongruence between the real world of policy making and the rational model of risk assessment and risk management, we nevertheless offer it as an ideal. While it is true that both scientific and policy judgments are involved at each stage, we believe that it is worthwhile to distinguish between factual and ethical questions, however imperfect our available knowledge and institutions may render the answers. Thus we do not go as far as the so-called "social constructivist" school that emphasizes the extent to which risks are a social construct, with values so inevitably clouding risk estimation that any effort to separate the factual and value bases of decision making is fruitless.[19]

In doing so we place ourselves in a camp of "neoseparationists"[20] who continue to emphasize a distinction between risk assessment and risk management. There are two reasons for this. First, we begin from the premise that some substances do present greater risks than others and that the norms and methods of science, while imperfect, constitute our best bet for distinguishing among them. Second, we believe that some allocations of risks and benefits are more just than others, and that democratic institutions and processes are our best hope to approximate equitable solutions. While there is undoubtedly a grey area between conventional science and politics in which the two are inseparable, if we define the entire policy-making enterprise as within the grey area, we leave ourselves vulnerable to political decisions made by scientists and scientific judgments made by politicians. Our preference would be to acknowledge that policy and scientific judgments are both made at each step of the process, while encouraging regulatory scientists and political decision makers to make explicit the basis for their decisions so that we can explore the boundary where scientific advice ends and value judgments begin.[21]

PATTERNS OF POLICY MAKING IN CANADA AND THE UNITED STATES

While the policy problems the two countries face are very similar, they have often addressed them in very different ways. A growing comparative policy literature suggests that there are different "national styles of regulation."[22] The U.S. style has been characterized as open, adversarial, formal, and legalistic. Conflict occurs not just between rival interest groups, but also between the executive, legislative, and judicial branches of government. The constitutional system of checks and balances, in combination with a deep-seated culture of distrust of arbitrary power, leads Congress to write very detailed statutes to restrict the discretion of executive agencies.[23]

These detailed rules and procedures in turn give interest groups the legal ammunition to challenge agency decisions in courts, where judges are more than willing to subject agency decisions to careful scrutiny under what is known as the "hard look" doctrine. Within this legalistic process, agencies are required by both statutes and judge-created administrative law doctrines to provide elaborate rationales for their decisions.

In contrast to this uniquely American approach, European and Japanese policy making has been described as closed, informal, and co-operative. Although differences between Japan and Europe and among European countries have been noted, they are less pronounced than the differences between these countries and the u.s. Agencies operate with extremely broad delegations of authority from legislatures, and regulatory policies traditionally have been negotiated by the government and interest groups behind closed doors. Because discretionary statutes do not establish clear obligations for government decision makers that can be enforced in court, potential litigants simply have fewer opportunities to sue the government, and as a result the judiciary plays only a minor role. Free from the constraints imposed upon their American counterparts, regulators in other countries rarely provide more than perfunctory rationales for their decisions.

While Canadian policy making seems to fit within this alternative pattern,[24] relatively little comparative research has been published on the Canadian regulatory style. Yet the Canadian-u.s. comparison offers insights into a number of other issues relevant to scholars and policy makers on both sides of the border. While in the United States there is growing interest in more cooperative approaches to regulation,[25] in Canada there is growing interest in opening up the regulatory process to increased public involvement, in many ways making it more similar to the u.s. one.[26] A comparison thus has the potential to yield important lessons for reformers in both countries.

In addition conflicts over international trade agreements – the u.s.-Canada Free Trade Agreement (FTA), the North American Free Trade Agreement (NAFTA), and the recent round of negotiations on the General Agreement on Trade and Tariffs (GATT) – have raised questions about the consequences of increasing economic integration for environmental, health, and safety protection.[27] Some sections of the agreements, such as the pesticides component of the u.s.-Canada Free Trade Agreement, explicitly encourage the harmonization of risk assessment procedures and regulatory standards. As a result there is a growing interest on both sides of the border in the similarities and differences in the two countries' regulatory processes.

REGULATORY FRAMEWORKS

The divergent regulatory styles are apparent in the two countries' legal frameworks for regulating risks, particularly in the design of regulatory statutes and the political control of regulation. As table 1 shows, the case studies examined in this book involve a total of thirteen regulatory statutes, administered by nine different agencies in the two countries. At the most general level the u.s. and Canadian statutes collectively cover the same subjects, and they provide regulators in both countries with similar regulatory instruments and authority.[28] In no case do regulators in one country have statutory authority absent in the other.

Regulating toxic substances is an extremely complex activity. It is thus not surprising that legislatures in both countries have delegated the task to expert agencies, in many cases with relatively little guidance. For instance the u.s. Toxic Substances Control Act merely requires regulation to prevent "an unreasonable risk of injury to human health or the environment," while the Canadian Environmental Protection Act (cepa) authorizes regulation of substances that "may have an immediate or long-term harmful effect on the environment" or "may constitute a danger in Canada to human life or health."

While statutes in both countries grant substantial discretion to regulators, the exercise of that discretion is significantly more constrained in the u.s. than in Canada, as u.s. legislators have provided increasingly detailed directions to regulatory agencies. As a crude but illustrative measure of the specificity of u.s. statutes, the six regulatory statutes covered in the case studies fill a total of 1216 pages in the u.s. Code, whereas the seven Canadian counterparts amount to only 298 pages.[29]

The statutory limits on discretion fall into three categories: substance, timing, and procedures. With respect to substance, both countries' food safety laws ban the sale of food that is "adulterated" and delegate to regulators the task of determining what should be considered adulterated. However in the u.s., the infamous Delaney clause prohibits the use of any food additives that have been shown to cause cancer in laboratory animals. Canadian regulators have greater flexibility to weigh the risks and benefits of food additives.

Table 1
Regulatory Statutes and Implementing Agencies

Statute	Implementing Agency	Case(s)
CANADA		
Canada Environmental Protection Act	Health and Welfare Canada, Environment Canada	dioxin
Food and Drug Act	Health and Welfare Canada	dioxin, Alar, saccharin
Fisheries Act	Environment Canada (DFO)	dioxin
Hazardous Products Act	Health and Welfare Canada (Cons. Corp. Affairs)	UFFI, asbestos
Pest Control Products Act	Agriculture Canada	alachlor, Alar
Ontario Occupational Health and Safety Act	Ontario Ministry of Labour	asbestos
Quebec Act Respecting Occupational Health and Safety	CSST	asbestos
UNITED STATES		
Toxic Substances Control Act	Environmental Protection Agency	dioxin, asbestos
Federal Water Pollution Control Act	Environmental Protection Agency	dioxin
Food, Drug, and Cosmetic Act	Environmental Protection Agency (Food, Drug Administration)	dioxin, Alar, saccharin
Occupational Safety and Health Act	Occupational Safety and Health Administration	asbestos
Federal Insecticide, Fungicide, and Rodenticide Act	Environmental Protection Agency	alachlor, Alar
Consumer Product Safety Act	Consumer Product Safety Commission	UFFI

Constraints in timing are illustrated by the Federal Insecticide, Fungicide, and Rodenticide Act (FIFRA), the u.s. pesticides statute. Both countries prohibit the sale of pesticides unless they are registered with the federal government, and both give regulators the authority to register new products, reevaluate existing pesticides, and remove those judged to be harmful from the market. While the Canadian statute leaves the reevaluation process to the discretion of the minister of agriculture, the u.s. process is governed by a strict timetable that demands its completion by 1998.

u.s. regulators are also more constrained by procedural requirements. First, they are required to adhere to the Administrative Procedures Act, a sort of quasi-constitution of the u.s. regulatory state. The act authorizes citizens to petition agencies for regulatory action, contains elaborate requirements for public consultation before an agency makes regulatory decisions, and authorizes judicial review of administrative actions. In addition to these general procedural requirements, many u.s. environmental, health, and safety statutes specify additional procedures for agencies to follow. For instance, before the u.s. Environmental Protection Agency (EPA) can proceed with any pesticide regulation, it must submit its proposal to a science advisory panel for review. Agriculture Canada is under no such obligation.

Canadian regulatory procedures historically have been far less formal. There is no Canadian equivalent to the Administrative Procedures Act to provide a general procedural framework. When consultation occurred, it was at the discretion of the responsible minister. Recently, however, regulatory reform has led to increasing procedural formality in Canada. Since 1986 federal regulatory agencies have produced annual regulatory agendas to alert the public to actions they are considering, published regulatory proposals in the *Canada Gazette* to solicit public comments, and prepared "regulatory analysis impact statements" to accompany regulatory proposals.[30] These changes have moved Canada closer to the u.s. "notice and comment" rulemaking model. However because they are only a matter of Cabinet policy, there is no way for interested parties to force agencies to abide by the new procedures.

Another major trend in the Canadian regulatory style is the increasing use of "multistakeholder consultations" designed to foster consensus among the relevant interests at stake in a particular regulatory initiative. While less formal than the notice and comment style procedures, these consultations also serve to open the regulatory process to greater public input and scrutiny. Despite their increasing formality and openness, however, Canadian regulatory procedures are still far more flexible and informal than their u.s. equivalents.

As a result of the fragmentation of authority in the u.s., constraints on regulatory discretion go well beyond the language of statutes written by Congress. First, Congress uses its oversight powers to scrutinize agency implementation of risk statutes, as we will see in the cases of saccharin and asbestos, among others. Second, u.s. presidents have sought to reign in regulators by exercising more careful executive oversight of agency actions. The asbestos case reveals the efforts of the White House Office of Management and Budget (OMB) to constrain EPA regulation. In Canada political control over regulation occurs through ministerial supervision of departments, Cabinet-wide review of major regulatory proposals, and legislative oversight during question period or in Parliamentary committees. In light of Cabinet secrecy it is difficult to assess the effectiveness of executive oversight of the bureaucracy. But as the case studies to follow demonstrate, the Canadian Parliament has played a much less significant role in overseeing regulation than the U.S. Congress.

Finally, perhaps the most significant difference between the regulatory frameworks of the two countries is the pivotal role of the judiciary in the U.S. Perhaps the most significant court-initiated procedural change was reinterpreting the Administrative Procedures Act to give environmental and other representatives of diffuse interests legal standing to challenge regulatory decisions in court.[31] According to one estimate, 80 percent of the Environmental Protection Agency's significant regulations have ended up in court.[32] The courts have played a central role not only in reviewing specific regulatory decisions – such as overturning U.S. regulatory agency decisions to ban urea-formaldehyde foam insulation and asbestos products – but also in infusing new meaning into both the substantive and procedural requirements of statutes. For instance, as discussed in the asbestos chapter, Supreme Court interpretations of the Occupational Safety and Health Act (OSHA) clarified the act's vague standards by requiring the agency to demonstrate the presence of significant risk, but not to perform a cost-benefit analysis. In effect, judges rewrote the statute.[33] In contrast, Canadian courts played virtually no role in any of the cases of risk regulation presented here. In the one case where industry challenged an agency decision – alachlor – the courts readily dismissed the suit with a bow to administrative expertise.

OUTLINE OF THE BOOK

The purpose of this book is to explore these differences in regulatory style and to evaluate their consequences for the regulation of toxic substances. Chapter 2 provides an overview of some of the controversies in cancer risk assessment that arise throughout the case studies. Chapters 3 through 8 examine seven toxic substances controversies: dioxins, alachlor, Alar, saccharin, urea-formaldehyde foam insulation, asbestos, and radon. Although these seven substances represent only a small fraction of the number of potential carcinogens that have been evaluated by the two countries, the cases do cover a variety of problem areas, including food contaminants (dioxins, saccharin, Alar), consumer products (UFFI), environmental contaminants (dioxins, alachlor, asbestos), indoor air pollutants (UFFI, radon), workplace hazards (asbestos), and naturally occurring carcinogens (radon).

These cases do not constitute a random or representative sample of toxic substances. Rather the case studies were chosen largely because each was highly controversial in at least one country. It is therefore necessary to be cautious about drawing conclusions about the regulation of other, less "political" toxic substances. We will return to the issue of the representativeness of the case studies in the conclusion.

All the cases examined in the following chapters reflect the fundamentally different regulatory styles at work in the two countries. Many of them nonetheless offer a special contribution to the u.s./Canadian comparison. For instance the dioxins case focuses on the incorporation of science in the regulatory process and the policy consequences of different approaches to risk assessment. The asbestos case emphasizes the intense politicization of science that can occur when science is uncertain and economic and political stakes are high. The saccharin case offers insights about the role of elected representatives in making science-based policy decisions and the relevance of different political institutions in the two countries. The formaldehyde case explores the unique role of the courts in the u.s. regulatory system. Differences in communication of risks to the public are most clearly elucidated by the radon case. Finally, the Alar and alachlor cases reveal the potentially significant role of interest groups in mobilizing public concerns for some risks over others.

We have adopted five criteria to compare the regulatory process and outcomes in the two countries for each case. With respect to outcomes, we compare the *stringency* and *timeliness* of standards. Since differences in regulatory standards could reflect different assessments about either the magnitude or acceptability of risks, we will also compare *how science was incorporated in regulatory decision making* and *how decision makers balanced risks and benefits.* Our intent is not to evaluate the quality of regulatory science in either country, a task for which we do not claim adequate expertise, but rather to explore differences in the two countries' approaches to regulatory science and to consider the implications of those differences for public policy. Finally, with respect to the decision-making process, we examine the question of *interest representation.* Each case study will discuss the extent to which those with different interests in the outcome had opportunities to participate and the mechanisms by which their interests were represented in each country.

It is important to emphasize what this study is not. It is not designed as an investigation of an exhaustive list of variables contributing to divergence or convergence in regulatory outcomes, including economic forces, interest group pressures, political institutions, science and technology, and other variables that shape the decisions of policy makers.[34] Instead we have adopted the approach of comparing the decisions made by the two countries on the basis of the five evaluative criteria described above. Because of our focus on regulatory styles, however, we inevitably do examine the impact of regulatory styles as a causal variable, and our study produces some important results on that point. As we emphasize in the concluding chapter, however, our concentration on regulatory styles is not intended to privilege that one explanatory factor over others in influencing policy outcomes.

Each chapter follows a common format. After a brief overview of the case, we describe the regulatory framework in each country. Collectively the chapters provide a portrait of the major laws governing toxic substances in the two countries. We then provide a detailed reconstruction of the regulatory decisions in each country, taking care to distinguish the various stages in the risk assessment and management process delineated earlier in this chapter. The discussion then addresses how the various stakeholders participated in the process. Finally, each chapter concludes with a summary assessment of the case based on our five criteria: stringency, timeliness, incorporation of science, balancing of risks and benefits, and interest representation.

2 Cancer Risk Assessment: Concepts and Controversies

In this chapter we survey several important controversies in cancer risk assessment and management, which arise time and again in the case studies we have chosen. While some of the material that follows is necessarily technical, it is so fundamental to the policy disputes in toxic substance regulation that it is essential to our discussion. We have attempted to make the information as accessible as possible to a lay audience. The focus of this and subsequent chapters is assessment of risks to *human* health; assessment of environmental hazards and risks to animals are beyond the scope of this volume.

Cancer risk assessment illustrates many of the controversies associated with regulatory science. In light of the current incomplete understanding of the mechanisms of cancer, it is necessary to draw inferences at each step of the analysis. In this chapter we introduce some of the controversies by proceeding through the first two analytical steps in the risk management process: hazard identification and risk characterization. In the final section we consider the advantages and disadvantages of formal risk assessment policies.

HAZARD IDENTIFICATION: DOES THE SUBSTANCE CAUSE CANCER?

The first step in a risk assessment is a qualitative evaluation of a substance's carcinogenicity. In other words: Does the substance cause cancer? While the question seems straightforward, the answer often requires interpretation of ambiguous, if not conflicting, evidence.

The strongest form of evidence of carcinogenicity is a positive epidemiological study, which shows that exposure to a particular substance is associated with elevated rates of cancer in humans. For ethical reasons experiments cannot be performed on human subjects to determine if a substance is harmful. Thus epidemiologists must rely on imperfect experiments designed by history and nature.[1] Their objective is to confirm whether there is a statistically significant association between exposure to a substance and incidence of cancer, after controlling for other factors that can cause cancer.[2]

Unfortunately the statistical power of epidemiology to confirm human carcinogenicity is limited for a number of reasons. First, in contrast to animals in controlled laboratory experiments, people lead complex lives in which they engage in risky behaviour, such as smoking and drinking, and come into contact with numerous hazardous substances. It is thus difficult to statistically control for all other potential causes of cancer in order to confirm the effect of the single factor under study. For instance in the asbestos and radon cases discussed in chapters 7 and 8, regulators were concerned about the potential for lung cancer. However in both cases interpretation of the epidemiological evidence was greatly complicated by the prevalence of smoking-related lung cancer in the populations under study.

Second, retrospective studies often are constrained by flawed human memory or incomplete historical records, particularly with respect to exposure. This problem is exacerbated by latency periods, which may be as long as several decades, between exposure and the appearance of many types of cancer. In the saccharin case, discussed in chapter 5, epidemiological studies did not confirm the cancer risk suggested by animal studies. However many scientists argued that the negative epidemiological studies offered little reassurance, because widespread consumption of saccharin in diet sodas had only begun a few years earlier. It simply may have been too soon to detect adverse human health effects associated with saccharin consumption.

Third, high background rates of cancer in the population make it difficult to statistically confirm anything but rare types of cancers or relatively large increases in the incidence of more common types of cancer in study populations.

Finally, epidemiology can only assess human health risks after exposure has occurred. It is thus of limited utility for prospective evaluation of the risks posed by new substances or processes. In light of the many limitations of epidemiology, it is perhaps not surprising that the International Agency for Research on Cancer has concluded that there is "sufficient" evidence of human carcinogencity for only some 50 chemicals or processes.[3]

Animal experimentation is an alternative source of evidence of carcinogenicity. In bioassays for carcinogenicity whole animals are exposed to a test substance under controlled laboratory conditions.[4] A control group of animals receives identical treatment in all respects except exposure to the test substance. As animals die or are killed at the end of the experiment, they are examined to compare the incidence of tumours in the experimental and control groups. Two or three groups, each comprised of 50 animals, are typically exposed to different doses, in addition to the control group at zero dose. Since tumours can develop long after exposure, experiments are continued for as close as possible to the animals' full lifetime. Rats or mice are most often used as test animals because they are small, inexpensive, and have relatively short lifespans, allowing completion of an experiment in about two years.

The biological similarity between cancer in humans and animals is the basis for reliance on animal testing to assess human health risks.[5] With the exception of arsenic, all proven human carcinogens are also known to be animal carcinogens.[6] Moreover recent work suggests a strong correlation between rankings of carcinogenic potency in humans and animals.[7] The fact that virtually all known human carcinogens are also animal carcinogens, however, does not necessarily imply the reverse, that all animal carcinogens are human carcinogens. There are hundreds of substances for which there is evidence of carcinogenicity in animal studies but no evidence of carcinogenicity in humans.

A final source of indirect evidence of carcinogenicity is short-term tests conducted with either microorganisms or animal tissues rather than whole mammals. Many short-term tests are designed to indicate mutagenicity, an essential step in the process of carcinogenesis. For instance the most common of these, the Ames test, measures a substance's ability to cause mutations in a certain type of bacteria. While these tests are attractive because they are faster and less expensive than whole animal experiments, the results are even further removed from human biology and experience than those from animal bioassays.

Conclusions concerning the carcinogenicity of a particular substance thus may be based on various kinds of direct and indirect evidence. However the assessment is often complicated by conflicting or ambiguous results. Legal concepts of proof offer a useful analogy to illustrate dilemmas in evaluating evidence of carcinogenicity. In criminal law the defendant is assumed innocent until proven guilty, placing the burden of proof on the prosecution. Analogously, should a substance be assumed safe unless proven hazardous or hazardous unless proven safe?

In assuming that defendents are innocent until proven guilty, the judicial system accepts the possibility that some guilty people will go free in order to avoid sending even a single innocent person to jail. Similarly, if we assume that a substance is hazardous unless proven safe, we minimize the likelihood of falsely assuming that a carcinogenic substance is safe (a false negative), but at the expense of a greater likelihood of assuming that the substance is hazardous when in fact it is not (a false positive).[8] The alternative assumption of safe unless proven hazardous avoids false positives at the expense of false negatives. The problem policy makers face is that both false positives and false negatives can be costly. Falsely assuming that substances are safe can cost lives, while falsely assuming that substances are carcinogenic can have tremendous economic consequences. An alternative decision-making criterion often suggested is to adopt a neutral initial position and allow the weight of evidence to suggest conclusions in either direction.

A related question concerns the appropriate standard of proof, which specifies the weight of evidence required to support a decision. In criminal law cases defendants must be proven guilty "beyond a reasonable doubt," while a less onerous requirement, that a particular action be found "more likely than not" to have caused the impugned damage, suffices in common law cases. In regulating toxic substances, will a single positive animal study be considered sufficient, or is further evidence of human carcinogenicity required?

The standards of proof of research science typically are very high. Before publishing their results researchers must ordinarily demonstrate with statistical confidence of 95 percent that the findings are not merely due to chance. While such high standards effectively maintain the credibility of research science, they may be less appropriate when one is considering the potential for substances to present serious public health risks.[9]

In several of the cases discussed in this volume, including saccharin, Alar, and urea-formaldehyde foam, there was evidence of carcinogenicity in animals but no confirmation of risks to humans from epidemiological studies. Historically, policy makers have often adopted a risk-averse position when faced with this dilemma. In light of the insensitivity of epidemiology for the many reasons discussed above, negative epidemiological studies are seldom accepted as proof that a substance is not a human carcinogen, particularly if there is positive evidence of animal carcinogenicity.

RISK CHARACTERIZATION: HOW DANGEROUS IS THE SUBSTANCE?

The outcome of the hazard identification step is a conclusion about whether or not a substance is likely to cause cancer in humans. The objective of the next step, risk characterization, is to refine that conclusion by estimating the severity of the risk the substance presents. The magnitude of cancer risk depends on two factors: the inherent potency of the carcinogen and the nature and extent of human exposure. Even a very weak carcinogen may be a source of concern if people are exposed to high levels or if many people are exposed, while a strong carcinogen may pose negligible risk if there is little human exposure.

Potency Estimation

Gold, Sawyer, et al. have reported that the carcinogenic potency of substances tested in animals vary by a factor of more than 10 million.[10] Clearly all carcinogens are not equal. However the attempt to predict the extent of risk to humans is fraught with uncertainty. In the absence of evidence of human carcinogenicity, how can carcinogenic potency in humans be estimated based on potency in animals, and which animal species should be used to approximate human sensitivity? How can one account for differences in sensitivity within the human population? We will illustrate the nature of the underlying debates by reviewing one particularly controversial question in greater detail: How should evidence of carcinogenicity obtained at high doses be extrapolated to lower doses of greater relevance to human exposure?

Both epidemiology and animal bioassays typically provide evidence of carcinogenicity at relatively high doses, thus demanding understanding of the relationship between dose and carcinogenic response in order to project the severity of risk at lower doses. Epidemiological studies are best able to observe a statistically significant increase in cancer if they focus on a highly exposed population. Thus epidemiologists often study workers who were historically exposed to much higher levels of contamination than are contemporary workers or the general population. In the radon case, evidence of human carcinogenicity was derived from studies of uranium miners who, decades ago, were exposed to relatively high levels of radon in the workplace. Similarly, much of our understanding of the hazards of asbestos is based on historical studies of miners and other workers who made little effort to limit their exposure to asbestos fibres because they were unaware of the risks. However when a positive association is found from such epidemiological studies, questions arise as to whether the substance is also carcinogenic at current levels of occupational exposure and the even lower levels faced by the general population. Thus controversy remains about the risks presented by relatively low levels of radon in homes and asbestos in the ambient environment.

The need for extrapolation to lower doses is particularly acute in the case of animal studies. Experimental animals must serve as surrogates for the exposed human population, which can number in the millions. However the extreme expense of animal testing necessitates limiting the number of animals used. Even then, bioassays, which typically involve only 50 or 100 rodents per experimental group, can cost $300 thousand to $1 million per chemical tested.[11]

The central problem is that negative findings among small experimental populations provide only limited assurance of safety. For instance, if no excess tumours are observed in a group of 100 animals, one can state with 95 percent confidence only that the actual incidence of tumours is less than 4.5 percent (that is, 4.5 tumours per 100 animals)[12] – small consolation if thousands or even millions of people are exposed. In order to increase the chances of observing a carcinogenic effect in a limited number of animals, experimental animals typically are exposed to relatively high doses. Many bioassay protocols recommend use of the "maximum tolerated dose" (MTD) as the highest experimental dose, where the MTD is defined as the highest dose that will not shorten the animals' lives from effects other than cancer.[13]

While reliance on higher doses increases the likelihood of detecting carcinogenicity, it also necessitates extrapolation to much lower doses typical of human exposure. In several of the cases studied in this volume, including dioxin, saccharin, Alar, and alachlor, regulators had to estimate human health risks based only on evidence of carcinogenicity from animal testing at relatively high doses.

Extrapolation to lower doses demands assumptions about the shape of the dose-response function. A hypothetical plot of the likelihood of exposed individuals' contracting cancer at different dose levels, figure 1, illustrates several alternative assumptions. Although supralinear (line A), linear (line B), and sublinear (lines C and D) curves could all be used to extrapolate from experimental doses to zero dose, the linear and sublinear hypotheses historically have been considered most biologically plausible.[14] At the limit, the sublinear curve takes on the "hockey stick" shape of line D, which implies that the substance presents zero risk of cancer below some threshold dose.

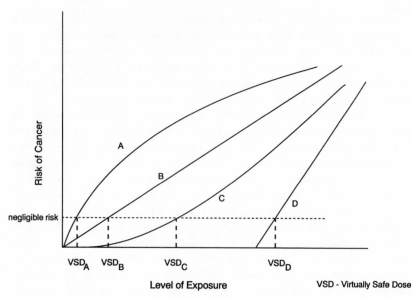

Fig. 1   Alternative Dose-Response Functions

Safety Factors vs Mathematical Models

Two main competing methodologies for extrapolation have emerged – safety factors and mathematical models – reflecting different assumptions about the underlying mechanism of carcinogenesis. The safety factor approach emerged in the 1950s as a technique to estimate safe levels of exposure for humans based on experimentation with animals.[15] It is widely held that acute and chronic toxins cause adverse effects only if the dose is sufficient to overwhelm the body's defense mechanisms, a mechanism consistent with the existence of a threshold (i.e., line D). As the dose is decreased in animal studies, there typically is some level at which no adverse effects are observed experimentally. That dose, referred to as the "no observed adverse effects level" or NOAEL, often is accepted as experimental evidence of a threshold. Toxicologists attempt to estimate the comparable threshold for humans by dividing the NOAEL by an arbitrary safety factor to allow, among other factors, for the possibility that humans may be more sensitive to the substance than animals and that some humans may be more sensitive than others. Thus, reliance on a typical safety factor of 100 leads to the conclusion that 1/100th of the NOAEL represents an "acceptable daily intake" (ADI) for humans.[16]

Reliance on safety factors is a well-established practice for traditional toxins. However, a fundamental problem with the approach is that an experimental observation of no adverse effects does not prove the existence of a threshold.[17] If no adverse effects are observed in a group of 50 experimental animals, there is no assurance that none would be observed if 500 or 5000 animals were tested. In fact it is impossible to experimentally confirm the existence of a threshold since there is always a possibility that adverse effects would be observed if more animals were tested.

The application of the safety factor approach to carcinogens has been particularly controversial, since many scientists believe that carcinogens are unlikely to exhibit thresholds. Current understanding of the mechanism of carcinogenesis is that tumours arise as a result of a series of changes to the genetic material within cells, some of which can be expected to be irreversible. If, as some scientists have suggested, even a single molecule of a carcinogen can cause irreversable DNA damage, which ultimately could lead to the formation of a tumour, the notion of a threshold of safety is highly problematic.[18]

The initial response of toxicologists was simply to use a larger safety factor in evaluating carcinogens.[19] The leading alternative is reliance on mathematical models, which extrapolate from high to low doses by making assumptions about the shape of the dose-response function. The most widely used model is based on a mechanistic assumption of linearity at low doses (i.e., line B).[20] Contrary to the threshold assumption implicit in the safety factor approach, the linear model assumes that there is a finite, though diminishing, risk at all doses above zero.

The assumption that there is no threshold for carcinogens has important implications for public policy. It implies that even at extremely low levels of environmental contamination, the number of projected cases of cancer could be significant if a sufficiently large population is exposed. Non-threshold models thus can raise questions about a large number of substances that would not be of concern if it were assumed that thresholds are present. The modelling approach also has implications for the very use of the word "safe." Rather than speak in qualitative terms of safety or hazard, those who rely on mathematical models offer probabilistic estimates of risk. Rather than declare a particular level of exposure "safe," with the implication that there is zero risk, they instead offer a quantitative estimate of the degree of risk, such as one in a million or one in a thousand.

In practice those who rely on quantitative risk assessment usually define some low level of risk as negligible or "virtually safe." U.S. regulatory agencies typically have settled on a virtually safe dose corresponding to a lifetime risk of one in a million in cases where a large population is exposed.[21] However higher levels of risk often are tolerated when smaller populations are at risk.[22] In one respect the choice of some quantitative level of risk as negligible is similar in effect to relying on an "acceptable daily intake"; in both cases, lesser exposures are tolerated. The level of exposure corresponding to the "virtually safe dose" based on mathematical models, however, can be significantly different from the "acceptable daily intake" based on safety factors. Reliance on safety factors typically results in higher estimates of acceptable doses than those derived by the most widely used mathematical models.[23] In the dioxin case, discussed in chapter 3, risk estimates derived from safety factors and mathematical models differed by a factor of 1700, with the safety factor approach resulting in the higher estimate of the acceptable level of exposure.

It is not a simple matter to choose the most appropriate model for extrapolation. With few data points, often only two or three at relatively high doses, different models may fit the data equally well in the experimental region but diverge widely in the region of interest to policymakers. Figure 1 illustrates that the virtually safe dose suggested by different models can greatly differ – differences of a factor of 1000 are not unusual.

The Initiator/Promoter Debate

The choice of methodology for extrapolation hinges on judgment about which model best approximates the mechanism of carcinogenesis for the particular substance in question. Scientific uncertainty about the mechanisms of carcinogenesis has fueled an often heated debate over extrapolation methodologies. It is widely accepted that cancer develops through a multistage process. In the first stage, initiation, exposure to a carcinogen directly or indirectly causes irreversable damage to a cell's genetic code. During the subsequent promotion stage cells divide, passing on their damaged DNA to the next generation of cells. Reproduction of mutated cells eventually can lead to uncontrolled cell growth. In the final stage, progression, cancerous tumours form and spread to other tissues.

There is evidence that different substances act at different stages in the process. Some carcinogens may act as initiators, others as promoters. Still others may be complete carcinogens, capable of acting at both the initiation and promotion stages. It is widely held that since initiators cause irreversable DNA damage, they would not be expected to exhibit thresholds. In contrast promotion appears, to a point, to be reversable, leading some scientists to argue that it is plausible that promoters have thresholds.[24] Those researchers stress a distinction between the "genotoxic" (i.e., DNA damaging) effect of initiators and the non-genotoxic or "epigenetic" effect of promoters and other indirectly acting carcinogens, and argue that a safety factor approach may be appropriate to assess the risks of promoters even if a linear model is used for initiators.

Other scientists have been more cautious in distinguishing between initiators and promoters. The u.s. Office of Science and Technology Policy concluded in 1986 that there was little evidence to suggest that promoters exhibit thresholds.[25] To date u.s. agencies have relied on linear models for substances suspected of being initiators and promoters alike for a number of reasons.[26] First, the linear model often is supported on the grounds that the most conservative approach should be adopted since the mechanisms of neither initiators nor promoters are well understood. Second, many promoters persist in body tissues. Thus even if a sustained effect is required, a single exposure may be sufficient. Third, the high background rate of cancer in the general population suggests that we are all exposed to many carcinogens. Even if promoters do have thresholds, if different carcinogens can have a combined effect (an important and controversial assumption), it is conceivable that the body's defense mechanisms are overwhelmed all the time. Thus even if carcinogens exhibit thresholds individually, their collective effect could ensure that those thresholds are exceeded all the time.[27] Finally, some individuals may be more sensitive than others. Even if each individual has her or his own characteristic threshold, the population threshold may nevertheless approach zero.[28]

Other scientists have reservations about the entire extrapolation exercise. They argue that the mechanism by which substances cause cancer may be qualitatively different at high doses than at low doses.[29] In particular, irritation of tissues that occurs at doses near the maximum tolerated dose may contribute to mechanisms of carcinogenicity that would not be expected to occur at lower doses. For instance damage to cells caused by high doses could lead to an increased rate of cell division, thus enhancing carcinogenesis. By performing most animal experiments at high doses, these scientists argue, we obtain evidence of little relevance in predicting carcinogenicity at levels of human exposure. Such arguments were central to the debate over the carcinogenicity of formaldehyde gas that is released by urea-formaldehyde foam insulation. Many scientists argued that the evidence of formaldehyde's carcinogenicity in rats was not relevant to human exposure, since the animal tests were performed at doses that caused acute irritation of the animals' nasal passages.

Exposure Assessment

In addition to assessing a carcinogen's potency, risk assessors must evaluate the nature and extent of human exposure. In light of the tremendous uncertainties surrounding potency estimates, it might seem surprising that exposure assessment has been described as the "weak link" in risk assessment.[30] To date the value-based assumptions embedded in exposure assessments have largely escaped the degree of scrutiny accorded to potency estimation.

Ideally, exposure estimates should be based on measurements of the actual doses received by members of the exposed population or by a representative sample of that population. However such information is costly to obtain and thus is seldom available. At best measurements of ambient concentrations of contaminants in the air, water, or soil may be available. In many cases ambient levels are only estimated using mathematical models of environmental dispersion. Reliance on measurements or projections of ambient levels demands additional information or assumptions about the number of people exposed and the nature and duration of their exposure. If the ambient air in the vicinity of a factory is more polluted than air elsewhere, for instance, how many people live there and how much time do they spend there? How much contaminated water do people drink and how much contaminated air do they breathe?

Exposure to some substances may occur via use of hazardous or contaminated products. Even if the amount of the substance in the product is known, additional information or assumptions are required about who uses the product, how often, and what exposure they receive in doing so. As is the case with potency estimation, disagreements among risk professionals often revolve around the appropriate degree of conservatism. Should a worst-case scenario be used, in which workers are assumed to be exposed to the highest conceivable levels of a substance for 40 hours per week for 40 years, or should estimates be based on a more typical exposure scenario? The implications of different sets of assumptions about the duration and extent of exposure can be very significant. As discussed in chapter 4, in the alachlor case Canadian regulators, relying on different assumptions about workplace practices and duration of exposure, derived an estimate of the exposure received by pesticide applicators that was as much as a thousand times greater than the comparable u.s. estimate.

Because not all individuals receive the same exposure, the risk assessor must attempt to convey information about both the magnitude and distribution of exposure throughout the population.[31] In addition to identifying populations that are vulnerable by virtue of greater exposure, it is important to estimate the exposure of specific subpopulations that may be biologically more sensitive to exposure. In the Alar case, for instance, the risks children faced were of particular concern, by virtue both of the children's potentially greater sensitivity and their greater consumption of contaminated apple products, particularly apple juice, relative to body weight. In the past risk assessments often have implicitly assumed that all members of the population were equally susceptible. While such an assumption may be reasonable for genetically homogeneous strains of laboratory rats, it is likely to understate the risks for more diverse human populations.[32]

In the final step of risk characterization, potency and exposure estimates are combined to characterize the severity and distribution of human health risks. Many risk assessors argue that it is also important to characterize the extent of uncertainty associated with their estimates.[33] Depending on the choice of methodologies, the risk assessors' advice may be qualitative or quantitative. Mathematical models derive quantitative estimates of the likelihood of risk experienced by different members of the population corresponding to the extent of their exposure. On the other hand the safety factor approach produces a qualitative assessment of risk. Those whose exposure is less than the assumed threshold are considered to face no risk of cancer, while those with exposures above the "acceptable daily intake" are considered to face an unacceptable, but unquantified, risk of cancer.

Quantitative risk assessment typically distinguishes between population risks and individual risks. The population risk is an estimate of the total number of cancers that are projected in an exposed population, while the individual risk is an estimate of the likelihood that any one exposed person will develop cancer. For instance, risk analysts might estimate that a factory discharging a potential carcinogen into the air could present a population risk of up to 10 cases of cancer per year among the population of 100,000 in the surrounding community, equivalent to an average individual risk of one in a thousand. However some people within the exposed population would be expected to face higher risks than others, whether by virtue of greater exposure or greater sensitivity. Thus an attempt might be made to develop more detailed estimates of the individual risks faced by workers in the factory, residents living near the factory fence, and those living in remote sections of the community.

ADVANCES IN RISK ASSESSMENT

Historically, risk assessment models have treated the human or animal as a "black box," focusing only on the relationship between "inputs" (exposure) and "outputs" (disease). However in recent years the level of scientific analysis has moved from the whole animal to the cell.[34] Research on the component processes of carcinogenesis has led to the development of more sophisticated biologically based models. For instance physiologically based pharmacokinetic models (PB-PK models) have been offered to describe the transport and transformation processes that occur between an applied (external) dose and the effective (internal) one. Such models offer promise for improving both high dose to low dose extrapolation and interspecies extrapolation.[35] Advances have also been made in exploring the multiple mechanisms of carcinogenesis and in developing techniques to more fully characterize uncertainty in risk assessments.[36]

The boundary between science and trans-science is not fixed; many trans-scientific questions can be expected to yield to systematic investigation and eventually to be met with something approaching scientific consensus.[37] Although scientific progress offers promise that many outstanding questions of fact will be resolved in the future, at present the policy debate rages on. In fact the new models may actually generate more controversy, since they offer a larger number of parameters and mechanistic assumptions for various interests to dispute.

At present scientists can seldom state with any certainty the risk of cancer a substance presents at doses typical of human exposure. Representatives of different interests or institutions offer widely divergent advice. Yet the costs of choosing the wrong advice can be high. If a linear model is used to evaluate a substance that in reality has a threshold, the resulting estimate of the acceptable level of contamination could be thousands of times more stringent than necessary – at tremendous cost. On the other hand if the safety factor approach is used to evaluate a substance that actually has a linear dose-response function, the level of risk could be substantially underestimated – at a cost of human lives. The challenge for policy makers is to weigh the scientific plausibility of these scenarios as well as the human and economic costs of error in either direction.

RISK ASSESSMENT POLICY

If one could estimate the magnitude of risks with certainty, it would be possible to clearly distinguish between risk assessment and risk management, leaving the value-laden comparison of risks and benefits to the risk management stage. However since risk assessment is uncertain, the analyst must at various steps in the analysis draw inferences from among plausible alternatives. There has been heated debate among those who advocate risk-averse assumptions,[38] risk-tolerant assumptions,[39] and risk-neutral assumptions.[40]

In general risk-averse assumptions have prevailed on the grounds that human lives are more important than dollars. It is a standard public health principle to "err on the side of safety." Thus risk assessments have often relied on a number of "conservative" assumptions, including using evidence from the most sensitive animal species tested, assuming linear dose-response functions for substances suspected of being initiators and promotors alike, reporting statistical upper confidence limits rather than most likely estimates, and making cautious assumptions about exposure.

In recent years there has been something of a backlash against this conservatism in risk assessment. Some critics argue that we do not face a simple choice between lives and dollars. Rather, we must ask: What is the most effective way to allocate society's resources to save the most lives? Wildavsky has argued that "richer is safer"; overly stringent regulations cripple the economy by restricting innovation and, in doing so, ultimately harm our health.[41] These critics argue that consumers who pay higher prices as a result of overly stringent environmental regulations may be less able to afford good nutrition and health care, while firms that are harmed by over-zealous regulations may be less able to invest in development of new and safer processes.

Another argument against risk-averse assumptions (or for that matter, against risk-tolerant assumptions) is that they can accumulate.[42] What begins as a prudent choice among scientifically plausible alternatives becomes less and less plausible as the most conservative alternative is selected at each inference juncture. For instance critics charge that exposure assessments often have focused on an implausible scenario for the "most exposed individual," who is assumed to spend 24 hours a day for 70 years at the factory fence.

Finkel has argued that the critics of conservatism in risk assessment tend to selectively emphasize overprotective assumptions while underemphasizing assumptions that are likely to understate risks.[43] For instance most risk assessments have overlooked individual differences in susceptibility and the potential for different substances to cause synergistic effects. Finkel recommends that, rather than providing a single numerical estimate of risk, whether more or less conservative, risk assessments should routinely report the full probability density function, conveying both the best estimate and richer information on the extent of uncertainty.

A related matter is the question of whether agencies should adopt explicit cancer-risk assessment policies to ensure that consistent value-based inferences are made in each risk assessment. An influential report of the u.s. National Reserch Council (NRC) recommended adoption of explicit "inference guidelines," defined as statements of predetermined choices among alternative methods.[44] The report offered several advantages of such a formal "cancer policy." First, making explicit the unavoidable value judgments in assessment of the magnitude of risk reduces opportunities for political interference under the guise of science. This openness can enhance both public and scientific credibility. Second, fairness is served by consistent and predictable policy judgments. Third, public understanding of risk assessments is enhanced by explicit cancer policies. Finally, formal cancer policies can promote administrative efficiency by eliminating the need to repeat the same debates with each new regulatory decision.[45]

However the NRC report also acknowledged several disadvantages associated with formal cancer policies. First, since policy and scientific judgments are inseparable in risk assessment, the attempt to impose consistent policy judgments could lead to simplistic, "boilerplate" science. Rigid policies not only limit opportunities for political manipulation, they also constrain scientists' flexibility to use their best judgment in resolving uncertainty. Second, formal policies may be difficult to amend, thus "freezing" science at an earlier stage of development. Third, if risk assessment becomes routinized, it may be difficult to attract the most creative scientific minds to the discipline.[46] While cookbooks are helpful in guiding those of us with limited culinary skills, they neither appeal to the best chefs nor advance the culinary arts. Fourth, in considering each inference choice separately, there is a strong chance that the most conservative assumptions will be adopted at each opportunity. As cautious assumptions are made at each inference juncture, the resulting estimate of the risk becomes less and less plausible. Finally, consistent application of conservative assumptions ironically does not ensure consistent results.[47] Because the evidence for some substances fits the predetermined set of assumptions more closely than for other substances, the resultant estimates of risk are not equally conservative in all cases. It is noteworthy that the purported advantages of explicit cancer policies all concern democratic values, such as openness, accountability, and fairness, while the disadvantages all concern scientific merit.

In the last decade several U.S. regulatory agencies have adopted formal cancer policies.[48] With the exception of a period early in the Reagan adminstration, these policies have relied on conservative (i.e., cautious) assumptions.[49] However the impact of those cancer policies is arguable. Graham, Green, and Roberts note that despite formal policies, scientists advising regulatory agencies still tend to draw their own case-by-case conclusions.[50] Moreover cancer policies do not lessen the degree of conflict between political interests. Once a generic risk assessment policy is in place, the debate simply shifts to questions of whether and how the guidelines apply to the particular case at hand.[51] And as we will argue in the final chapter, the cautious assumptions in u.s. agencies' cancer policies ensure that, as uncertainty is reduced, future revisions to risk assessments often will be in the direction of decreasing the risk estimate.[52] Such revisions *appear* to provide less protection for the public, and thus are politically difficult to make.

In contrast to the u.s., Canadian authorities have not adopted formal cancer policies. As the case studies that follow will demonstrate, Canadian regulators typically have taken a flexible, case-by-case approach to risk assessment rather than constraining themselves with a uniform set of inference guidelines. The following chapters will explore both the political factors that lead to these two different approaches and the implications of the alternative approaches for public policy.

3 Between Science and Politics: Assessing the Risks of Dioxins

INTRODUCTION[1]

The very mention of the word "dioxin" ignites public concern over environmental and public health issues. Dioxin's reputation as the most toxic substance known to humanity has ensured that controversy closely follows identification of each new source of dioxins, including municipal incinerators, Agent Orange, and pulp mill effluents. Despite the controversy, there have been few regulations to date in either Canada or the United States to control environmental releases of dioxins. This chapter therefore differs somewhat from those that follow in placing greater emphasis on the risk assessments performed in the two countries than on final regulatory standards. In that sense it provides the most complete illustration of many of the risk assessment controversies introduced in the preceding chapter.

The chemical usually referred to simply as "dioxin" is properly known as 2,3,7,8-tetrachlorodibenzo-p-dioxin (2,3,7,8-TCDD), one member of a family of structurally similar chlorinated dioxins and furans. Animal studies have shown 2,3,7,8-TCDD to be the most toxic of the dioxins and furans. As a result most government attention in both countries has focused on TCDD. Although both Canada and the U.S. have relied on the same body of scientific evidence, and in particular on the same study of TCDD's carcinogenicity in rats, Health and Welfare Canada has derived an acceptable level of exposure to the chemical that is about 1700 times greater than the comparable figure derived by the U.S. EPA.[2]

Since the mechanism by which toxic substances, including dioxins, cause cancer is a subject of considerable uncertainty within the scientific community, it is not surprising that risk assessments for the same chemical can differ by several orders of magnitude. However this chapter argues that there is a pattern to the divergence. The regulatory science positions adopted by the two countries reflect the cultural, legal, and political environments in which their regulatory scientists work. The dioxin case suggests that there may be national styles of regulatory science akin to the national styles of regulation identified by other authors.[3] In other words, not only do the political choices and processes differ between countries, but the way that government scientists answer questions of fact in the face of scientific uncertainty also can differ in important ways.

THE LEGAL FRAMEWORK

Dioxins are unintended byproducts of industrial processes such as bleaching of wood pulp, manufacture of certain chlorinated chemicals, and incineration of municipal or industrial wastes. Trace quantities of dioxins and furans also may be produced by such natural sources as forest fires.

A variety of regulatory responses is available to control multimedia contaminants like dioxins. Source-specific regulations can be used to control releases of dioxins to air, water, and soil. Product quality regulations can be used to limit the dioxin content of products such as pesticides, wood preservatives, or bleached paper. Finally, once dioxins are present in the environment, governments can limit their potential impact on human health by regulating the harvest or sale of dioxin-contaminated foods.

Both the Canadian and u.s. federal governments have a variety of regulatory instruments at their disposal. Air and water pollution control legislation in both countries authorizes regulations to control environmental release of dioxins. In particular, water pollution control legislation is available in both countries to control dioxins discharges from pulp mills. Water pollution control by the Canadian federal government has historically been accomplished indirectly through the Fisheries Act, which authorizes regulations to protect fisheries. Federal regulations for pulp and paper effluents, which were based on an assessment of "best practicable technology," were initially issued in 1971, and revised to include dioxin limits in 1992.

The u.s. Clean Water Act combines uniform national regulations with an element of state discretion in water quality planning.[4] EPA has issued technology-based national standards for various source categories, including pulp mills. Recognizing that technology-based standards may not be sufficient in all areas, the 1987 amendments to the act also established a planning process to ensure that water quality objectives are achieved. Subject to EPA's approval, states are required to adopt ambient water quality criteria for toxic pollutants and to devise control strategies for individual sources to achieve those criteria by deadlines specified in the act.

The U.S. Toxic Substances Control Act and the Canadian Environmental Protection Act both authorize a wide variety of regulatory control measures on a chemical-specific, rather than media-specific, basis. Other statutes control the disposal of hazardous waste, at the federal level in the U.S. and primarily at the provincial level in Canada. Pesticide and consumer product legislation also could be used to limit dioxins in products.

Finally, food and drug statutes in both countries provide authority to control the sale of contaminated foods and food packaging. Both governments have established advisory levels for dioxins in foods. When new sources of environmental contamination are discovered, one of the first questions government officials face is whether contaminated foods are safe to eat. Thus determination of acceptable levels of dioxins in foods has been the "front line" regulatory response in both countries.

The regulatory frameworks established by food and drug legislation in Canada and the U.S. are very similar. In Canada Section 4 of the Food and Drugs Act prohibits the sale of any food that is "adulterated."[5] Cabinet is authorized by the act to issue regulations declaring foods to be adulterated if they contain prescribed substances or classes of substances. This authority has been used to ban some substances from foods altogether and to specify concentration limits for others.

Similarly the U.S. Food, Drug and Cosmetic Act prohibits the adulteration of any food sold in interstate commerce.[6] The Secretary of the federal Food and Drug Administration is authorized to issue regulations or "tolerances" specifying levels of specific substances, below which foods will be deemed exempt from the definition of adulteration.[7] The statute also contains the "Delaney clause," which prohibits the use of any food additives "found to induce cancer when ingested by man [sic] or animal."[8] However FDA considers that clause to apply only to substances that are intentionally added to foods.[9] In the case of environmental contaminants, like dioxins, the statute grants FDA somewhat greater discretion in establishing tolerances. The statute states that the Secretary "shall take into account the extent to which the use of such substance is required or cannot be avoided in the production" of certain food products.[10] FDA interprets this provision as requiring that the agency balance the risks to public health against the availability of the food supply.[11]

In both Canada and the United States, jurisdiction is shared between federal governments and state or provincial governments. The primary focus of this chapter will be on federal activities. Responsibility is also divided among the regulatory bodies that have authority to implement different statutes. In Canada, Health and Welfare Canada and Environment Canada have been most involved in assessing the risks posed by dioxins. In the u.s., the Environmental Protection Agency and Food and Drug Administration (fda) have been particularly active with respect to dioxins.

CHRONOLOGY OF EVENTS IN CANADA

In the late 1970s Canadian and u.s. scientists reported that they had detected dioxins in fish and the eggs of fish-eating birds in the Great Lakes region.[12] The discovery was cause for concern, since the extreme toxicity of dioxins was already well documented. In Canada the task of deciding whether the detected levels of contamination posed a threat to human health fell to Health and Welfare Canada. Since the contaminated fish were found in international waters, Canadian officials worked closely with their counterparts in the u.s. Food and Drug Administration, ultimately arriving at very similar conclusions.[13]

Health and Welfare Canada has issued two regulations concerning dioxins under the Food and Drugs Act. The first, promulgated in 1980, prohibits the sale of foods containing any level of chlorinated dioxins.[14] The regulation is characteristic of the regulatory approach that prevailed at a time when less sensitive detection techniques still allowed both the public and regulators to think of contamination in qualitative rather than quantitative terms. After TCDD was detected in Great Lakes fish, the standard was revised in 1982 to allow up to 20 parts per trillion (ppt) of 2,3,7,8-TCDD in fish.[15] The amendment had the illogical effect of allowing a higher level of only the most toxic dioxin, while maintaining a complete prohibition of all other dioxins in foods.

In late 1987 both the Canadian and u.s. press reported that pulp mills using chlorine bleaching were a source of dioxins in the environment.[16] u.s. government and industry studies had confirmed the presence of dioxins, including TCDD, in paper products and in fish caught downstream from mills. The discovery dramatically raised the profile both of dioxins and of pulp mill pollution in Canada, and sparked efforts to revise existing regulations concerning pulp mill effluents and dioxins in foods.

After the u.s. discovery the Canadian government undertook extensive sampling of fish, shellfish, and sediments in the vicinity of pulp mills using chlorine bleaching. The Department of Fisheries and Oceans subsequently closed fisheries in the vicinity of several B.C. mills on the advice of Health and Welfare Canada, based on levels of TCDD contamination in shellfish. Although the 20 ppt standard is still embodied in formal regulations, Health and Welfare Canada actually relies on a "tolerable daily intake" of TCDD of 10 picograms per kilogram of body weight per day (pg/kg/day) in evaluating the degree of hazard posed by contaminated foods.[17] (A picogram is one trillionth of a gram.) This tolerable daily intake is about twice the level of exposure to TCDD Health and Welfare originally considered acceptable in establishing the 20 ppt standard for fish. However the higher figure is used to evaluate the acceptability of exposure to all dioxins and furans by translating their risks into "TCDD equivalents," while the earlier standard was used to evaluate exposure to TCDD alone.

It is noteworthy that much of the food currently sold commercially in Canada violates the existing Food and Drug regulations, which prohibit any level of dioxins other than 2,3,7,8-TCDD, and any level of TCDD in foods other than fish. Studies have confirmed the presence of trace levels of dioxins and furans in many common foods, including fruits, vegetables, meat, fish, and milk.[18] A spokesperson for Health and Welfare Canada explained that "to apply the regulation as it now stands would really mean that such food couldn't be sold. The health department is considering whether to introduce a new dioxin standard to get around this problem."[19] Health and Welfare is likely to raise the acceptable levels, if not to revoke the regulation completely and replace it with nonbinding guidelines.

In 1990 Environment Canada and Health and Welfare formally placed dioxins and furans on the "List of Toxic Substances" under the new Canadian Environmental Protection Act (CEPA).[20] In doing so the federal government indicated its intent to develop regulations to limit dioxin releases from both incinerators and pulp mills. A draft CEPA regulation for pulp mills was subsequently circulated for public discussion in April 1990, formally proposed in December 1991, and finalized in May 1992.[21] The regulation requires that pulp mill effluents contain levels of TCDD that are "nondetectable" when measurements are made according to a protocol appended to the regulation.

In light of public concern with dioxins as well as international obligations under the Great Lakes Water Quality Agreement, there were strong incentives to write the pulp mill regulation so that it could be described as achieving "virtual elimination" of dioxins. In practice, however, the regulation is comparable to a numerical standard.

Environment Canada has indicated that it will only undertake enforcement actions if a polluter violates a standard of 20 parts per quadrillion (ppq), which represents federal chemists' estimate of the level of
contamination that can be measured with sufficient reliability to stand
up in court.[22] Interestingly the proposed regulation includes a numerical limit of 50 ppq for a structurally similar, but less politically controversial chemical, reportedly in response to the industry's
technological limitations.[23]

Although the regulation is worded such that the regulated industry
could face a moving target as advances in detection technology permit
measurement of increasingly low levels of dioxins, government officials
have publicly promised that amendments to the testing protocol are
not foreseen.[24] Moreover the 20 ppq limit for TCDD can be met with
control measures that the industry had already committed to install
"voluntarily." Technologies such as oxygen bleaching, which would further reduce releases of dioxins and other toxic substances, will not be
required in order for mills to meet the proposed federal regulation.

Several provinces have adopted their own regulations to control
dioxin releases from pulp mills. British Columbia and Alberta finalized
their regulatory requirements for the industry in advance of the federal
government, while Quebec took action shortly after the May 1992 publication of the federal regulations. Ontario finalized its own much-
delayed regulations in late 1993. Although only Ontario, Alberta, and
Quebec regulate dioxins directly, they and British Columbia all regulate
adsorbable organic halogens (AOX), which is a measure of total chlorinated organics in pulp mill effluents and thus an indirect limit on dioxins.[25] In contrast several of the smaller provinces have chosen to rely on
the federal regulations rather than develop their own.

Although all provinces have thus promised "virtual elimination" of
dioxins, the economic implications for the pulp and paper industry
in different provinces differ substantially. More stringent controls on
chlorinated discharges, including dioxins, will be required in provinces that have adopted stringent AOX standards than in those relying
only on the federal dioxin regulations.[26] For instance mills in Alberta
and British Columbia will be required to adopt oxygen bleaching,
while those in Atlantic Canada, which are covered only by the proposed federal regulations, will not.

CHRONOLOGY OF EVENTS IN
THE UNITED STATES

The U.S. Food and Drug Administration is responsible for regulating
contaminants in foods and food packaging. FDA worked with Health

and Welfare Canada to assess the risks after dioxins were detected in Great Lakes fish. In late 1981 FDA issued an advisory to Great Lakes states in response to a query from the governor of Michigan concerning the safety of fish caught in the Great Lakes.[27] FDA recommended that consumption of fish contaminated with less than 25 ppt of TCDD need not be restricted, but fish contaminated with between 25 and 50 ppt should be consumed at most twice per month, and fish contaminated with more than 50 ppt should never be consumed. The advisory was not binding; it merely represented federal guidance to state governments.

To date FDA has resisted issuing an enforceable standard under the Food and Drug Act. In late 1983 the agency was petitioned by a public interest group to set an enforceable 5 ppt tolerance for TCDD in foods. In denying the petition FDA argued that the 25 ppt advisory was adequately protective of public health, and that contamination of fish was a regional problem, which did not warrant federal action.[28] An agency official argued before Congress that scientific understanding of the risks posed by dioxin was insufficient to support FDA action in court.[29]

While FDA is responsible for establishing tolerances for foods once dioxins are present in the environment, the U.S. Environmental Protection Agency has primary responsibility for control of sources of dioxins. As yet there are no U.S. air or water pollution control regulations for sources of dioxins. However, EPA's assessment of the cancer risks posed by TCDD has greatly influenced numerous agency decisions and programs, most notably cleanup of abandoned hazardous waste disposal sites.

In 1984 EPA issued a water quality criteria document for TCDD.[30] The agency was required to do so by the Clean Water Act amendments of 1977, which specified that EPA publish criteria documents for TCDD and 64 other pollutants. In issuing that directive Congress effectively codified the terms of an earlier court-sanctioned settlement between the agency and an environmental group that had sued EPA for failure to implement the original 1972 act.[31] The TCDD criteria document offers EPA's advice to state water pollution control agencies, which are delegated authority to set ambient water quality standards, subject to EPA's approval, under the Clean Water Act.

In the criteria document, EPA estimated a lifetime cancer risk of one in a million at a TCDD concentration in ambient water of 0.013 parts per quadrillion.[32] The corresponding virtually safe dose of 0.006 pg/kg/day was roughly 1700 times less than Health and Welfare Canada's tolerable daily intake of 10 pg/kg/day.

There was pressure from within the agency for change soon after the risk assessment was first published. Staff in the hazardous waste division, in particular, were constrained by EPA's risk assessment for dioxin, since estimates of the carcinogenic risks of TCDD frequently overwhelmed estimates of risks posed by other chemicals and thus drove the entire decision-making process. In 1988 EPA proposed to increase its estimate of the dose corresponding to a one in a million risk by a factor of about 17, to 0.1 pg/kg/day, thus decreasing its assessment of the cancer risks posed by TCDD.[33] However the agency's Science Advisory Board subsequently rejected the proposal, and it was never adopted as agency policy.[34]

In 1988 EPA reached a settlement with two environmental groups that had sued the agency over its regulatory inaction concerning dioxins.[35] EPA agreed to take various actions to address dioxin releases from pulp mills, incinerators, and other sources according to a strict court-sanctioned timetable. One of the first actions the settlement required was publication of a multimedia risk assessment for TCDD in April 1990.[36] In preparing the risk assessment, EPA relied on its original potency estimate for TCDD rather than on the revised figure that had been proposed in 1988. Based on the risk assessment the agency concluded that control of disposal of TCDD-contaminated sludge from pulp mills is warranted, and has since published a proposed regulation under the Toxic Substances Control Act.[37] EPA also indicated that it would revise its existing regulations for pulp mill effluents, in addition to overseeing state implementation of TCDD water quality standards under the Clean Water Act.

The promised draft regulation for the industry was published in November 1993 and is expected to be finalized in 1995.[38] In the absence of a final dioxin regulation, however, there was nonetheless considerable activity at the state level as a result of the water quality planning requirements of the federal water pollution control statute. Under the 1987 amendments to the Clean Water Act states were required in 1990 to submit for EPA's approval strategies to achieve water quality criteria in problem areas within three years. Most States chose to adopt EPA's proposed criterion for TCDD of 0.013 ppq, corresponding to a one in a million risk. However, several southern states challenged EPA's risk assessment and proposed TCDD criteria that were approximately 100 times greater. Although EPA refused to approve Georgia's proposed standard of 7.2 ppq, the agency did accept two other states' standards of 1.2 ppq.[39] Both states relied on FDA's, rather than EPA's, assessment of the potency of TCDD, and also accepted risks of greater than one in a million.

The new state water quality standards prompted EPA regional offices and individual states to revise many pulp mills' discharge permits to include requirements for control of releases of dioxins. The water quality criteria adopted by different states have significant implications for the stringency of individual pulp mills' permits. In devising control strategies, state agencies must estimate the maximum loading of toxic pollutants consistent with their water quality criteria and allocate them among known sources. Thus states with more sources will be required to impose more stringent requirements.

This approach effectively caps total dioxin releases – in contrast to technology-based regulations proposed by the Canadian government, which would allow dioxin releases to increase as production increases. In fact water-quality-based standards could potentially be more stringent than technologically or economically achievable by individual mills. Mills in states with more lenient water quality criteria than EPA expect to satisfy their permit requirements with readily available control technology.[40] Mills in other states will be required to adopt costly additional technologies, including oxygen bleaching. It is noteworthy that there have been court challenges to most, if not all, of the permit revisions issued to date to control dioxin releases from pulp mills.[41]

It appears that the stricter water-quality-based state requirements will be reinforced by the forthcoming technology-based national regulations. In addition to proposing "virtual elimination" of dioxin discharges by 1998, a standard comparable to the Canadian regulation (albeit three years later), the U.S. agency has proposed additional process changes with the intent of further reducing formation of dioxins and other chlorinated toxins. As many as 127 of 350 U.S. mills will be required to install oxygen bleaching, and a small number of sulphite mills currently relying on chlorine bleaching will be required to completely eliminate the use of chlorine in their operations.[42]

FDA has neither taken regulatory action nor updated its original regional advisory to state governments since the discovery that pulp mills located throughout the United States are a source of dioxins. The agency collaborated with EPA in preparing the 1990 multimedia risk assessment for TCDD. Among the many sources of exposure to TCDD evaluated, TCDD-contaminated food containers, such as cardboard milk cartons, fall within FDA's jurisdiction. Both EPA and FDA concluded that, although the risk to consumers from contaminated packaging is small, it nevertheless can and should be reduced. However the news release and subsequent statements by FDA officials have promised to oversee only *voluntary* measures undertaken by paper manufacturers rather than regulation of food packaging.[43]

ASSESSING THE HEALTH RISKS
OF DIOXINS

The TCDD case illustrates many of the controversies surrounding cancer risk assessment. Two factors exacerbate the uncertainties concerning TCDD's effects on humans. First, TCDD is never intentionally manufactured; it is only produced as an unwanted byproduct of certain manufacturing processes. As a result human exposure inevitably involves concurrent exposure to other substances that may also be toxic, making it difficult to ascertain the effects of TCDD alone. Second, because it is an unintended trace contaminant, levels of TCDD in products or waste streams often have not been carefully controlled or even measured. This further complicates epidemiological studies, since after the fact it is difficult to know who was exposed and to what degree.[44]

One clearly demonstrated effect of exposure to dioxins is chloracne, a disfiguring skin condition that can persist for years after exposure.[45] Other symptoms reported to be associated with exposure to dioxins include nausea, headaches, depression, sexual dysfunction, reproductive problems, and cancer. Numerous epidemiological studies have focused on the incidence of cancer and birth defects among humans exposed to TCDD, with conflicting and highly controversial results.[46] Epidemiological studies of cancer rates among the population exposed to dioxins after an industrial explosion in Seveso, Italy, and among Viet Nam veterans exposed to dioxin-contaminated Agent Orange generally have been negative. However other epidemiological studies of populations exposed during spraying of forests with dioxin-contaminated pesticides have reported elevated rates of miscarriages and rare forms of cancer.[47]

Recent charges of deliberate evidence manipulation in two earlier industry-sponsored studies of workers exposed to dioxins raise questions about those studies' conclusions that there were no detectable increases in rates of disease.[48] In 1991 the largest study to date of industrial workers exposed to dioxins found positive evidence of human carcinogenicity among those with relatively high exposures to dioxins, but the results were equivocal for those with lower exposures.[49] It is too early to draw conclusions about the impact of these recent developments on government policies concerning dioxin.

In the absence of conclusive epidemiological evidence government scientists have historically relied heavily on animal studies. TCDD is extraordinarily toxic to laboratory animals in both acute and chronic studies. It has been identified as the most potent carcinogen and teratogen ever tested to date in rodents.[50] The relevance of animal studies to humans, however, is clouded by the fact that TCDD's toxicity varies greatly among animal species – the acutely lethal dose of TCDD for guinea pigs is thousands of times less than that for hamsters – and different health effects have been observed in different species.[51]

The mechanism by which TCDD causes cancer in animals has been the subject of heated debate. As discussed in chapter 2, there is disagreement within the scientific community about how one should assess the risks of cancer initiators and promoters. There is convincing experimental evidence that TCDD is a potent cancer promoter. However the question remains whether it also is capable of initiating carcinogenesis,[52] or whether it causes cancer via some other indirect mechanism.[53] The assumed mechanism has important implications for the choice of risk assessment methodology and thus for resultant estimates of acceptable levels of exposure.[54]

In animal studies an increased incidence of cancer is typically observed only among groups of animals exposed to higher experimental doses. The "safety factor" approach to risk assessment, reviewed in the preceding chapter, assumes that the absence of adverse effects among groups of animals exposed to lower doses provides evidence of a threshold below which a substance presents no risk.[55] A safety factor, typically between 10 and 1000, is applied to the highest dose at which no adverse health effects were detected in laboratory animals (known as the "no observed adverse effects level") in order to estimate a safe level of exposure for humans. The safety factor allows for the possibility of greater sensitivity in humans than in the experimental animals and for differences in sensitivity among humans. Scientists who have concluded that TCDD acts only as a cancer promoter generally advocate the use of the safety factor approach to derive an "acceptable daily intake" for dioxins.

The leading alternative for assessing the risks posed by carcinogens involves reliance on mathematical models to predict a dose-response function. The model U.S. regulatory agencies have traditionally used assumes a linear dose-response relationship at low doses.[56] Those scientists who believe that TCDD may be an initiator generally support reliance on this approach. Others favour reliance on a linear mathematical model in the absence of conclusive evidence one way or the other concerning the mechanism of TCDD's effects, simply because the approach provides more conservative (i.e., risk averse) estimates in the case of TCDD.

The two approaches lead to very different estimates of acceptable levels of exposure. Using the safety factor approach, Health and Welfare Canada arrived at an estimate of an acceptable daily intake of

TCDD that is approximately 1700 times greater than the estimate of the "virtually safe dose" derived by the U.S. Environmental Protection Agency using a linear mathematical model. The discrepancy is of more than theoretical interest: estimates of current levels of human exposure fall between these two estimates.[57] Thus the choice of risk assessment methodology could determine regulators' conclusions concerning the need for costly control measures.

RECONSTRUCTING THE CANADIAN RISK ASSESSMENT

When it originally promulgated regulations under the Food and Drugs Act, Health and Welfare Canada did not publish its rationale. An advisory committee on dioxins, subsequently appointed by the federal government, reported that Health and Welfare used a safety factor of 218 in arriving at the 20 ppt standard for TCDD in fish.[58] Reliance on such an unusual safety factor strongly suggests that factors other than health risks were taken into account in setting the standard.

Health and Welfare Canada more recently arrived at a "tolerable daily intake" of 10 pg/kg/day TCDD by applying a safety factor of 100.[59] The report on dioxins recently issued by the federal government relies on the safety factor approach based on two assumptions: that TCDD is not genotoxic, and that a threshold exists for non-genotoxic carcinogens.[60] It seems unlikely, however, that this was Health and Welfare's original reasoning in the early 1980s when it first used the safety factor approach to derive the 20 ppt standard for TCDD in fish. At that time mathematical models were just being introduced, and reliance on safety factors simply was the standard toxicological approach. It is interesting that the 1990 report discusses neither alternative assumptions concerning TCDD's mechanism of impact nor other methodologies for assessing risks of carcinogenicity. Nor does it mention that U.S. estimates of acceptable exposures to TCDD are substantially lower.

The Ontario provincial government also has rejected the mathematical modelling approach.[61] Like Health and Welfare Canada, the provincial government applied a safety factor of 100 to arrive at an allowable daily intake of 10 pg/kg/day. Although Canadian government scientists at both the federal and provincial level have relied exclusively on safety factors in assessing the risks of dioxins, other Canadian scientists have been more receptive to other risk assessment approaches. A 1981 National Research Council report on dioxin used a variety of models to estimate a range of tolerable doses 100 to 300 times less than Health and Welfare's recommended maximum daily intake.[62] A federally appointed expert advisory committee, which relied on both safety factors and mathematical models, was also more cautious than Health and Welfare Canada in recommending tolerable daily exposures.[63]

RECONSTRUCTING U.S. RISK ASSESSMENTS

In contrast to Health and Welfare Canada, both FDA and EPA ostensibly relied on mathematical models that assume linearity at low doses in estimating cancer risks from TCDD. However, there were significant differences between the approaches of the two U.S. agencies.

Like Health and Welfare Canada, FDA originally did not publish a rationale for its advisory level for TCDD in fish. Subsequent statements by FDA representatives estimated the lifetime risk of cancer from consumption of fish contaminated with 25 ppt TCDD to be three in a million based on a linear mathematical model.[64] This conclusion relies on an elaborate set of exposure assumptions.[65]

It is striking that FDA and Health and Welfare, working cooperatively, arrived at similar standards at the same time, yet subsequently offered widely different rationales. There is reason to believe that FDA, like the Canadian agency, initially relied on the safety factor approach and only later constructed the alternative rationale. An early paper by an FDA official justified the 25 ppt TCDD advisory level based on application of a safety factor of 70 and slightly different exposure assumptions.[66] A 1984 letter responding to a public interest group, which had argued that FDA had relied upon a safety factor, stated: "The agency acknowledges that at one time it held the views attributed to it in the petitions. However as the petitions also acknowledge, FDA has established the risk of cancer from exposure to TCDD in fish and has used a linear extrapolation model to do so. Therefore, the agency has revised its views on TCDD risk assessment, but, as dictated below, it still finds no basis for changing the advisory."[67]

FDA's reluctance to take regulatory actions may be explained by evidence that agency scientists simply are not convinced by their own risk assessments. In 1989 one FDA scientist stated, "Nobody knows the risk (of TCDD), so the consumers and the environmentalists can make a day of it and the toxicologists can't say they're wrong ... But none of us believe it."[68]

EPA was the first regulatory agency worldwide to rely on a mathematical model to estimate the risks posed by TCDD. Although other U.S. agencies subsequently followed suit, EPA's risk estimate remained the most conservative due to minor differences in assumptions. Among U.S. agencies, EPA and FDA differed by the greatest amount.

FDA's estimate of the dose corresponding to a one in a million risk is approximately nine times higher than EPA's figure.[69] (In other words FDA estimates the risk of cancer to be nine times less.) The fact that other countries, including Canada, established even higher acceptable daily doses than FDA using the safety factor approach made EPA's risk assessment vulnerable to criticism as overly conservative.

In 1988 EPA proposed to increase its estimate of the virtually safe dose of 2,3,7,8-TCDD by a factor of about 17, to 0.1 pg/kg/day. The agency's proposal acknowledged that other countries rely upon a safety factor approach, but concluded that in the absence of an understanding of the mechanism of TCDD's effects, an "approach that recognizes the possibility of linearity at low doses and presents estimates in terms of plausible upper bounds would be preferable."[70] EPA acknowledged divergence among equally plausible non-threshold models for estimating cancer risks at low doses and selected a figure amid the range of available estimates. The proposal described the new value as a "reasonable science policy position."[71]

The EPA proposal generated considerable publicity. Many of the agency's critics did not agree that selecting the mid-point of a variety of plausible models was an appropriate way to deal with scientific uncertainty.[72] One of EPA's most visible critics was Dr Ellen Silbergeld, a scientist with the Environmental Defense Fund (EDF), which at the time was suing EPA over its lack of regulatory action on dioxin.[73] Dr Silbergeld was well placed to register her objections, since she was a member of the EPA Science Advisory Board (SAB) panel that reviewed the dioxin proposal. The review panel's report agreed with the agency that the original linear model is flawed and uncertain. However it refused to condone EPA's proposal to deviate from the model's predictions in the absence of an accepted alternative. The panel concluded that the agency could revise its risk assessment "for policy reasons," but that there was "no scientific basis for such a change at this time."[74]

The panel limited itself to reviewing the merits of the 1988 proposal, as EPA had requested, without reevaluating the 1984 risk assessment that the agency sought to revise. Although the panel chair insisted that the SAB review did not reflect an endorsement of the existing standard,[75] the panel's rejection of the proposed revision nevertheless buttressed the status quo. The panel in effect subjected the proposed revision to a more stringent standard of review than the original risk assessment.[76] Their conclusion that EPA could still make the change as a "policy" decision, while denying the scientific defensibility of the proposed revision, effectively discredited the proposal. In essence the reviewers offered an informed "science policy" position of their own that differed from that of EPA.

Although the rebuff from the Science Advisory Board led EPA to rely on its original risk assessment in recent decision making, the agency subsequently began to marshal evidence for another attempt to revise its dioxin potency estimate. In 1991 the EPA administrator launched another review of the 1985 risk assessment after a meeting of 38 scientists cosponsored by EPA, FDA, and the industry-affiliated Chlorine Institute reached consensus that dioxin acts through a receptor-mediated mechanism, which many of those present argued was consistent with the existence of a threshold.[77] The agency has proposed to develop an alternative to the linear model used previously to better reflect current understanding of the biological mechanism.[78] Initial indications are that, although EPA may downgrade its estimate of cancer risks at very low levels of exposure, there is increasing concern with respect to the potential reproductive and immunological effects of dioxins.[79]

BALANCING THE RISKS AND BENEFITS

Whether risk assessors rely on safety factors or mathematical models, they cannot avoid introducing value judgments. Policy decisions are embedded both in the assumptions underlying mathematical models and in the choice of a safety factor. However an important difference between the two approaches is that, in practice, safety factors are chosen on a case-by-case basis, while the assumptions underlying computer models are identified once and for all when the model is developed.

While the modelling approach strives for explicit assumptions and sequential risk assessment and risk management decisions, these two steps can be readily fused in the selection of a safety factor. Policy makers not only have greater flexibility to take factors other than health risks into account in the choice of safety factors, they can do so invisibly. Health and Welfare's reliance on an unusual safety factor of 218 in setting the standard of 20 ppt TCDD in fish leads one to ask which was selected first – the safety factor or the standard?

It is likely that health and economic factors were considered simultaneously. Interestingly FDA stated at the time that Health and Welfare Canada had chosen a standard of 20 ppt, slightly below the U.S. standard of 25 ppt, "in order to help assure that fish imported into the U.S. from Lake Ontario [would] not contain dioxin at levels believed by the FDA to be unsafe."[80] Even though factors other than health risks appear to have been influential in setting the 20 ppt standard, it nevertheless has been widely depicted by government spokespersons and the media as Health and Welfare Canada's judgment of what is "safe."

Early statements by Canadian government representatives indicated a preference for persuasion and guidelines, rather than enforceable regulations, to control sources of dioxins. One paper by government officials stated, "In the case of pentachlorophenol [a wood preservative commonly contaminated with dioxins], it was particularly important to consider the effect of any regulations on a billion dollar lumber industry ... the already restricted use pattern in Canada combined with some encouragement to the wood industry to be more prudent with respect to environmental and occupational exposure by the development of Codes of Good Practise, would alleviate many potential problems."[81]

The 1990 decision to list dioxins and furans as "Toxic Substances" under CEPA and to develop enforceable federal regulations for certain sources, however, reflects a trend toward a more formal and open regulatory process in Canada. The rationale for the federal government's decision to list the chemicals was well documented and released for public discussion. Extensive stakeholder consultations and public information meetings were subsequently held on the proposed pulp mill regulations.

In the United States FDA also considered factors other than health risks in establishing its advisory level for TCDD in fish as authorized by its statute. One agency representative suggested that 25 ppt "represented a level of risk acceptable to public health while resulting in minimal impact on the availability of Great Lakes fish as a food source."[82] FDA chose an advisory level of 25 ppt, which happened to be higher than the typical levels of TCDD detected at the time in samples of commercial fish species collected from the Great Lakes.[83] The state of detection technology apparently also was considered. The same spokesperson argued that "to set the concern level much lower than 25 ppt would in fact be forcing the technology beyond its current state of the art and thus could not provide a scientific basis for legal actions that might be taken."[84] The fact that U.S. and Canadian officials worked together suggests that these same factors influenced Health and Welfare Canada's choice of a 20 ppt standard.

INTEREST GROUP INVOLVEMENT IN REGULATORY SCIENCE

Environmental controversies involving dioxin have been heated in both countries. One might question whether pressure from politicians, industry, or environmental groups has influenced regulators' risk assessments. There have been occasional allegations of political or industry interference in EPA's science policy decisions concerning dioxins. Greenpeace has argued, "It would be naïve to think that the chlorine- and organochlorine-producing industry ... have had no influence on the colour of dioxin science."[85] However two controversial attempts to weaken EPA's risk assessment were defeated, through Congressional oversight in one case and by EPA's own science advisors in another.[86] In Canada regulation of dioxins in pesticides, wood preservatives, and pulp mill effluents has important implications for the economically significant forest industry. Yet there is no evidence that either environmental groups or industry have *directly* influenced government scientists' risk assessments. Nonetheless government scientists in Canada and the U.S. operate within very different political environments, a factor that *indirectly* influences their decisions.

Regulatory science clearly is much more politicized in the U.S., where legislators, interest groups, and the media are attentive to the scientific basis of government decisions. As Weinberg observed, in the United States, "the debates on trans-scientific issues are particularly noisy."[87] A draft version of EPA's proposal to revise its dioxin risk assessment received front-page coverage in the *New York Times* even before it was made public.[88] And virtually every assumption underlying EPA's cancer risk assessment models has been the subject of intense public scrutiny.[89]

In contrast the scientific basis for Health and Welfare Canada's original food regulations for dioxins was never explained to the public, let alone challenged, and the fact that the department is currently reviewing those standards has received almost no public attention. Although the Canadian federal government did publish the scientific rationale for its recent decision to regulate various sources of dioxins and furans under CEPA, the report was prepared and finalized internally, with no opportunity for public input. There was no acknowledgment that policy decisions could enter into the risk assessment stage of regulatory decision making. Moreover the concise 60-page CEPA report is a striking contrast to the 600-page EPA Health Assessment Document for TCDD.

Differences in risk communication strategies also are evident. Canadian officials clearly place greater emphasis than their U.S. counterparts on avoiding undue public alarm. One government official offered that "there will always be some level of concern associated with any chemical, but it serves no purpose to worry people."[90] In their public statements about dioxins, Canadian government officials repeatedly promised absolute safety, even at the expense of exaggerating the degree of scientific certainty. When the Department of Fisheries and Oceans released evidence of dioxins detected in salmon, for example, the press release stated that "there is nothing in there that poses a potential risk to the health of anyone who consumes salmon harvested in the commercial fishery."[91] Another Canadian official commented on dioxins in human breast milk, "It has no relevance to human safety when you get down to these extremely low levels."[92] In contrast an EPA spokesperson couched his conclusions in double negatives and caveats in commenting on dioxins in paper products that "there is no basis to conclude at this time that these products are unsafe."[93] Another EPA representative testified before a Congressional committee that "EPA professionals do not use the word 'safe.'"[94]

EVALUATION

Incorporation of Science

The case study reveals that Canadian and U.S. regulators relied on different methodologies to derive risk estimates amid scientific uncertainty, with divergent results. The "virtually safe doses" of TCDD calculated by EPA and FDA are 0.006 pg/kg/day and 0.057 pg/kg/day, respectively. Other U.S. agencies have reported VSD's between those two figures. All U.S. agencies have relied on mathematical models to estimate statistical risks of cancer, and all normally report the "one in a million" dose. In contrast, Health and Welfare Canada has estimated an acceptable daily intake of TCDD of 10 pg/kg/day, based on a safety factor of 100. Ontario, the Netherlands, New York State, and Germany also have relied on safety factors in arriving at ADIs of 10, 4, 2, and 1 pg/kg/day respectively.[95]

Given the uncertainties, it is not surprising that there are discrepancies between risk assessments for TCDD. The distribution of scientists supporting the two methodologies for assessing the risks of TCDD, however, is not random. While risk assessment professionals within U.S. government agencies all support a modelling approach for TCDD, at least publicly, scientists at Health and Welfare Canada support the safety factor approach. Scientific opinion within each country has not been unanimous, however. Within Canada, scientific advisors outside the federal government were more receptive than Health and Welfare to mathematical models. In the U.S., industry scientists and some academics have criticized EPA's approach as overly cautious. Yet among regulators in each country, only one methodology has prevailed. It is the *regulatory science* that has differed between the two countries, not the research science.

Jasanoff and others have suggested that the countries' divergent approaches to evaluating the risks of toxic substances reflect broad differences in political culture.[96] They argue that EPA places greater emphasis on explicit scientific rationales for its decisions because, operating in a more adversarial political environment, it needs the credibility offered by science. Jasanoff suggests that U.S. regulators must find the methodological rigour of formal mathematical models particularly appealing, since the models rely on explicit assumptions at each step and provide a quantitative estimate of risk that at least appears less subjective than that derived with safety factors.[97] It is noteworthy that in its current effort to revise its dioxin risk assessment, EPA is attempting to develop a new computer model to replace its linear model rather than simply adopting the safety factor approach used by other countries to evaluate TCDD.

Brickman, Jasanoff, and Ilgen note that in Europe science reinforces the traditional authority of the state, while in the U.S., it is used as a replacement for authority.[98] Ironically, EPA's efforts to derive credibility from science often backfire, since the adversarial nature of U.S. politics spills over into discussions of regulatory science. The dioxin case suggests that Canadian regulators may behave more like their European counterparts.

Although political culture can help to explain the divergence between national styles of regulatory science, it cannot account for differences within countries, such as those observed between EPA and FDA. FDA operates within the same untrusting American political culture as EPA, yet FDA officials' behaviour and regulatory science decisions in many respects were closer to those of Health and Welfare Canada than of EPA.[99] The differences between FDA and EPA lie in different statutory mandates, which can either shield an agency or expose it to its critics.

Many of the statutes that EPA administers direct the agency to set standards to provide absolute protection of human health – without regard to cost or even technological feasibility. Those statutes typically limit the agency's discretion by providing specific directives to protect human health, while at the same time empowering interest groups to sue EPA to compel performance of non-discretionary actions. This fact explains why EPA was first to publish a risk assessment for dioxin: EPA's 1984 water quality criteria document was mandated by the terms of an earlier legal settlement with a public interest group.

Although FDA avoided challenging its sibling agency by ostensibly adopting an approach similar to EPA's, it nevertheless maintained an advisory level for TCDD in fish that is even higher than Health and Welfare Canada's. The relevant provisions of the statute that FDA administers were passed in an earlier era of greater Congressional deference to regulatory agencies, and thus allow the agency considerable discretion to control environmental contaminants in foods. After the fact, FDA was able to construct an alternative rationale for its original advisory that at least appeared consistent with the EPA approach only because it had not been required to offer a justification for its advisory level in the first place. Moreover because FDA has statutory discretion, interest groups have not been able to use litigation to force the agency to issue regulations.

Timing and Stringency

Does it matter that the two countries' regulatory science policies differ? Differences between risk assessments can be significant because they can lead to differences in regulatory standards. However risk assessment is not the only factor that influences the setting of standards.

There are few regulatory standards for dioxin in either country to serve as a basis for comparison. Environment Canada has revised its regulations for pulp mill effluents to require nondetectable concentrations of dioxins. Although EPA's deliberations are clearly proceeding at a slower pace, it seems likely that the U.S. standards ultimately will be most stringent. EPA has indicated its intent not only to match the Canadian nondetectability requirement for dioxins by 1998, but to require additional process changes comparable to those of the stricter Canadian provinces and stricter than the Canadian national standards. Moreover even in the absence of a final U.S. regulation, strict water quality planning requirements of the U.S. statute have forced state regulators to revise mills' permits to incorporate requirements comparable to, if not stricter than, the Canadian standard.

The one area where both countries have already finalized standards is for dioxins in foods. FDA and Health and Welfare Canada's conclusions about acceptable levels of TCDD in fish were similar in both timing and stringency, which is not surprising since the Canadian and U.S. standards were developed jointly. One difference is that FDA's standard is only advisory, while the Canadian regulations for dioxins in food are enforceable. However, this difference has had no impact since the Canadian regulations have not been enforced. FDA and Health and Welfare Canada justified comparable TCDD limits in fish, despite widely different potency estimates, by adopting different exposure assumptions. (In contrast, in recommending its water quality criterion for TCDD, EPA implicitly judged the acceptable level of TCDD in fish to be 350 times less than FDA's recommended limit.[100])

In some respects it is striking that the regulatory initiatives taken to date by the U.S. and Canadian governments have not differed more widely in light of the tremendous disparity between their estimates of the risks posed by TCDD. One reason for the substantial degree of convergence is that even the less stringent Canadian risk assessment led regulators to conclude that regulatory controls for pulp mills are warranted. Although *average* levels of exposure to dioxins fall below the Canadian tolerable daily intake, many subpopulations are exposed to levels of dioxin that exceed even the Health and Welfare Canada guidelines.[101]

Another explanation may lie in U.S. regulators' lack of faith in their own risk assessments. EPA's approval of less stringent state objectives for TCDD and the agency's efforts to revise its original risk assessment reflect rising pressure both from within EPA and from scientists in other agencies to reconsider the conservative assumptions underlying EPA's original risk assessment.[102] The fact that Canadian and U.S. regulators have developed comparable standards for dioxins in foods and also displayed relatively similar intentions to regulate pulp mill effluents, despite divergent risk assessments, indicates that one should not overstate the significance of differences in risk assessments, since it is still possible for agencies to adopt more or less stringent regulations by taking other factors into account.

Risk-Benefit Balancing

Although only Canada has issued final standards for dioxins in pulp mill effluents to date, it is possible to comment on risk-benefit balancing in establishing recommended Canadian and U.S. tolerances for TCDD in fish. FDA and Health and Welfare Canada weighed costs and benefits similarly in arriving at comparable recommendations for TCDD in fish in the early 1980s. Later statements by FDA representatives imply that an advisory level just above average levels of contamination in commercial species sampled at the time was selected to avoid adverse economic impacts on the Great Lakes' commercial fisheries and on consumers that rely on those products. Interestingly, although subsequent Congressional inquiries forced FDA to offer a public explanation for its advisory level, Health and Welfare Canada has never explained the basis for its regulations.

Representativeness

Neither FDA nor Health and Welfare Canada consulted the public or interest groups in establishing their advisory levels for TCDD in fish in the early 1980s. Canadian authorities were not required by statute to invite public input, and FDA was not bound by the U.S. requirements for notice and comment rulemaking because it was issuing an unenforceable guideline rather than a formal regulation.

In contrast, there have been avenues for public involvement in both countries' recent efforts to develop dioxin regulations for pulp mill effluents, though it has taken different forms in Canada and the United States. In the u.s. lawsuits by environmental groups were instrumental in committing EPA to issue new pulp mill regulations. The agency's recent regulatory proposal will be subject to a formal process for public review, and if experience is any judge, to eventual litigation by both the affected industry and environmental groups. Dozens of lawsuits have already been launched challenging recent revisions of pulp mills' permits. Canadian regulators have departed from the closed industry-government bargaining of the past in holding public information meetings and consensual "multistakeholder consultations" on their new pulp mill regulations. It is noteworthy, however, that the Canadian regulations were not challenged in court.

Although the extent of public involvement in risk *management* decisions in the two countries has been similar, public involvement in risk *assessment* has been much greater in the United States. Canadian and u.s. government scientists interviewed for this chapter all volunteered a caveat that risk assessment is not "science." Typical comments include, "It's not science at this stage," and, "It's all smoke and mirrors."[103] Yet it is striking that in Canada, regulatory science is left to government scientists, who remain relatively insulated from interest group politics, while u.s. government scientists conduct their risk assessments under the watchful eye of the media, interest groups, and Congressional committees.

Although EPA's dioxin risk assessment was prepared by agency scientists, their methodological assumptions had previously been subjected to extensive public review. Moreover their conclusions were subjected to a rigourous critique by external scientists, which carried sufficient weight to veto EPA's 1988 proposal to revise its risk assessment for TCDD. In contrast, the regulatory science that underlay Health and Welfare Canada's decisions remained shielded from public debate. It is interesting that there is little evidence that Canadian interest groups sought greater involvement at the risk assessment stage. With the exception of Greenpeace, which has rejected formal risk assessment by any methodology, Canadian environmental groups did not challenge Health and Welfare Canada's evaluation of the health risks of dioxins, even while engaged in an extensive campaign for control of pulp mill effluents.

Regulators' risk communication strategies reflect the different approaches. The tone of the 1990 Canadian assessment of dioxins under CEPA is one of *explaining* scientific information to a trusting lay public. In contrast, EPA's health assessment document seeks to *justify* policy decisions to a skeptical and scientifically sophisticated audience.

CONCLUSIONS

Many features of the dioxin case reinforce the general themes of this study. In the cases of formaldehyde, saccharin, alachlor, and Alar, U.S. regulators relied on mathematical models to assess the risks of potential carcinogens, while Health and Welfare Canada relied on the more traditional safety factor approach.[104] The growing body of evidence is suggestive of national styles of regulatory science. Features of the U.S. style include publication of explicit scientific rationales for regulatory decisions, reliance on consistent and explicit risk assessment principles, and open public debate over the scientific aspects of public policy. The Canadian style is exemplified by closed decision making, case-by-case review, and the absence of public debate over the scientific basis for government decisions. The Canadian style tends to treat the hybrid endeavour, regulatory science, like research science, while the U.S. style stresses the policy, and thus political, aspects of regulatory science.

The differences observed between FDA and EPA in this case study suggest an important caveat, however. The "U.S. style" is most clearly reflected in the implementation of the non-discretionary environmental, health, and safety statutes passed by the U.S. Congress since 1970. However more closed and traditional styles of regulatory decision making survive within the U.S. as vestiges of a more deferential past.

The history of U.S. and Canadian risk assessments for dioxin is an increasingly familiar tale of debates within the scientific community played out in the political arena. Uncertainty among scientists creates the possibility of large disparities between different governments' policies. However the pattern of differences that emerges reflects the context in which regulatory science decisions are made within each agency and within each country. The political environment has implications not just for how regulatory science is received, but for how it is conducted.

4 Forbidden Fruit: Regulating the Pesticides Alachlor and Alar

INTRODUCTION

Pesticides confront regulators with a classic risk-benefit trade-off. While pesticides can greatly increase agricultural productivity, they can also pose threats to the environment and to human health, such as cancer and birth defects.[1] Humans are exposed to pesticides during application, through residue on food, and through groundwater contamination. This chapter examines two regulatory controversies involving pesticides. The first, alachlor, is a clear case of policy divergence.[2] Canada banned the substance, while the United States kept it on the market with minimal restrictions. The second case, Alar, is less straightforward. After a great deal of negative publicity, the manufacturer withdrew the product from the market in North America, obviating the need for regulatory action in either country. Nonetheless the u.s. was much more aggressive in its regulatory stance toward the product.

This chapter highlights a number of important themes. First, like other chapters in this volume, this one reveals the fundamentally different styles of regulatory science used in the u.s. and Canada. However, unlike other cases studies in this book, in the case of alachlor the Canadian approach resulted in a more stringent decision by regulators. Second, this chapter explores the different approaches the two governments use to communicate information about risks to the public, and the consequences of those approaches. Finally, the Alar case demonstrates both the extraordinary role interest groups and the media can play in shaping public risk perceptions and the vulnerability of the Canadian system to actions that occur south of the border.

REGULATORY FRAMEWORKS

The basic structures of pesticide regulation in Canada and the U.S. are similar. Both countries regulate pesticides through two approaches. The "front-end" approach is based on controlling the introduction of new products into the marketplace. The U.S. Federal Insecticide, Fungicide, and Rodenticide Act (FIFRA) prohibits the sale of pesticides unless they are registered with the federal government.[3] In Canada the same basic restriction is imposed by the Pest Control Products Act (PCPA).[4] Jurisdiction over pesticide regulation, however, is different in the two countries. In the U.S. pesticides are regulated by the Environmental Protection Agency; in Canada they are regulated by Agriculture Canada, although Health and Welfare Canada also plays an important role.[5] Under a 1982 inderdepartmental agreement, Health and Welfare assesses the safety of pesticides, and Agriculture determines whether the identified risks are "acceptable."[6]

The second, "back-end," approach is the regulation of food quality through restrictions on food adulteration. This approach originated in the U.S. in the Pure Food and Drug Act of 1906, but the most recent restrictions are contained in the 1954 amendments to the Federal Food, Drug, and Cosmetic Act.[7] This act requires EPA to set limits on the amount of pesticide residues in food, called "tolerances." In Canada similar restrictions are imposed by Health and Welfare Canada under the Food and Drugs Act. While occasional references will be made to various aspects of this "back-end" approach, this chapter focuses primarily on the "front-end," pesticide registration.

Both Canadian and U.S. front-end statutes give their respective governments the authority to remove chemicals from the market when new information raises health, safety, or environmental concerns. EPA's "special review" program involves the intensive scrutiny of chemicals that are considered to have the potential to pose unreasonable risks. Once the agency concludes that certain risk triggers – such as a finding that the chemical produces cancer in mice – have been exceeded, it initiates a special review. However if the registrant successfully rebuts the agency argument, or if other data alleviate the agency's concern, the special review is terminated. If the agency's concerns are not alleviated it formulates a proposed regulatory position. This can take the form of label changes or cancellation of the pesticide's registration. This procedure is similar to an informal rulemaking under the Administrative Procedures Act, where all decisions are extensively documented, opportunities for comment by all interested parties are provided at several stages, and the agency is required to respond to comments in making its final determination.

The Canadian government does not have a similar formal program of special review. Like the u.s. statute, however, the Canadian PCPA allows the minister of agriculture to remove a product from the market when "the safety of the control product or its merit or value for its intended purpose is no longer acceptable to him [or her]."[8] In the u.s., FIFRA gives EPA the authority to remove pesticides from the market if they are found to present an unreasonable balance of risks and benefits.

Both countries have elaborate review procedures to protect the interests of registrants. Canadian regulations provide for appeal of that suspension or cancellation by the registrant within 30 days of the agriculture minister's notice of intent. If an appeal is made, the minister must establish a review board, which must then conduct hearings and file a report containing recommendations with the minister. The minister can accept or reject the recommendations of the review board.[9]

In the u.s. the administrative procedures for revoking a pesticide registration are even more cumbersome. FIFRA gives registrants the right to appeal EPA cancellation decisions to an administrative law judge, who conducts the proceedings like a formal trial. The administrative law judge's recommendations are then reported to the EPA administrator, who has the discretion to accept or reject the recommendations.[10] The appeal procedures in both countries are available only to the registrant. Once an appeal is launched, however, other actors – such as farm groups or environmentalists – may participate in the hearings in both countries.

ALACHLOR

Alachlor, which is used to control weeds, was first registered for use in Canada and the United States in 1969 by the Monsanto Chemical Company. By the early 1980s alachlor had become the most widely used herbicide in the world. Approximately 80 million pounds are used in the u.s. annually. About 91 percent of alachlor use is on two crops, corn (63 percent) and soybeans (28 percent).[11] In the late 1970s the tests upon which alachlor was originally registered were shown to be invalid.[12] Monsanto submitted replacement studies in 1982, which raised concerns about the carcinogenicity of the chemical.

As a result the u.s. EPA initiated a "special review" of alachlor in January 1985.[13] In October of 1986 the agency announced a regulatory proposal to place relatively minor restrictions on the use of the chemical. The most significant proposed change was to reclassify the chemical in the category of "restricted use," which requires that only certified applicators apply the product. In the array of regulatory instruments available to the agency, this is the least restrictive. Despite the objections of environmentalists, the agency adopted this proposal as law on 31 December 1987.[14] Surprisingly, environmentalists declined to challenge the decision in court, claiming that limited resources and other priorities discouraged them from doing so.[15]

The Canadian government followed a markedly different path. After reviewing the 1982 toxicology studies, Health and Welfare Canada recommended that Agriculture Canada cancel alachlor's registration. On 5 February 1985 the minister of agriculture, John Wise, adopted Health and Welfare's recommendation. In response, Monsanto took advantage of its right to request the establishment of a review board.[16] As required by statute, the minister of agriculture appointed the Alachlor Review Board in November 1985. It consisted of five people, four of them scientists, and conducted an extensive review, with 41 days of public hearings and 53 witnesses.[17]

In October 1987 the report of the Alachlor Review Board recommended that the decision of the agriculture minister to cancel alachlor be overturned. The Alachlor Review Board was highly critical of the decision-making process leading to the ban, especially Health and Welfare's evaluation of the safety of alachlor. However, the agriculture minister rejected the Alachlor Review Board's recommendation in January 1988, and the ban continued.

Monsanto filed for judicial review of the minister's decision in the Federal Court of Appeal, claiming that the minister was bound by law to adopt the Alachlor Review Board's recommendation, and that the decision was based on an "egregiously erroneous finding of fact" and policy considerations beyond the scope of the minister's jurisdiction. In a decision issued in December 1988, the court had little difficulty rejecting the manufacturer's arguments, and the ban was upheld.[18] Monsanto appealed the decision to the Supreme Court of Canada, but its leave to appeal was dismissed in May of 1989, bringing the alachlor decisions in both countries to a close.

Risk Assessment

Why, given the same scientific evidence, did Canada ban the pesticide while the u.s. returned it to the market with minimal restrictions? This section reconstructs the two decisions by scrutinizing risk assessments, benefits estimates, and the way the two countries balanced risks and benefits in the alachlor decision.[19]

There was no substantial difference between the two countries' interpretations of the laboratory studies. The Monsanto studies showed a statistically significant increase in cancer in two experiments on rats and one on mice. On the basis of this information both countries classified alachlor to be a proven animal carcinogen and a "probable human carcinogen."[20]

Despite this initial consensus the two countries interpreted the animal data in very different ways. The U.S. EPA applied its formal "cancer policy" for the interpretation of such data for risks to humans.[21] Using a mathematical model EPA derived a quantitative estimate of human cancer risks.[22] Unlike EPA the Canadian government does not have a formal cancer policy, and it provided strikingly little supporting rationale for its decision to ban the chemical. It is thus difficult to reconstruct Canada's position, which in fact seems to have shifted over time. In the original cancellation recommendation Health and Welfare Canada appeared to disagree with the use of quantitative risk assessment methodologies, and thus did not derive quantitative estimates of human risk.

The most important difference between the two governments' risk assessments lay in their assumptions about human exposure to alachlor. Both countries developed estimates of the exposure of the group most at risk, those who actually apply the herbicide.[23] Using assumptions designed to estimate the upper bound of exposure, Health and Welfare Canada estimated exposure of 2.7 milligrams per kilogram body weight per day (mg/kg/day).[24] The U.S. EPA developed its estimate based on a more elaborate methodology. EPA's estimate ranged from a low of 0.0012 mg/kg/day to a high of 0.12 mg/kg/day, depending upon the circumstances of exposure.[25] Thus even the upper bound of EPA's estimate was a factor of 23 less than Canada's, while EPA's lower bound was 3 orders of magnitude less.

EPA combined its exposure estimate with a potency estimate to derive an estimate of excess cancer risk of between one in 10,000 and 1 in a million over the lifetime of alachlor applicators. Canada did not develop comparable quantitative estimates. Instead Health and Welfare compared the laboratory studies on animals directly to human exposure estimates. The animal studies on alachlor showed tumour-producing effects at exposures as low as 2.5 mg/kg/day. Exposure of applicators of alachlor was estimated to be up to 2.7 mg/kg/day. On the basis of this comparison, Health and Welfare Canada concluded that there was no margin of safety, and recommended cancellation.[26]

The Alachlor Review Board was extremely critical of Health and Welfare's exposure estimates. Based on many of the same studies used by EPA but not included in Health and Welfare's analysis, the Alachlor Review Board derived what it considered to be a more reasonable estimate of human exposure. It then compared that estimate to the lowest dose causing excess cancer in the animal studies, and claimed the presence of a margin of safety ranging from 1,000 to 10,000.

Prior to the agriculture minister's final decision to reject the Alachlor Review Board's recommendation, Health and Welfare responded to some of the Alachlor Review Board's criticisms in a brief three-page letter. Here the confusion over Health and Welfare's policy on interpreting cancer risks is magnified. First, Health and Welfare rejected the Alachlor Review Board's exposure estimates as based on studies with "significant protocol deficiencies," without elaborating on the nature of those deficiencies. But the agency was willing to revise its earlier exposure estimate downward to a "margin of safety ranging from an upper limit of 63 to a lower limit of 334."[27]

In the next paragraph, however, Health and Welfare rejected the use of the concept of margin of safety – a concept it had employed throughout the regulatory proceedings – claiming that it "does not represent the generally accepted approach to carcinogen risk assessment."[28] The agency then proceeded to provide a probabilistic risk assessment of 1 in 1000 to 1 in 10,000. (This compares to EPA's range of 1 in 10,000 to 1 in 1,000,000.) The letter provided neither the potency nor the exposure figures on which it based these risk estimates. While the cancer policy of Health and Welfare Canada is certainly unclear, it is clear that when the agriculture minister made his final decision to uphold the alachlor ban, he did so based on risk estimates that were significantly greater than those derived by EPA.

The Benefits of Alachlor

Another element in the regulatory decision-making process is the evaluation of benefits. The regulatory schemes of the two countries are different in their requirements for the consideration of benefits. The U.S. EPA is required by law to balance risks and benefits. In contrast the Canadian scheme does not require such balancing, but it also does not preclude it. As in the U.S., the consideration of benefits is standard practice.[29]

There were important differences between the two countries' assessments of the benefits of alachlor. The key issue was the comparative cost and effectiveness of the main alternative to alachlor, a herbicide called metolachlor, manufactured by Ciba-Geigy. Again the Canadian decision is difficult to evaluate because of absence of documentation.[30]

Nevertheless testimony of Agriculture Canada officials suggests that the agency believed alachlor and metolachlor to be equally effective in controlling weeds. The Agriculture Minister concluded that "the aggregate loss to Canadian society from continued cancellation of alachlor would be relatively small."[31] While the Alachlor Review Board was critical of the department's analysis, it too concluded that the effects of banning alachlor would be "relatively minor, as long as metolachlor remains available at reasonable cost."[32]

EPA performed a more elaborate evaluation of alachlor's benefits. Based on field studies, the agency concluded that alachlor was "slightly more effective" than metolachlor in controlling weeds. As a result it concluded that there would be a 5 to 7 percent loss of net income for farmers using alachlor on corn, and a 1 to 2 percent loss for corn and soybean crops.[33]

When considering the benefits of alachlor it is necessary to consider not only the effectiveness of alternatives but also the risks they present. Although Canada and the U.S. reached similar conclusions about the relative safety of the two chemicals, they used that information in very different ways in reaching a regulatory decision. A key component of the Canadian decision was the conclusion that metolachlor was significantly safer than alachlor. Health and Welfare Canada concluded that metolachlor was not an animal carcinogen, and the agriculture minister accepted Health and Welfare's analysis, despite the vehement objections of the Alachlor Review Board. EPA concluded that metolachlor is significantly less toxic than alachlor. Based on analysis of animal studies, EPA concluded that metolachlor was a carcinogen, albeit one nearly 30 times less potent than alachlor.[34] An important difference between the two countries' decisions was how the estimates of the risks posed by metolachlor were incorporated into the decisions (see below).

Balancing Risks and Benefits

The final step in risk decision making is determining the acceptability of the risks involved. Agriculture Canada considered estimates of alachlor's risk, metolachlor's relative safety, and their equivalent effectiveness to conclude that "the use of alachlor represents an unacceptable risk of harm to public health ... The appreciable cancer risk to applicators seen by Health and Welfare Canada with respect to alachlor, and the availability of metolachlor were the principle factors in the Minister's decision to keep alachlor off the market."[35]

EPA reached a substantially different conclusion. While acknowledging the risks to applicators from exposure to alachlor, EPA concluded, "Upper bound levels of risk of this order of magnitude do not outweigh the substantial benefits of alachlor use."[36] Canada's estimate of risks posed by alachlor was substantially larger than EPA's, and Canada's estimate of benefits was lower than EPA's, thus leading to different assessments of the risk-benefit balance.

Consideration of the toxicity of the alternative metolachlor constituted an important difference in the balancing process. While both countries concluded that metolachlor was significantly safer than alachlor, this conclusion was highly salient in Canada but apparently ignored in the U.S. Although nothing in the regulatory framework precluded them from doing so, EPA officials were convinced that it was not necessary to compare metolachlor's toxicity to make a regulatory judgment on alachlor. Instead they used their conclusion that alachlor by itself posed an acceptable risk-benefit balance to justify the neglect of metolachlor's smaller risk.[37] Thus despite their remarkably rigorous documentation of the risks and benefits of alachlor, the ultimate decision was flawed by the failure to consider an important factor that may have tipped the balance toward more stringent regulation of alachlor.

Interest Representation

There are four basic stakeholders in pesticide politics: (1) chemical companies that manufacture pesticides, (2) farm groups that rely on pesticides, (3) environmental and consumer groups concerned about health and environmental risks from pesticides, and (4) farmworkers who are directly exposed to pesticides during their application. In almost all pesticide regulatory disputes, farmers and manufacturers have been on the same side of regulatory disputes, opposed by environmentalists and consumer groups. Manufacturers and environmentalists have in most cases played the dominant roles. Farmworkers historically have been the least well represented of these interests, but when involved they typically have been allied with environmentalists and consumer groups.

As discussed above, industry interests have a strong procedural advantage in both countries. Both the Canadian and U.S. regulatory schemes grant a statutory right of appeal to manufacturers but deny it to pro-regulation interests. In Canada, Monsanto took full advantage of these rights in the alachlor case, although without success.

While both countries provide comparable guarantees of industry access, mechanisms for environmental group representation differ. In Canada consultation is within the discretion of the minister and is usually restricted to the manufacturers and user groups.[38] In the U.S., in contrast, the procedure is open to the public through notice and comment rulemaking. Canadian environmentalists were not involved in the process prior to Agriculture's decision to ban alachlor; they were not even aware of the fact that the government was considering a ban until it was announced by the agriculture minister in February 1985.[39] Once the Alachlor Review Board was established, however, they played an active role in the proceedings.

In contrast, American environmentalists were involved as soon as EPA initiated its special review process. While there was no formal public hearing as in Canada, EPA conducted a more routine "paper hearing" under its special review process. Environmental groups commented on EPA's regulatory proposal, and in the final regulatory documents the agency was required by law to respond in detail to the major objections raised by environmentalists.[40]

Despite the broader guarantee of participation by pro-regulation interests in the U.S., the alachlor case shows that greater rights to participation do not necessarily produce more pro-environment decisions. In fact, the alachlor case highlights the importance of ministerial discretion in the Canadian system. In many ways the decision of the agriculture minister seems quite surprising. The review board report was highly critical of the initial decision, and the department's constituents – farmers who rely upon pesticides – would be expected to favour continued use of alachlor. The pressures to overrule the ban were counteracted by the minister's desire to appear aggressive on health regulation in a political environment that was beginning to pose a challenge to Agriculture Canada's jurisdiction of pesticide regulation.[41]

Whatever the ultimate motivations for the decision, the key fact is that once the minister is committed to action, there are few constraints. In this case he could ban alachlor despite the clear recommendations of the review board established to advise him, and despite being challenged in court the decision was only given cursory review. We will return to a discussion of the significance of these issues after an analysis of the Alar case.

ALAR

Daminozide, more commonly known by its trade name Alar, is a "growth regulator." Applied to apples and other orchard crops, it promotes product uniformity, reduces pre-harvest losses, increases firmness, reduces bruising, and extends storage life.[42] When treated apples are processed into apple sauce and apple juice, Alar breaks down into a chemical known as unsymmetrical dimethylhydrazine, or UDMH. Both Alar and UDMH have been linked to cancer in laboratory animals. As a result of an extraordinarily effective publicity campaign by a U.S. environmental group, the Alar case exploded into a major media issue in early 1989. Uniroyal, the chemical's sole manufacturer, was forced to withdraw the product from the market when the adverse publicity caused severe damage to the market for apples and apple products. This voluntary withdrawal of the product preempted regulatory action in both countries. In contrast to alachlor, however, U.S. regulators displayed much greater interest and willingness to take aggressive regulatory action than their Canadian counterparts.

Chronology: U.S.

Alar was first registered in the U.S. in 1963; tolerances were established in 1968. The first study suggesting a cancer risk for Alar appeared in 1977, and in 1980 it was discovered that UDMH is produced when Alar-treated apples are cooked. This heightened concern about the chemical, because UDMH had been shown in 1973 to have carcinogenic effects in animals. In 1980 EPA notified Uniroyal that it was considering issuing a special review notice for the product.

The regulation of Alar was affected by the Reagan administration's early efforts to relax environmental regulations.[43] When John Todhunter, EPA's Assistant Administrator for Pesticides and Toxic Substances and the administration's leader on reforming cancer policy, came into office, he held a number of private meetings with Uniroyal to discuss the product's status. As a result of these meetings EPA agreed to forego the special review process, and instead issued a "data call-in" notice in 1983 requesting that Uniroyal generate additional data. EPA's decision not to initiate a special review was one of the 13 decisions on pesticides subject to a legal challenge based on alleged procedural improprieties.[44]

In 1983 there was an intense backlash against the Reagan administration's regulatory policies, and virtually all of Reagan's early EPA appointees were forced to resign. After this "purge," EPA staff renewed their search for special review candidates, and Alar was one of the first selected. On 18 July 1984 EPA formally initiated a special review of Alar.[45] A year later the agency issued its proposed decision. The quantitative cancer risk assessment suggested that the dietary risk to consumers was quite high, in the range of 1 in 10,000 to 1 in 100. Based on this assessment EPA proposed to cancel all food uses of Alar and specified restrictions for the minor non-food uses that would be allowed to continue.[46]

EPA's regulatory proposal ran into trouble when, as required by FIFRA, it was submitted to the agency's Science Advisory Panel for review.[47] The science panel concluded that the animal studies the agency relied upon were flawed and inadequate to support its quantitative risk assessment.[48] The advisory panel urged the agency to perform additional studies before taking regulatory action.[49] EPA's scientific staff acknowledged problems with some of the studies, but disagreed with the science panel's conclusion that the studies were an inadequate basis for the regulatory action they proposed.[50]

Its scientific credibility undermined by the science panel's decision, EPA withdrew its proposed ban on Alar in January of 1986. In its place the agency required that Uniroyal perform more long-term toxicity studies, gather additional data on residue levels, and change the product's label to reduce application rates to apples by one half. The agency also took action to reduce tolerances for Alar on apples from 30 parts per million (ppm) to 20 ppm.[51] Environmentalists and some state health officials were outraged by EPA's about-face. In a letter to EPA the National Coalition Against the Misuse of Pesticides (NCAMP) claimed that the reversal "makes a mockery of those very regulatory programs that your staff often point to as a measure of success."[52]

Private Regulation: The Legacy of the EDB Scare

After witnessing the multi-million dollar losses incurred by food companies during the public alarm over ethylene dibromide (EDB),[53] some food companies attempted to preempt similar losses by voluntarily eliminating Alar from their products. Tree-Top, Inc., the world's largest apple juice processor, announced in March 1986 that it would cease using apples treated with Alar, citing "unacceptable and unreasonable business risks" as the basis for its decision.[54] Soon after, makers of Motts, Very Fine, and Red Check apple juice followed Tree-Top's lead. Three prominent manufacturers of baby foods, Heinz, Beech Nut, and Gerber, also announced they would join the boycott.

Frustrated by EPA inaction, consumer groups took it upon themselves to eliminate Alar from the food supply. In a 6 July 1986 letter to EPA administrator Lee Thomas, Ralph Nader announced that he would begin using his network of citizen groups to pressure supermarkets, apple processors, and consumers to refuse to accept Alar-treated apples. As a result of these threats Safeway, the country's largest food retailing chain, announced it would no longer purchase apples treated with Alar.[55]

While their pressure was insufficient to move EPA to take action, environmentalists still had sufficient influence in the media to use the threat of creating massive public fear to persuade powerful members of the food industry to take unilateral action. It is important that the

Nader efforts were effective in the absence of widespread public knowledge or concern about Alar residues. According to a Washington Apple Commission poll, only about 10 percent of the public at the time was aware of any publicity regarding the health concerns of apples. As one apple industry official said, "Two or three calls around the country from Ralph Nader threw the marketplace into a tizzy."[56] The campaign was quite successful, leading most apple growers to abandon the use of the pesticide in 1986. EPA figures show that Alar use dropped by about 60 percent from 1985 to 1989.[57] However, the industry had yet to see Nader and his allies at their best.

The Crisis Emerges

In early 1989 the politics of Alar were transformed as a result of two coincident factors. First, the additional laboratory studies EPA requested had produced interim results. One of the five studies showed statistically significant increases in cancer, leading acting EPA administrator John Moore to declare, "There is an inescapable and direct correlation between exposure to UDMH and the development of life-threatening tumors in test mice." As a result the agency announced it was accelerating the process to cancel the registration of Alar. However, it did not view the new evidence as alarming enough to warrant immediate suspension.[58]

Second, the Natural Resources Defense Council (NRDC), a major U.S. environmental group, launched a public campaign to remove Alar from the market. On 24 February 1989 the group issued a report warning, "Our country's children are being harmed by the very fruits and vegetables we tell them will make them grow up healthy and strong." While the report implicated a number of pesticides, virtually all of the excess risk estimated by NRDC was attributed to Alar's by-product, UDMH. According to the NRDC report, 1 in every 4200 children could contract cancer through exposure in their first six years to UDMH.[59]

The NRDC strategy was very effective. First, the report was presented with strong scientific credentials. Its peer review committee consisted of nine scientists affiliated with prestigious medical centres or universities. Second, it utilized two potent symbols: the apple – long mythologized as the quintessence of pure, healthy food – and the threat to infants and young children – the most innocent and vulnerable members of the population. Third, it extended its image and visibility beyond the traditional environmentalist community by recruiting actress Meryl Streep to lead an ad hoc group called Mothers and Others for Pesticide Limits.

The campaign garnered a tremendous amount of publicity. *60 Minutes* ran a feature story on the issue, with an extensive followup several months later. Streep appeared on talk shows, at Senate hearings, and in a TV ad campaign; her activities were even reported in the widely circulated *People* magazine. The public reaction was dramatic. Sales of apples and apple products plummeted.[60] In what was the most dramatic response, dozens of school systems, including New York, Los Angeles, and Chicago, stopped distributing apple products in school lunch programs.[61]

While Alar was taking a beating on the market, the product's legal status was assaulted from three directions. On 13 May EPA formally proposed to cancel Alar's regulation. On 15 May NRDC filed suit in an attempt to force EPA to invoke an emergency suspension, which would have a more immediate effect than EPA's proposed withdrawal of registration. Three days later five U.S. senators introduced a bill to ban the chemical.[62]

The trade group for apple growers, the International Apple Institute, announced in late May that its growers would no longer use Alar, effectively destroying its domestic market. On 2 June 1989 Uniroyal announced that it was temporarily withdrawing Alar from the U.S. market. A Uniroyal spokesperson stated: "While there is no scientifically valid reason to stop using it, [Alar has] become the focus of a needless controversy that is causing doubt and confusion about the safety of America's food supply, a needless controversy that is hurting the industry and the American public."[63]

After further results from the laboratory studies added to EPA's concerns, the agency announced in September 1989 that it would revoke all tolerances for Alar on crops.[64] The following month Uniroyal announced that it was halting worldwide sales of the product, and actually requested that EPA formally cancel the product's registration.[65] The agency obliged, and the Alar case was brought to a close in the U.S. – a dramatic victory for environmentalists.

Chronology: Canada

In Canada the Alar controversy shadowed developments in the United States. When Alar was registered in Canada in 1973, 95 percent of its use was on apples. Regulatory concern in Canada first emerged when EPA proposed to ban the product in 1985. Unlike the alachlor case, however, Canada adopted a wait-and-see attitude toward developments in the U.S. After EPA withdrew its proposal in response to the Science Advisory Panel's criticism, Agriculture Canada followed EPA's lead in requiring growers to reduce their application rates.[66] In response to

Nader's consumer boycott efforts, some Canadian growers stopped using the product. Beginning with the 1988 growing season, the B.C. Fruit Growers Association required their growers to sign an affidavit claiming they were not using Alar.[67]

In late February 1989 widespread media coverage of the NRDC study spilled over into Canada, leading to questions in Parliament and demands for action by Canadian environmentalists. Canadian government officials downplayed the concerns, stating that the existing data did not warrant regulatory action.[68] As measured by the number of newspaper stories on the subject, the issue was not nearly so controversial in Canada as it was in the U.S.[69] Nonetheless, in response to market-inspired pressures from growers the Canadian subsidiary of Uniroyal withdrew the chemical from the Canadian market in June 1989, a week after its parent company took the same action in the United States.

Assessing the Risks in the United States

The Alar debate differed from others in this book in that it focused almost exclusively on the risks posed by the chemical. There was remarkably little discussion about the benefits it offered.[70] Thus the approach of this section departs from others in the book in that we will focus on the intense disputes over risk assessments, and will not discuss the risk-benefit tradeoffs. In the chapter's conclusion we will return to the question of why benefits played such a small role in the conflict.

The NRDC report gave rise to a major debate about the health effects of Alar and UDMH. A full-page ad in the *New York Times* by the International Apple Institute claimed that NRDC's conclusions "have absolutely no basis in scientific fact." The industry belittled NRDC's concerns with the following statement: "To approach the exposure levels that produce ill effects in the laboratory, a person would have to consume more than 28,000 pounds of Alar-treated apples every day for 70 years."[71]

The U.S. EPA was also highly critical of NRDC's risk estimates, especially when schools began banning apple products. Agency officials sought to calm the alarmist tone of public debate. At a press conference, the agency announced that "the Government believes it is safe for Americans to eat apples."[72] This statement reflects a conscious departure from the traditional position of the EPA's pesticide staff that it was inappropriate to use the word "safe" in reference to a probable human carcinogen.[73] The press release also stated, "There is not an imminent hazard posed to children in the consumption of apples at this time, despite claims to the contrary."[74] This position was difficult for EPA to maintain, however, because the previous month they had declared that Alar posed a sufficiently large cancer risk to warrant cancellation proceedings.[75]

There were significant differences between the risk assessments of NRDC and EPA, but it is important to place them in context. EPA estimated a risk of 1 in 22,000 over a lifetime.[76] The agency acknowledged that because infants consume a proportionately higher quantity of apple products, they are at greater risk. EPA estimated that for the year and a half that it would take the agency to remove Alar from the market via cancellation proceedings, infants faced a lifetime excess risk of 9 in a million (this compares to approximately 1 in a million for adults over the same period).[77]

NRDC's figures were somewhat higher. Its estimate of a lifetime risk average from birth to age 5 is 1 in 4200, a factor of 5 higher than EPA's 1 in 22,000 estimate for all age groups. In the uncertain world of quantitative risk assessment, this is not a particularly significant difference. There were a number of differences between the two group's methodologies, including the way exposure was averaged over time and the dietary surveys upon which the exposure estimates were based. However the biggest difference was the fact that NRDC relied on a potency factor for UDMH EPA had calculated in 1986 on the basis of studies that were subsequently discredited by the Science Advisory Panel. The potency factor from that discredited study was an order of magnitude higher than the one used by EPA in 1989 based on the new animal studies. While these differences did not produce dramatically divergent risk assessments, they did allow EPA and others to claim that NRDC's calculations were based on faulty science.[78]

Assessing the Risks in Canada

The approach taken in Canada was profoundly different. First, Canada adopted a different approach to the communication of Alar risks to the public. When widespread media coverage of the NRDC study spilled over into Canada, the Canadian government downplayed the concerns, relying on arguments much closer to those of the industry than those of either EPA or NRDC. In a letter to members of Parliament, Health and Welfare Canada claimed that "it is estimated that a child would have to consume 250,000 to 2,000,000 times more than their present daily intake of apples/apple products" in order the reach the dosage level that caused tumours in laboratory animals. The department claimed, "There is no reason to conclude that Canadian consumers, including preschool children, are exposed to hazardous levels of Alar."[79]

Second, Canada adopted a different standard of proof with respect to the scientific evidence. Its published documents revealed a great deal more skepticism about the significance of the cancer findings in the interim test results. Health and Welfare Canada placed greater emphasis on the negative findings in the other interim studies (only one of five studies had produced a positive interim result), and raised doubts about the significance of the findings of malignancy in the highest dose in the one positive study: "The finding of malignancy at the highest dose is inconclusive. Malignancy may have been due to certain 'confounding' factors other than UDMH which make the findings of malignant tumors difficult to interpret. Further analysis is required to determine the significance."[80] Health and Welfare Canada required a much higher burden of proof before it was willing for policy purposes to consider UDMH a carcinogen with implications for human exposure at low doses.

Third, the Canadian approach also differed in its assumptions about the mechanisms of carcinogenesis. Health and Welfare Canada raised particular doubts about whether it is appropriate to apply a linear dose-response model to UDMH exposure. Environmentalists wrote a letter to the government demanding that it ban Alar and calling for a clarification of the federal government's views on thresholds for carcinogens.[81] In response Health and Welfare Canada described its approach as follows: "For example, a chemical that increases the tumour incidences in male mice but not in female mice or rats of both sexes, occurs at one site and only after high doses, must be viewed quite differently from a chemical which produces malignant tumours, in a dose dependent fashion, at more than one site, in both sexes of mice and rats and at low doses. *Thus, it is not meaningful to give a simple yes or no answer to your question as to whether 'Health and Welfare holds the view that there are no safe levels for carcinogens.'*"[82] This statement reveals a direct contrast between Health and Welfare Canada's risk assessment and both EPA's general policy for cancer risk assessment and its views on the implications of these particular interim studies on UDMH.

Rather than perform a quantitative risk assessment like those of EPA or NRDC, Health and Welfare Canada relied on the more traditional safety factor approach. As in the case of alachlor Canada relied on a comparison of the dose that showed carcinogenic effects in laboratory animals with its estimated exposure in humans, leading to the conclusion that human exposure was 250,000 to 2 million times lower than the dose associated with cancer in mice. Implicit in this approach is the assumption that there is a threshold below which exposure does not present a cancer risk – in stark contrast to EPA's approach, which assumed a linear dose-response relationship.

Health and Welfare Canada's assessment was not only based on a different methodology, but also on different exposure estimates. Canada estimated that UDMH exposure in children was about an order of magnitude less than EPA's estimate.[83] NRDC and EPA relied on residue samples collected in 1986, while Health and Welfare Canada's samples were collected in 1988. Canada's data, while more up to date, were not necessarily more appropriate for regulatory purposes. After EPA had initially proposed a ban in 1986, a number of Canadian growers stopped using Alar. If Alar's regulatory status were to be vindicated, usage and exposure patterns could reasonably be expected to revert to pre-1986 levels. Regardless of the appropriate exposure figures the difference in approaches to risk assessment is clear. Based on the same laboratory data EPA produced a quantitative estimate of human risks, while Canada relied on the margin of safety approach.

Epilogue

While the voluntary bans on Alar brought the regulatory controversy to a close, neither the political fallout from the conflict nor the scientific controversy has yet ended. Despite a full recovery of apple sales, in November 1990 a group of apple growers launched a lawsuit against the CBS, NRDC, and the environmental group's media advisors for the damages the growers incurred as a result of what they alleged were "false, misleading, and scientifically unreliable statements" about their products.[84]

While an extraordinary success on its own terms the NRDC campaign against Alar appears to have provoked a backlash by the group's traditional allies in the media. After being burned by the Alar scare, the next several times issues about pesticide contamination of the food supply emerged, EPA was exceptionally careful in crafting its press releases. After anticipating that public alarm would follow announcements of contamination of potatoes and bananas with the controversial pesticide aldicarb, agency officials were stunned by the absence of public reaction. Officials attribute the difference to lack of interest on behalf of the media.[85] Revelations that NRDC relied on a professional public relations firm to devise a campaign to saturate the media with NRDC's message have jeopardized the group's credibility with journalists.[86]

EPA also has been subjected to severe criticism for its interpretation of the interim results of the animal experiments.[87] A number of critics have claimed that the only interim result that produced statistically significant increases in tumours was conducted at a dose that exceeded the maximum tolerated dose.[88] Based on the interim studies, the

British government concluded that there was "no risk to health," and a United Nations scientific panel reached essentially the same conclusion.[89]

The completion of the study and the analysis of the results clarified the science of Alar somewhat, but did not do much to calm the regulatory science controversy surrounding Alar and the more general issue of how animal studies should be used in chemical regulation. The full studies confirmed that UDMH was carcinogenic in laboratory animals; statistically significant cancers appeared in more species and at more doses than observed in the interim studies. In addition Alar itself was shown to produce cancers in animals.[90] While the completed studies strengthened EPA's position that Alar and UDMH are animal carcinogens, it also led the agency to reduce its potency estimate by a factor of 2, a relatively minor change in light of the uncertainties surrounding risk assessment.[91] Everything else being equal, this would change EPA's risk assessment from a 1 in 22,000 lifetime excess cancer risk to 1 in 44,000.

While certainly not cause for the extent of alarm that surrounded the Alar scare of 1989, this level of risk could be cause for concern if population exposure is as widespread as is the case for apple products. While EPA may feel vindicated that its interpretation of the interim results was not far off the mark, some scientists and other governmental agencies continue to disagree with the way EPA extrapolates animals studies to humans.[92]

CONCLUSION

Stringency and Timeliness

In the case of alachlor Canada's decision was unquestionably more stringent: the product was removed from the market altogether, whereas it remained on the U.S. market with minimal restrictions. In contrast the nod for regulatory stringency in the Alar case would appear to go the U.S., although that case was complicated by the manufacturer's voluntary withdrawal of the product in both countries. However the differences in the two governments' apparent willingness to take regulatory action on the same data demands qualification. EPA was willing to initiate the process partly because the agency knew it would take an estimated 18 months to complete, during which the final results from the ongoing animal studies would be issued. If the final results supported EPA's interim assessment, its position would be vindicated. If not, the agency could withdraw the action. Canada on the other hand might have been more willing to wait for the final results because if they showed more cause for concern, the government could act swiftly to ban the product.[93] Nonetheless it is fair to say that Canada was far less risk averse in interpreting the scientific data and demanded a greater weight of evidence of harm before it was willing to act.

With alachlor the Canadian decision was more drawn out because of the elaborate Monsanto appeals. However, one of the reasons the Canadian process took longer was that it banned alachlor. Had EPA done so Monsanto would almost certainly have appealed the decision, postponing the resolution of the case.

The regulatory history of these two pesticides reveals the extent of economic and social integration between the two countries. With Alar similar consumer concerns and integrated markets for apple products produced convergence despite differences in the positions of regulatory agencies. In the end, Meryl Streep had a greater impact on the regulatory outcome in Canada than did Canadian regulators. However the alachlor case demonstrates that Canada does retain some regulatory independence – it was able to ban the product despite the U.S. decision to leave it on the market.

Incorporation of Science

These two pesticide cases are revealing examples of the two countries' different styles of risk assessment. In both cases the U.S. adhered to its general cancer policy. A risk averse approach was taken to the interpretation of animal data, a linear dose response relationship was assumed, and quantitative risk assessments were performed. EPA risk assessments were explained in exhaustive detail in publicly available documents.

In contrast both cases reveal the Canadian government's case-by-case approach to risk assessment. Health and Welfare Canada's risk assessments were less clearly documented and rigorously argued. The government persistently relied on the margin of safety approach in the alachlor case, only to later acknowledge that such an approach does not reflect contemporary understanding of the mechanisms of carcinogenesis. Yet in the Alar case Health and Welfare scientists once again adopted the margin of safety approach with its implicit assumption of thresholds for carcinogens. No doubt government scientists had their reasons for interpreting the data in a particular way, but the manner in which the results are presented makes it extremely difficult for others to understand the basis for decisions.

The Canadian government also adopted significantly different standards of proof in the two cases. In the Alar case the government was highly skeptical of the animal studies and applied quite risk tolerant assumptions, but Health and Welfare scientists applied extremely risk averse assumptions in the alachlor case, especially in the area of exposure assessments. The strong views of one government scientist, Dr Len Ritter of Health and Welfare, seemed to play an essential role in the alachlor case.

As explained in chapters 1 and 2, risk assessments contain implicit value judgments. The sparsely documented, case-by-case approach used in Canada makes it difficult to discern the mix of facts and values employed in risk assessments.

The Alar case also reveals the consequences of the two countries' different strategies of communicating risks to the general public. EPA acknowledged that there were cancer risks but argued that they did not constitute an imminent hazard warranting an immediate ban. The public and the media had difficulty either accepting or understanding this distinction, leading to the extreme reaction of banning apple products in schools. To EPA officials this was an overreaction, but their strategy of risk communication runs this risk. Health and Welfare Canada, on the other hand, dismissed the risk from the outset. Canada avoided the alarmist behaviour of consumers in the U.S., but at the cost of potentially misleading the public concerning the nature of the risk.

Risk/Benefit Balancing

Both countries weighed the benefits of alachlor use against the risks but came to opposite conclusions. The most important difference was EPA's failure to carefully consider the safety and efficacy of alternatives to alachlor, and for that reason its decision-making process was less comprehensive. It is interesting that the benefits of Alar played a much smaller role in the regulatory dispute than in the case of alachlor. In that case little informed discussion about benefits took place in either jurisdiction.

The explanation for this is not entirely clear. The debate in both countries focused on whether or not Alar or its breakdown products caused cancer, not whether any of the benefits of Alar use justified the potential elevated cancer risk. Both industry and the Canadian government focused on discrediting the arguments that the substance caused cancer. This contrasts with the alachlor case, where consideration of benefits consumed much of the debate. The most plausible explanation for this difference is the nature of the population at risk. The alachlor case focused on applicator exposure, a relatively small group, while with Alar the focus was on exposure to the general public, particularly young children. When such widespread and vulnerable segments of the populations are exposed, it is apparently much less acceptable to admit the existence of a cancer risk, no matter how small.

Interest Representation

Interest group participation in both pesticides cases was widespread. In the alachlor case u.s. environmentalists were involved earlier in the process, but their Canadian counterparts got a careful hearing once the Alachlor Review Board opened the process. This case is also testimony to the discretion of the minister in the Canadian system. The minister had the freedom to reject the review board's highly critical report, and was effectively insulated from judicial review. If the administrator of EPA had given the same reasons for rejecting expert scientific advice, the decision almost certainly would have been overturned by the u.s. courts.

The Alar case was subject to a far broader scope of conflict than was the case for alachlor. The Alar issue exploded beyond the normal range of participants in risk management decisions to include the public as a whole. As a result of the successful NRDC media campaign, environmental and consumer interests had no trouble being heard. Industry and apple growers responded, but were overwhelmed by the opposition.

In fact the Alar case circumvented the normal process of risk regulation, in which various stakeholders make their case to a regulatory agency, which then decides the case, subject to the potential for judicial or other forms of review. Consumer reaction, based largely on environmental group publicity, led directly to a self-imposed ban by the manufacturer. The u.s. agency was left merely to ratify the action. In Canada the regulatory agency barely had time to consider taking action before the issue became moot.

Industry groups no doubt feel that they were not given a fair hearing in the heated public debate. In fact the media presented their case in both countries. The problem was that in disputes about apples, cancer, babies, and mothers, the industry was at an overwhelming symbolic disadvantage. Indeed the Alar case is testimony to the immense scientific and political sophistication of u.s. environmental groups. While Canadian environmentalists occasionally participate in regulatory science debates, they have far less influence on regulatory science than their American counterparts.

These two pesticides cases clearly show the two countries' contrasting regulatory styles at work. The results are mixed: in one case

Canada regulated more aggressively, in the other less so, although in the latter case the outcomes were ultimately the same in the two countries. In the context of the risk controversies surveyed here, the alachlor case is unique. In other cases discussed in this volume where the U.S. has acted less stringently, saccharin and urea formaldehyde, the weaker U.S. regulations resulted from courts and Congress overruling the actions of U.S. regulators. Alachlor is the only case in our sample where Canadian regulators took action to ban the substance but U.S. regulators did not. We will return to explanations for this anomaly in the concluding chapter.

5 Paternalism vs Consumer Choice: Regulation of Saccharin in Canada and the United States*

In 1977 a Canadian laboratory study revealed that saccharin – a widely used artificial sweetener – causes bladder tumours in rats. In Canada this resulted in the enactment of a regulation drastically limiting the availability of the only non-caloric sugar substitute available at the time to the diet food industry and diet food consumers. While the decision sparked only moderate controversy in Canada, announcement by the U.S. Food and Drug Administration of a proposed ban in the United States, based primarily on the Canadian study, precipitated a public outcry that the loss of saccharin would have a devastating impact on diabetics, dieters, and the diet food industry. Letters opposing the ban flooded Congressional offices, and Congress responded with a moratorium on FDA's proposed ban.

The U.S. debate over saccharin illustrates the tension between uncertain risks and benefits. As the public outcry indicated, many consumers perceived significant benefits from saccharin. The tension was particularly pronounced since the risks faced by individual saccharin consumers were relatively low. Most Americans apparently felt that the benefits outweighed the slight risks. However since millions of people were exposed to saccharin, the projections of the number of cases of cancer per year that might be caused by saccharin were actually quite high.[1]

---

* Co-authored with Colleen Rohde

The saccharin case also reveals a tension between expertise and popular opinion or, put another way, between technocracy and democracy. Regulatory scientists in both countries advocated a ban on saccharin, but in the U.S., consumers rebelled against the ban and ultimately prevailed. The regulatory history of saccharin raises questions about the appropriate role of experts, on the one hand, and the lay public and their elected representatives, on the other hand, in making public health decisions that involve both scientific and policy questions.

This chapter uses the saccharin case to illustate the problems associated with the regulation of carcinogenic food additives and the methods of resolving those problems in the two countries. A discussion of the regulatory framework in each country will be followed by a review of the chronology of events. The chapter will then focus on the factors that influenced decision making in each country, including the nature of the scientific and political debate. Finally, we will compare the regulatory process and outcomes based on our five criteria: protectiveness, timeliness, incorporation of science in the regulatory process, balancing of risks and benefits, and representation of societal interests.

CANADIAN REGULATORY FRAMEWORK

The Canadian federal minister of health and welfare is formally responsible for regulation of food additives under the authority of the Food and Drugs Act, which authorizes the minister to add or remove food additives from a list of permitted substances.[2] In practice the responsibility for regulation of sweeteners, such as saccharin, cyclamates, and aspartame, and other food additives falls to the Health Protection Branch of Health and Welfare Canada.

The statute authorizes the Cabinet to make regulations concerning food additives in order "to prevent injury to the health of the consumer or purchaser."[3] If the minister of health and welfare decides that a substance ought to be removed from the list of permitted food additives, a recommendation is made to Cabinet that the use of the substance be prohibited or restricted. In effect, Cabinet's decision on the matter is final.

The statute neither requires nor precludes the weighing of costs and benefits. In fact the minister is not "required" to propose any regulations at all, since the legislation only states that Cabinet "may make regulations."[4] Apart from publishing the final regulation in the *Canada Gazette*, the minister is not required by the statute to hold public hearings or in any other way invite public input. Historically, informal consultations have been conducted with select participants at the discretion of the minister and departmental officials. Since 1986, however, government policy has required prepublication of regulatory proposals and more extensive public consultation.[5]

UNITED STATES REGULATORY FRAMEWORK

The language of the corresponding u.s. legislation is more specific. The Food and Drug Administration's authority to regulate food additives is found in the federal Food, Drug, and Cosmetic Act.[6] Section 409 of the act, also known as the Food Additives Amendment, was passed in 1958. Under its general provisions FDA is granted authority to issue regulations permitting the conditions and quantity in which an additive may be used, provided that the agency considers such uses to be "safe." FDA cannot permit continued use of a substance at levels that have been shown to be unsafe. The agency has interpreted the legislation to mean that it cannot approve a substance even if its benefits outweigh the health risks.[7]

The so-called Delaney clause, which is part of the Food Additives Amendment of 1958, stipulates that "no additive shall be deemed to be safe if it is found to induce cancer when ingested by man [sic] or animal, or if it is found, after tests which are appropriate for the evaluation of the safety of food additives, to induce cancer in man [sic] or animal."[8] FDA has characterized the clause as redundant, since the general safety provisions of the Food Additives Amendment already require that the agency ban any food additive that has been shown to be unsafe.[9] While it is true that the Delaney clause and the general provisions of Section 409 both preclude weighing of risks and benefits, the clause nevertheless greatly restricts FDA's discretion to determine just what constitutes "safety."

The act requires that FDA publish a notice of proposed rulemaking at least 30 days before finalizing a regulation it has initiated. (Requirements differ somewhat if the agency is acting in response to a private citizen's petition.) Any person adversely affected by the regulation has a right to a public hearing, and FDA is required to respond publicly to any objections raised at that hearing. The agency also must respond to written comments received on the proposed rule. FDA's final decision can be appealed to the United States Court of Appeals.[10] In contrast judicial review is not specifically provided for in the Canadian act.

CHRONOLOGY

Saccharin was first synthesized in 1879 by U.S. chemist Constantin Fahlberg. From 1911 to 1938 saccharin was available in the U.S. as a drug, but it was not allowed in the general food supply except during World War I, when sugar shortages resulted in a temporary lifting of this ban. Between 1938 and 1959 saccharin was available both as a drug and special dietary supplement available to those with special medical needs. During this period Canadian availability appears to have been similar to that in the U.S. Consumption of saccharin and other artificial sweeteners began to increase in the 1950s in both countries, after manufacturers of artificially sweetened foods adopted a marketing strategy of appealing to dieters as well as diabetics, who previously had been assumed to constitute the only market for artificially sweetened foods.[11]

In 1969 both the Canadian and American governments took steps to restrict the availability of cyclamates, another artificial sweetener. Both countries banned cyclamates as a food additive. The Canadian government continued to allow the sale of cyclamates in drug stores as a table-top sweetener. In the U.S., FDA initially proposed to allow cyclamate products to be sold as non-prescription drugs to people who required them for medical reasons. In 1970, however, even medical uses of cyclamate products were prohibited in the U.S. At the time saccharin was the only other artificial sweetener available to food producers and millions of consumers.[12]

Because the cyclamate ban led to increased consumption of saccharin, regulators in both countries became increasingly concerned about the safety of saccharin as a food additive. When a 1977 study conducted by the Canadian government conclusively revealed that saccharin was an animal carcinogen, both Canadian and American officials found it necessary to act. On 9 March 1977 both countries announced their intention to prohibit the sale of foods containing saccharin.

The Canadian minister of health and welfare, Marc Lalonde, announced a ban on the use of saccharin in foods and other consumer products, such as drugs, toothpaste, mouthwash, and lipstick.[13] However the Canadian regulation provided for limited availability of saccharin as a table-top sweetener to be sold only in pharmacies as a non-prescription drug, a concession to diabetics and dieters.

The Canadian government also sought to accommodate the concerns of the food industry and retailers by phasing out saccharin gradually. As originally announced the sale of beverages containing saccharin was not to be permitted after 1 July 1977, while the sale of other foods containing saccharin would not be permitted after

1 November.[14] At the request of producers and retailers, these dead-lines were subsequently extended by several months.[15] In addition, commencing 1 June 1979 every saccharin sweetener had to be labelled to state that continued use of saccharin may be injurious to health and that it should be used by pregnant women only on the advice of a physician. The phase-out periods and the later extension of the deadlines were a direct response to the anticipated difficulty industry would have adjusting their production and product lines. Products already on store shelves could continue to be sold until the dates specified in the regulation in order that store owners and producers not be left with unsold inventory.

Information sessions for members of Parliament were held, where departmental officials were available to answer technical questions concerning the saccharin ban. In addition the ban was discussed on various occasions in the House of Commons and the parliamentary Standing Committee on Health, Welfare and Social Affairs. Although several members of Parliament were critical of the saccharin ban, there was no public outcry or organized lobbying campaign in Canada. As a result, apart from a 19 April 1977 announcement that the phase-out deadlines would be extended, the saccharin ban took effect as originally announced.

FDA also announced its proposed saccharin ban on 9 March 1977. Coordination appears to have been important to regulators in both countries. The Canadian government invited officials from the U.S. and other countries to a meeting on March 7 to seek consensus on the significance of its research results, and reportedly pressured U.S. officials to synchronize the announcements.[16] When the Canadian government advanced its announcement from the previously agreed-upon date of March 10 in response to leaks to the press concerning the forthcoming regulatory action, FDA hastily arranged its own late-afternoon press conference to ensure that the U.S. and Canadian decisions were announced on the same day, even though the requisite *Federal Register* notice would not be ready for weeks.[17]

On 15 April 1977 FDA published a formal notice of its intent to ban saccharin, indicating that in addition to the normal 60-day comment period for the receipt of written comments (later extended), it would hold an informal public hearing on May 18 and 19.[18] FDA proposed to revoke the interim food additive regulation under which saccharin was then permitted as a table-top sweetener and as an ingredient in prepackaged foods, such as soft drinks. Like Canada, FDA also proposed to ban the use of saccharin in drugs and cosmetics. It was anticipated that the final regulation would take effect in mid-July or August.

FDA also proposed to review applications for the marketing of saccharin as a non-prescription drug, in consideration of the needs of diabetics. The potential for continued availability of saccharin as a table-top sweetener followed from the fact that drugs are not covered by the food additives provisions of the federal Food, Drug, and Cosmetic Act, which prohibit balancing of risks and benefits. However under drug provisions of the act, in order for the FDA to allow restricted use of saccharin as a non-prescription drug, applicants for approval were required to provide scientific evidence of medical benefit. It was by no means obvious that applicants would be able to provide such evidence, since studies had yet to demonstrate medical benefits of saccharin to either dieters or diabetics.[19]

In light of the Delaney clause there was little point in pressuring the agency to change its decision. Rather than waiting for FDA's hearings, associations representing the 10 million American diabetics began to lobby members of Congress in opposition to FDA's proposed action almost immediately. More important, the diet food industry successfully mobilized individual consumers to lobby Congress as well. The lobbying efforts of American industry interests were coordinated by the Calorie Control Council, an organization wholly financed by the manufacturers of diet sodas and other low-calorie foods. The council published full-page advertisements in newspapers in most major U.S. cities discounting the scientific evidence on saccharin, emphasizing the plight of diabetics and dieters should saccharin be banned, and urging Americans to pressure Congress to prevent the ban.

Public response was overwhelming. Members of Congress were beseiged by letters opposing FDA's proposed ban. Congress reportedly received more mail on saccharin than on any issue since the Viet Nam war.[20] A leading Congressional critic of the ban claimed that one million Americans wrote letters to members of Congress or contacted the White House or FDA in opposition to the ban.[21] Senator Edward Kennedy charged that behind this deluge of mail was an "aggressive and indefensible media blitz" by the diet food industry.[22] National associations representing diabetics also organized successful letter-writing campaigns. Poignant letters describing the social stigma and perceived medical risks that diabetic children would suffer in the absence of saccharin were read into the Congressional record.

Debate in the House of Representatives began the day after FDA's announcement and continued off and on for eight months, when the Saccharin Study and Labelling Act was passed.[23] The act, signed by the president on 23 November 1977, denied the Secretary of the Department of Health, Education and Welfare (through whom FDA acts) authority to remove saccharin from the market for an 18-month period. The act also requested that the National Academy of Sciences examine the risks and benefits to health of saccharin and also study general issues concerning federal food safety policy. In the interim Congress required producers of foods and beverages containing saccharin to include warning labels on their packages alerting consumers to the possibility that saccharin could be a carcinogen.

The National Academy of Sciences (NAS) subsequently reported to Congress in November 1978. Although the NAS report declined to offer regulatory recommendations, it implicitly supported FDA's analysis in concluding that "saccharin must be viewed as a potential cause of cancer in humans" and that there was "no scientific support for the health benefits of saccharin."[24] Despite that fact Congress has repeatedly extended the Saccharin Study and Labelling Act. Products containing saccharin remain available in the United States, although since the late 1980s saccharin has largely been replaced by aspartame in diet foods.

In a development in November 1992, Health and Welfare Canada reversed its ban on saccharin in drugs and cosmetics, such as toothpaste and lipsticks.[25] The reversal of the Canadian government's position was in response to sustained pressure from the drug industry, which objected to the fact that products containing saccharin were allowed on the market in other countries, including the U.S. Interestingly although the federal government alerted drug and cosmetic manufacturers and consumer groups of its intentions through an information letter in December 1991, the government exempted itself from its own policy requiring that a draft regulation be published for public comment in the *Canada Gazette Part I* prior to being finalized.[26] The U.S. government clearly could not have obtained an exemption from the statutory requirements for notice and comment rulemaking in that country with such ease.

Although the Drugs Directorate of Health and Welfare Canada has reevaluated its position, no comparable review of the ban on saccharin in foods and beverages is anticipated by the Food Directorate at present. However the fact that the recent regulatory amendment bluntly stated as Canadian government policy that "it can be concluded that the evidence does not suggest that saccharin consumption increases the risk of bladder cancer in humans" certainly opens the door for such a review, if there was pressure from the food industry.[27]

HISTORY OF SACCHARIN STUDIES

Since saccharin was first synthesized in the late 1800s, its safety as a food additive has been subject to scientific review and controversy.

Saccharin was suspected of being a carcinogen in 1951, when the first long-term study of the effect of saccharin on rats was conducted.[28] Since then a variety of short- and long-term tests have been performed. The regulatory actions by the governments of Canada and the United States were precipitated by a study initiated in February 1974 and completed in 1977 by Health and Welfare Canada, which indicated that saccharin caused bladder cancer in rats.[29]

The Health and Welfare Canada study was originally designed to test the carcinogenicity of a chemical impurity in saccharin known as ortho-toluenesulforamide (o-TS), since two previous studies had confirmed that saccharin containing o-TS had caused cancer in rats. Those earlier studies had been conducted between 1970 and 1975 by the FDA and the Wisconsin Alumni Research Foundation (WARF). A consortium of sugar companies eager to discredit the safety of saccharin partially funded the second study.[30] In both studies, various doses of saccharin were fed to two generations of laboratory rats. The rationale for continuing the experiments through the second generation was to investigate the effects of exposure from the point of conception; in contrast, single-generation studies typically commence exposure only after the animals are weaned. Although elevated rates of bladder tumours were detected in the male animals in the second generation in both studies, uncertainty remained as to whether saccharin or o-TS was the carcinogen. A review of these studies and other available evidence by the U.S. National Academy of Sciences led the Academy to report to FDA in 1974 that the data then available had "not established conclusively whether saccharin is or is not carcinogenic when administered orally to test animals."[31] Further research was recommended.

The Canadian study thus was designed to determine whether o-TS or saccharin itself was the carcinogen. The study plan initially called for groups of rats to be fed varying levels of o-TS to investigate its carcinogenicity in the absence of saccharin. Prior to commencement of the study, however, a form of saccharin became available which contained no detectable levels of o-TS and fewer total impurities than present in the previously available saccharin. This new form of saccharin was fed to rats at a level of 5 percent in the diet for two generations, a level of exposure comparable to the doses used in the previous WARF and FDA studies.

Of a total of 200 rats fed saccharin, 21 developed bladder tumours. Seven male rats of the first generation developed bladder tumours while 12 male and 2 female rats in the second generation developed bladder tumors. Among the 100 control animals fed neither saccharin nor o-TS, only one developed a tumour. There was no significant increase in bladder tumours in any of the rats fed o-ts. Thus it was possible to conclude that saccharin, rather than o-ts, caused the rats' cancer. The increased incidence of tumours among male rats of the second generation was particular cause for concern, since it suggested that maternal exposure during pregnancy and lactation could be particularly harmful.

Upon receiving the results of the study Health and Welfare Canada convened an international panel of scientists to review the findings. That panel and subsequent reviewers were satisfied with the study's design and conduct, and concluded that the findings clearly indicated that saccharin caused the animals' bladder tumours.[32] It was widely accepted in the scientific community that saccharin is an animal carcinogen, albeit a weak one compared to other known carcinogens.[33]

At the time of the Canadian and FDA decisions several epidemiological studies of the effect of saccharin on human populations were also available.[34] The results generally were negative, a fact widely cited by opponents of the saccharin ban in the United States as evidence that saccharin does not cause cancer in humans, even though it may be harmful to rats. However, as FDA noted, the available epidemiological studies focused on relatively small populations, and thus could only detect relatively high risks. FDA estimated that up to 20,000 saccharin-related cases of bladder cancer per year in the u.s. could have gone undetected given the statistical insensitivity of the available epidemiological studies.[35] Moreover many cancers exhibit latency periods of 30 or more years, and it had been only about 15 years since consumption of saccharin increased in response to the introduction of diet soft drinks.

THE CANADIAN DECISION RATIONALE

The Canadian Risk Assessment

The Canadian decision was based on a risk averse policy that, since safe levels of saccharin could not be established, consumption should not be allowed. The Canadian announcement of the ban stressed the precautionary nature of the decision while attempting to downplay the cause for concern: "It must be stressed that the dose used in this study exceeded average human exposure by at least 800 times, based on consumption of one 12-ounce bottle of 'diet' soft drink per day. No cases of human cancer attributable to saccharin have been identified. Action to restrict the use of saccharin by the general public is being taken, however, as a precautionary measure, in the interest of prudence."[36]

An important factor in Health and Welfare Canada's decision apparently was that the highest users of saccharin were considered to be those most at risk.[37] These groups included women in their childbearing years, whose saccharin consumption might affect their children, and children themselves, who consumed more saccharin per kilogram of body weight than the average adult.

It does not appear that Canadian officials ever performed a quantitative risk assessment. One representative of the Health Protection Branch reported that the estimated levels of exposure of the high end of diet soda consumers (those who consume 3 or 4 cans per day) offered an unacceptable margin of safety of only about 200 compared to the level of exposure that caused cancer in rats. He implied that a safety factor of 5000 would be more reasonable.[38]

The recent reversal of the Canadian ban on saccharin in cosmetics and drugs represents a move toward a more risk tolerant posture. In an open letter circulated to solicit comments on the proposed change, Health and Welfare Canada suggested that "the observed effect in the animal carcinogenicity studies may be due to the very high and prolonged doses used in those studies."[39] That letter and the subsequent *Canada Gazette* notice also stressed the absence of positive epidemiological studies to corroborate the evidence in rats. Although there apparently are no plans to reconsider the ban in foods, the relatively minor amendment concerning drugs and cosmetics opens the door for a more far-reaching reversal of the Canadian position on saccharin.

Balancing the Risks and Benefits in Canada

Although the impact of a saccharin ban on industry and individual consumers may have been considered during the Canadian decision-making process, health concerns were clearly given greater weight. However the government did weigh the medical benefits of saccharin against the health risks, and fashioned a compromise that would allow limited availability for special needs groups.

One member of Parliament criticized the ban by arguing that without saccharin, Canadians collectively would gain 60 million pounds and suffer an additional 2500 heart attacks per year.[40] Health and Welfare Canada concluded, however, that the available evidence did not indicate that saccharin had any benefit in controlling obesity.[41] Available evidence suggested that dieters simply tended to replace the calories "saved" by saccharin by consuming more of other foods. Canadian regulators concluded that for the general population the risks of saccharin consumption outweighed the potential benefits.

However they were more willing to concede that saccharin played a role in management of diabetics' diet and health.

Consultations were held prior to the Canadian decision with the Canadian Medical Association, the Canadian Dental Association, the Canadian Diabetic Association and the Registrars of Pharmacy.[42] The intent was to strike a compromise that would balance the health risks with health benefits of saccharin for those with special needs. When the ban was announced, there was also an indication that further consultations would be held with medical experts and representatives of the food industry to assess the role of saccharin in special foods for diabetics and as a sweetener in drug preparations. These consultations were to consider exemptions from the ban for special food products.

The concession of limited availability of saccharin in pharmacies indicated Health and Welfare Canada's willingness to allow that there might be circumstances where benefits outweighed the health risks. The limited form of the ban offered political benefits as well. In December the minister of health and welfare responded to critics that "we are not banning saccharin as is the case in the United States; we are simply putting it where it belongs, in drug stores."[43]

Canadian decision makers were not prepared to accept that Canadian consumers could or should make their own decisions about whether to consume saccharin for three reasons.[44] First, the government rejected reliance on warning labels because Canadian officials believed that only 11 to 15 percent of people actually read labels. Second, officials argued that the amount of information required for a person to make an informed decision would require an impractically elaborate warning label. Finally, children, who were among the heaviest users of saccharin, could not be expected to read warning labels or make reasoned decisions based on such labels. In Canada, a greater degree of protection than that afforded by warning labels was considered warranted, however paternalistic that protection might be.

THE AMERICAN DECISION RATIONALE

FDA and Congressional Assessments of the Risk

Much of the u.s. debate focused on competing interpretations of the scientific evidence of saccharin's carcinogenicity. However since Congressional decision making does not follow the idealized model of sequential risk assessment and risk management steps, one cannot state with confidence whether members of Congress overruled FDA's decision because they arrived at a different assessment of the magnitude of the risks or because they considered the benefits of saccharin to outweigh the risks, a comparison FDA was statutorily precluded from making. It seems likely that both factors influenced American legislators.

FDA, wittingly or unwittingly, may have precipitated the u.s. regulatory controversy over saccharin by the way it initially announced its decision. *Consumer Reports* charges that the message originally released by FDA, which the press was quick to adopt, was that saccharin was essentially harmless but that the FDA had no choice except to ban the only non-caloric sweetener on the market.[45] FDA's announcement invited criticism of both its regulatory science and its legislative mandate.

FDA officials later explained that they chose to downplay the risks because they were concerned that their announcement might spark panic among saccharin consumers and that they were surprised when the public reaction was anger at FDA rather than fear of cancer.[46] In the press release announcing the proposed ban, FDA followed the Canadian government's example in emphasizing that the amount of saccharin fed to rats in the Canadian study was roughly equivalent to human consumption of 800 diet sodas daily over a lifetime.[47] In this initial announcement, the agency failed to explain the scientific rationale for such a dose level in research on animals or the levels of risk to humans that the results indicated. One report notes that "images of rats drowning in a sea of diet colas almost immediately appeared in newspaper cartoons and in the minds of millions of Americans."[48] Had the FDA originally presented their risk analysis as it was later explained in the *Federal Register*, the subsequent debate and ultimate decision on saccharin might have been very different.

FDA's announcement also may have been tempered by the prospect of having to defend its previous inaction on saccharin. In 1976 the u.s. General Accounting Office had criticized the agency for delaying a decision on saccharin.[49] Members of Congress and consumer advocates had been hounding the FDA to resolve the saccharin problem for several years.[50] In response FDA had made it clear that decisive action would be taken if the Canadian study results were conclusive.[51]

The *Federal Register* notice that followed the initial press announcement offered a more complete justification for the proposed ban. In fact FDA took pains to refute the impression that it was reluctantly proceding with the ban because it had no choice under the Delaney Clause.[52] FDA's formal notice differed from the Canadian announcement in offering a quantitative assessment of the risks. The agency estimated that lifetime consumption of one diet beverage per day presented a cancer risk of between zero and 4 in 10,000. Equivalently, if every resident of the United States drank one diet soft drink per day, the agency estimated that saccharin could cause up to 1200 additional cases of bladder cancer per year.[53] FDA arrived at these estimates by performing a very simple linear extrapolation from the doses the rats received and their corresponding rate of cancer to the human dose contained in one diet beverage. The FDA had to defend its decision against a lack of epidemiological evidence. The *Federal Register* notice maintained that the risks of saccharin consumption indicated by the animal studies could not have been detected by the available epidemiological studies; the study populations simply were too small to permit detection of relatively low individual risks, which nevertheless could constitute an unacceptable aggregate population risk.[54]

FDA concluded that "conscientious protection of the public health is not consistent with continued general use in foods of a compound shown to present the kind of risk of cancer that has been demonstrated for saccharin – regardless of the asserted benefits of its use for some individuals in the population."[55] Like Health and Welfare Canada, FDA concluded that the risks of saccharin outweighed the benefits.

Many members of Congress offered their own interpretations of the available scientific evidence which differed substantially from the FDA analysis. First, many members ridiculed the Canadian study as having little relevance to human exposure given the high dosages of saccharin administered to the rats. It was argued that the proposed ban was not warranted, since humans could not possibly consume comparable quantities of the substance. The leading opponent of the ban in the House of Representatives, James Martin, frequently decried the "massive overdoses" used in the Canadian research.[56] It even was suggested in the Congressional debates that *any* substance delivered in such high doses would cause cancer.[57] Senator Lloyd Bentsen's statement was representative of many members' remarks in focusing on FDA's own "800 can" analogy: "I am not a scientist but my commonsense tells me that the level of saccharin fed to the rats in the Canadian tests – an amount equivalent to human consumption of 800 cans of diet soda a day – is not even remotely likely to be consumed by any human being."[58]

Second, members of Congress argued that evidence of *human* incidence of cancer from saccharin consumption was needed to justify a ban. One widely quoted remark ridiculed FDA's reliance on studies of rats, rather than humans, in suggesting that an appropriate label for products containing saccharin would be, "Warning: The Canadians have determined that saccharin is dangerous to your rat's health."[59] Rather than accepting the FDA's explanation that the available epidemiological studies on saccharin were inconclusive, critics of the ban repeatedly cited the negative epidemiological studies as proof of saccharin's safety.[60]

The fact that the ban's opponents repeatedly emphasized that the study was foreign suggests a conscious strategy to discredit FDA's proposal by any available means. Some members of Congress argued that because the study was Canadian the results were inappropriate for evaluation of regulatory action in the United States.[61] Others pointedly referred to the "Canadian study" at every opportunity. Criticism was even implied for reliance on "Canadian rats"![62]

The few members of Congress who supported the saccharin ban decried the circulation of misinformation on the subject and repeatedly offered reasoned explanations for FDA's action.[63] One Representative reminded his colleagues that the Canadian tests were conducted "according to well-established and accepted scientific techniques. The data that they yield are very significant for human beings consuming saccharin in reasonable amounts. Yet the FDA has been ridiculed by the press and industry, who seem to refuse to look at the scientific basis for the agency's decision."[64] FDA's allies in Congress cited scientific opinion that there was no evidence to support a safe threshold for any cancer-causing chemical, and that not all substances cause cancer when consumed in large quantities. These legislators also stressed that virtually every substance known to cause cancer in humans also is known to be an animal carcinogen, suggesting a basis for prudent extrapolation from animals to humans.

Opponents of the ban apparently were not convinced. It is important to recognize that the questions at stake involved more than just science. In light of the scientific uncertainty surrounding risk assessment, scientific questions become intertwined with questions of policy. Elected representatives undoubtedly had an important voice to contribute to the debate over regulatory science. However, that reasoned voice could not be heard over the chorus of misinformation in the saccharin debate. Instead of addressing the question of an appropriate standard of proof, the arguments offered by opponents of the ban were often simplistic and scientifically unsophisticated. In fact the Congressional debates over saccharin revealed remarkably obdurate misunderstanding of the scientific basis and regulatory need for extrapolation from high to low doses and from rats to humans. U.S. legislators' apparent unwillingness to consider the rationale offered by FDA and its Congressional supporters leads one to ask whether they truly did not understand or whether they simply found it politically prudent to misrepresent FDA's logic.

To be fair it should be noted that U.S. legislators did not have a monopoly on misunderstanding of regulatory science. Canadian MPs who opposed the ban offered similar arguments to those of the Congressional critics. One of the more vocal critics of Health and Welfare Canada's proposal revealed misunderstanding of the nature of the scientific enterprise in stating, "The word 'scientific' is used very loosely. It is remarkable they should use the word 'may' and still call it a scientific reply. It is hardly scientific not to use absolutes."[65] However Canadian members of Parliament expressed much less interest in the saccharin issue. Only eight MPs from either the government or opposition sides of the House attended Health and Welfare Canada's briefing on the issue.[66]

Balancing the Risks and Benefits in the United States

One significant difference between the regulatory frameworks in the two countries is the fact that the responsible Canadian officials could weigh risk and benefits, but their U.S. counterparts were precluded from doing so. FDA is afforded little discretion under its legislative framework. As Merrill has observed, "In the final analysis, the Food Additives Amendment is binary; ultimately it allows only approval/disapproval decisions."[67]

The U.S. Congress faced no such restriction. Public opinion clearly persuaded members of Congress that the benefits of saccharin outweighed the risks. Apart from the fact that it was good politics to find a way to accede to overwhelming public opinion, there appeared to be genuine concern for the approximately 10 million diabetics in the U.S. who argued that they required a non-caloric sweetener to maintain their health. Also of concern were those people who claimed to need saccharin to control obesity. Arguments were made in Congress that if saccharin were banned, the number of deaths attributable to heart disease associated with obesity would dramatically increase. Although FDA's supporters in Congress noted that scientific studies had yet to establish medical need or benefits for diabetics or the population in general, either members of Congress remained convinced of saccharin's benefits or they were swayed by arguments that at least a psychological benefit existed. The latter was demonstrated in letters from parents of diabetic children that cited the social stigma which might accrue to young diabetics who could not consume readily available soft drinks.

A unique aspect of the U.S. saccharin debate was that the issue was often framed in terms of consumers' rights to make their own choices.

Congressional critics of the ban maintained that the public's right to choose whether or not to consume saccharin was an important benefit in itself. The industry-sponsored Calorie Control Council promoted the argument that citizens did not need government to make their choices for them by sponsoring newpaper advertisements with the headline "Government by the People, of the People, and for the People, except in the case of saccharin."[68] Cummings noted that the industry campaign ultimately succeeded in framing the issue as one of "the individual against big government" rather than "cancerous colas."[69]

Divergence between Canada and the U.S. is particularly evident on this question. That consumers' right to choose was not a prominent feature of the Canadian debate suggests greater Canadian deference and trust in government. However there is reason to question whether the U.S. opponents of the ban were really committed to freedom of choice or simply to saccharin's continued availability. Members of the public and Congress who expressed outrage at FDA's paternalism in the saccharin case did not appear troubled by the agency's role in evaluating the safety of hundreds of other food additives on Americans' behalf. Nonetheless the freedom of choice argument did enjoy greater resonance in the U.S., which allowed opponents of the ban to mobilize public opinion and members of Congress to justify the moratorium.

A related issue was the question of health warnings. While Congress recognized that consumers would require information on the risks of saccharin in order to make an informed choice, Congressional action also reflected concern for the rights of advertisers. A requirement in the Senate bill calling for warnings in radio and television advertisements was deleted based on "the inconclusiveness of the scientific and medical data relating to saccharin and its potential health risks, combined with the important ramifications of restricting commercial speech."[70]

INTEREST REPRESENTATION

The Canadian decision-making process was characterized by closed consultations, accommodation, and a striking absence of conflict. The Health Protection Branch conducted consultations with representatives of the medical and dental professions, pharmacists, and diabetics before making recommendations to the minister. Somewhat surprisingly Health and Welfare officials did not consult the affected industry prior to the decision, although the industry was *notified* of the department's decision in advance of the public announcement.[71] Subsequent meetings with the industry, however, did result in an extension of phase-out deadlines to accommodate producers' concerns. Nor were product safety advocates, consumer groups, or individual consumers provided with an opportunity for input before the regulatory decision was made. It is doubtful that they even were aware that the government was considering a ban.

In light of the absence of opportunities for public input to the decision, the low level of controversy that followed the Canadian ban is noteworthy. (The absence of resistance from consumer groups to the recent reversal with respect to drugs and cosmetics is also note-worthy.) It is particularly striking that the Canadian food industry offered little opposition after the fact. Unlike the u.s. industry, Canadian producers did not attempt to mobilize public opposition through newspaper advertisements challenging the ban. There was no court challenge, although the industry's resounding defeat in its earlier challenge of the cyclamates ban presumably discouraged another try.[72] The relatively small number of references in Parliamentary debates to the problems the industry anticipated suggests that it did not undertake an extensive lobbying effort with MPs. In fact the parliamentary secretary to the minister of health and welfare claimed, "I have not heard a great deal of fight in the business community against this [ban]. I have talked to a number of businessmen who feel they have been treated fairly and who feel they have been given enough time to make the necessary changes."[73] Most accounts suggest that industry did not challenge the government's intentions but rather sought ways to adjust to the new requirements.[74]

The Canadian industry's acquiescence is one of the most puzzling aspects of the saccharin story. Canadian rates of saccharin consumption were not markedly different from those in the u.s., and the low-calorie soft drink market represented a $60-million growth industry in Canada. It often has been suggested that Canadians are more deferential to government authority than Americans.[75] Moreover the diet food industry may have conceded defeat because it perceived little choice but to accept the decision of the majority party in the parliamentary system of government. It is nevertheless striking that the industry would accept substantial financial losses without a fight; certainly other Canadian industries have been quite willing to challenge government policies that adversely affect their interests. Producers may have been appeased by the limited availability the Canadian government offered and by the fact that the announcement held out the possibility that further discussion between the industry and officials might find a place on pharmacy shelves for saccharin-containing diet foods.[76] Coercion also might have played a role in the industry's acquiescence. The press release announcing the extension of the phase-out deadlines noted that the government granted the extension only on the condition that the industry not take advantage of the delay to campaign publicly for repeal of the ban.[77] In the end the flexibility of the Canadian regulatory process may have provided a safety valve that allowed the release of just enough pressure to avert an explosion.

The U.S. regulatory process offered formal opportunities for a broad range of interests to comment on FDA's proposed action. However those opportunities were virtually irrelevant since the restrictions of the Delaney clause left FDA with little choice but to ban saccharin as a food additive. Although FDA held out the possibility of approval of saccharin as a non-prescription drug, it seemed doubtful that the industry would be able to marshal evidence of medical efficacy as demanded by the statute. Thus lobbying efforts quickly moved to the legislative forum, where the affected industry and individual consumers who lobbied elected representatives met with great success. Congress responded to the majority of Americans that opposed the ban – an April 1977 poll reported that 76 percent of respondents opposed FDA's proposed action.[78] Interestingly the original sponsors of the saccharin moratorium legislation were defenders of the Delaney clause who chose to delay or even sacrifice the saccharin ban in order to avoid repeal of the clause itself, as prominent critics of the saccharin ban had advocated.[79] In a sense the saccharin moratorium itself was the safety valve that saved the Delaney clause, at least for a few more years.[80]

CONCLUSION

The final objective of this chapter is to compare the regulatory process and outcomes in Canada and the United States based on our five criteria.

Stringency

In the final analysis the Canadian decision was clearly more stringent in terms of protection of public health. Although saccharin remained available in pharmacies, Canadian decision makers resisted allowing consumers to make their own choices concerning most saccharin products because they felt that the people most at risk either would not read or could not understand warning labels.

Ironically, based on a reading of the two countries' statutes, one might have expected a more stringent decision in the U.S. In Canada substances are evaluated on a case-by-case basis in accordance with norms of administrative discretion and ministerial responsibility, rather than legislatively mandated formal procedures. In the case of saccharin, that discretion supported the product ban. In contrast acting under the authority of the highly restrictive Delaney clause, FDA had no choice but to ban saccharin as a food additive and to do so completely. Since FDA had no flexibility to accommodate producers' and retailers' concerns, those groups proceeded to lobby Congress and the public directly. Public opposition forced Congress to override the terms of its own legislation.

Timeliness

Regulatory officials in both countries reacted promptly to the release of the Canadian study results. In fact their announcements were made within hours of one another. Coordination of regulatory decisions and announcements clearly was important to officials in both countries. This may have reflected a concern that unilateral action by one country could spur either consumer panic in the other or an effort to "circle the wagons" to fend off criticism by acting jointly.

Nor can the U.S. Congress be criticized for inertia. If nothing else the saccharin case clearly demonstrates the responsiveness of the American system and of individual members of Congress to public opinion. Many members of Congress were quick to introduce their own bills to prevent or alter FDA's proposed ban, and others were anxious to add their names to the list of members of Congress supporting such legislation.

Incorporation of Science

Although there were minor differences in the risk assessment approaches officials took in the two countries – FDA staff reported a quantitative risk assessment while Health and Welfare Canada officials apparently relied on a margin of safety approach – those differences did not prevent regulators in both countries from drawing similar conclusions. The real contrast in the saccharin case was between FDA and Congressional risk assessments.

There is ample evidence that the public and many members of Congress misunderstood the scientific basis for the FDA proposal. Many apparently believed reports that they would drown from consumption of saccharin-containing diet sodas before consuming enough to cause cancer. FDA contributed to the public misunderstanding through the way it handled the original announcement, and an aggressive public campaign by the U.S. diet food industry served to reinforce that misunderstanding.

Although many policy assumptions embedded in FDA's risk assessment (and in the statute itself) were indeed arguable, the Congressional debate seldom achieved a level of informed discourse about policy making amid scientific uncertainty. A cynic might question whether the members of Congress really were incapable of grasping FDA's rationale or whether, in the saccharin case, good politics made for bad science. Whether members of Congress genuinely misunderstood or merely misrepresented the regulatory science issues, the saccharin case raises doubts about the appropriateness of the legislature as a forum for regulatory decision making concerning scientifically complex questions of public safety and health.

The U.S. experience also illustrates the dangers inherent in allowing consumers to choose, since the choice was often based on sensationalized or misunderstood information. Sapolsky has argued that consumers have difficulty sorting out risks given the distortions produced by the competition between groups who have a stake in product regulation.[81] In the saccharin case the American public was ill-informed initially by the FDA, later by the industry, and ultimately by Congress.

While misinformation was widely disseminated in the U.S., very little information at all made the rounds in Canada. No news was not necessarily good news. Saccharin remains available to Canadians who wish to purchase it at a pharmacy. Ironically, the warning labels on saccharin products available in pharmacies in Canada are less extensive than the U.S. warnings. Anyone not privy to the limited amount of debate concerning the scientific risk assessment was provided with little information to inform their decision.

Balancing Risks and Benefits

Although the Canadian government made some concessions to special needs groups and to retailers and the diet food industry, the Canadian saccharin ban clearly reflected a view that the risks outweighed the benefits. In contrast U.S. legislators placed greater weight on the benefits of saccharin as perceived by diabetics and dieters. While Health and Welfare Canada was skeptical of saccharin's medical benefits, members of the U.S. Congress were more willing to accept the public's claims of medical and other benefits at face value. Moreover members of Congress placed greater value on consumers' freedom of choice, an issue that received almost no attention in Canada.

The widespread reaction in the U.S. to FDA's proposed ban of saccharin offers insight into the lay public's weighing of risks and benefits. The degree of risk tolerance in the saccharin case is striking in comparison to Americans' risk aversion in the Alar case. Although the disparity could suggest that people are more willing to accept risks and to discount uncertain scientific claims when they perceive direct benefits, the contrast between the saccharin and Alar cases could also suggest that the lay public is vulnerable to whomever dominates risk communication. In the saccharin case the food industry successfully framed the issue by challenging FDA's science, while in the Alar case, a U.S. environmental group framed the issue in terms of risks to children.

Representativeness of Societal Interests

Both countries' regulatory decisions on saccharin appear consistent with public demand. The U.S. public demanded continued availability of products containing saccharin, and Congress responded accordingly. It is noteworthy that Congress chose to treat the symptom rather than the cause, the Delaney clause. Cummings has observed, "The saccharin moratorium legislation demonstrated both Congressional responsiveness to the crisis of the moment and distaste for dealing with tough long-term issues ... With the saccharin moratorium, Congress is saying that Americans can have their cake and eat it too, even if it is slightly carcinogenic."[82]

In Canada the virtual absence of public demands for continued availability of products containing saccharin allowed the government to follow through with ease on its decision to ban saccharin. Although the option to exert pressure directly on politicians also exists in Canada, it was not exercised on such a grand scale. The divergent role of the diet food industry in the two countries is one of the most striking elements of the saccharin story. While the Canadian industry moved quickly to adjust product lines, the U.S. industry took its case to Congress and the public – and won.

It is not clear whether the origins of these differences lie in different political cultures or political institutions in the two countries. Although Canadian consumers and industry reacted less strongly to the saccharin ban, it is not obvious whether that reflected greater trust in government or whether the closed Canadian regulatory system limited the scope of conflict and preempted conflict via concessions. And although American consumers strongly opposed the proposed saccharin ban, it is not clear whether that reflected distrust of government authority and concern for individual freedom or whether the open and divided U.S. system of government provided an opportunity for an aggrieved industry to mobilize the public and individual legislators.

Finally, the saccharin case reveals a tension between technocracy and democracy. In both Canada and the u.s. critics of the proposed bans were wary of the potential for tyranny by experts at the expense of responsiveness to the wishes of the public and their elected representatives. The regulatory history of saccharin in the u.s. demonstrates not only the democratic responsiveness of the u.s. political process but also the risks of relying on the lay public and their elected representatives in scientifically complex questions of policy. The strength of the Canadian parliamentary political system is that it can combine policy accountability with bureaucratic expertise; it was the elected minister who announced his department's decision and subsequently responded to critics in Parliament. However the corresponding weakness of "responsible government" is that one cannot know where expert advice leaves off and political decisions begin.

If the consumer's right to choose is to be the overriding value, then the American system reached the correct decision; if one accepts the premise that government possesses a mandate to protect the health of the public from both potentially harmful substances and competing vested interests, then the Canadian system resulted in the more appropriate decision in the saccharin case.

6 Political Insulation: The Rise and Fall of Urea-Formaldehyde Foam*

INTRODUCTION

Urea-formaldehyde foam insulation (UFFI) enjoyed a surge in popularity in both Canada and the United States following the "energy crisis" of the mid-1970s, as homeowners sought to avert rising energy costs by better insulating their homes. The history of the product followed a similar path in the two countries in many respects. Virtually identical product standards were developed in Canada and the U.S. in cooperation with UFFI manufacturers. Later, when evidence emerged of the hazards of formaldehyde gas released by the product, regulators in both countries moved to ban the product within months of each other in the early 1980s.

However the two regulatory histories also differ in important ways. The Canadian government successfully banned UFFI, while a U.S. ban was ultimately overturned by the courts. Also in contrast to the U.S., the Canadian government played a more active role in the UFFI story from start to finish. Not only did the federal government promote the product by subsidizing the majority of UFFI purchases in Canada, it was actually in the UFFI business as part owner of a leading Canadian manufacturer of the insulation.[1] In a final contrast with the U.S. government, only the Canadian federal government ultimately subsidized homeowners' expenses to have UFFI removed.

---

* Written with the assistance of Anjan Chaklader

Urea-formaldehyde foam is a shaving cream-like substance that is installed by pumping it through small holes drilled in a building's walls. It subsequently hardens to form a permanent insulation. The fact that the product can be installed readily in existing buildings made it popular with homeowners eager to avert rising energy costs in the mid-1970s. UFFI was installed in roughly 60,000 Canada homes and 500,000 homes in the U.S.[2] By the late 1970s, however, it was discovered that formaldehyde gas UFFI released into the home could cause health problems. At sufficient concentrations formaldehyde is an irritant to the eyes, nose, throat, and respiratory system.[3] A small fraction of residents of UFFI homes complained of health problems ranging from minor irritation to more severe symptoms – in a few cases, families were forced to leave their homes because of adverse effects of the product. Additional questions about the safety of UFFI were raised in 1979, when evidence emerged that formaldehyde causes cancer in laboratory animals.

Although UFFI constituted a relatively small fraction of formaldehyde use, the regulatory debate over urea-formaldehyde insulation became particularly heated when the North American chemical industry sought to defend the larger reputation of formaldehyde, an important chemical building block in the manufacture of a wide variety of consumer products. Formaldehyde is used in such diverse products as plywood, particle board, permapress fabrics, paints, cosmetics, and drugs. In fact U.S. manufacturers estimate that formaldehyde is a component of products comprising 8 percent of the gross national product.[4]

THE REGULATORY FRAMEWORK

In both Canada and the United States consumer product safety is controlled by two parallel mechanisms: a formal process to regulate hazardous products, and an informal process to develop voluntary product standards. In Canada, the ministers of Consumer and Corporate Affairs and of Health share responsibility for regulation of consumer products. Consumer and Corporate Affairs formally administers the Hazardous Products Act with advice from Health and Welfare Canada. Under the act, Cabinet is authorized to ban a product on the advice of either minister if it is satisfied the product "is or is likely to be a danger to the health or safety of the public."[5]

The vague wording of the Hazardous Products Act offers considerable flexibility. The act does not specify the degree of public risk necessary to justify a product ban. Nor does it indicate whether the potential costs of a ban to either consumers or the product manufacturer should be taken into consideration. The government is not required by statute to provide a rationale when it bans a product. In addition to allowing discretion with respect to the substance of regulatory decisions, the statute places few limits on the decision-making process. For instance the Hazardous Products Act requires neither public hearings nor that an opportunity be provided for written submissions prior to finalizing a regulation.

Although not required by statute, public consultation, regulatory impact analyses, and prepublication of proposed regulations have been required for new federal health and safety regulations since 1978 as a matter of government policy.[6] However the original requirement for extensive socio-economic impact analysis was satisfied by only 11 federal regulations between 1978 and 1985.[7] A policy calling for more modest regulatory impact analyses superceded the original policy in 1986, and it has been more routinely observed.[8]

The Hazardous Products Act does establish an indirect process for appeals. Within 60 days of the decision to ban a product the minister must establish a Hazardous Product Board of Review if requested to do so by any manufacturer or seller of the product.[9] Although a board of review can only be requested by the affected industry, once established it must provide an opportunity for input by *any* person affected by the decision. The minister must make the board's final report public unless the "public interest would be better served by withholding publication."[10] While the recommendations of the board of review have no legal force, the presumption of public disclosure would create considerable pressure for reversal if a board's report were critical of the original Cabinet decision. The ban remains in effect throughout the board's deliberations.

In a parallel, informal process to promote product standardization, the Canadian government relies less on its regulatory authority and more on its powers of persuasion. A federal government body, the Canadian General Standards Board (CGSB),[11] encourages development of "consensus standards" through numerous technical committees. CGSB committees typically are composed in varying proportions of representatives of the federal and provincial governments, industry, professional organizations, and consumer groups. The federal government participates in two ways. First, CGSB, itself a government agency, convenes and provides administrative support for the process. Second, representatives of federal departments normally participate as members of CGSB technical committees. Compliance with CGSB standards is strictly voluntary. It is simply assumed that manufacturers will comply with standards that they helped to develop.

The Canada Mortgage and Housing Corporation (CMHC) also plays a role in promoting product standards.[12] CMHC is a Crown corporation (i.e., a government-owned corporation) that insures a fraction of Canadian homeowner mortgages. As guarantor CMHC has an incentive to ensure quality construction, to limit the extent of its future liability. Thus CMHC specifies which materials may be used in the construction of homes in order to qualify for CMHC-insured mortgages. Products that qualify are issued CMHC "acceptance numbers." In deciding whether to accept individual products, CMHC relies heavily on standards developed by other bodies, particularly CGSB. However in contrast to CGSB standards, CMHC standards are in a sense enforceable. If a product fails to meet the conditions set by CMHC, the Corporation can refuse to guarantee mortgages for any homes that use the product. However CMHC's standards apply only to CMHC-insured homes – nothing prevents product manufacturers from selling or builders from using construction materials that have not received CMHC acceptance.

CMHC officials are careful to describe the process as one of product "acceptance," rather than "approval," for fear that the latter would be interpreted as an endorsement of particular products.[13] The fact remains, however, that CMHC only "accepts" a product if it is satisfied that it meets certain standards. Thus CMHC acceptance does indeed convey information about the federal government's evaluation of a product's quality.

In the United States the Consumer Product Safety Commission (CPSC) is responsible for regulation of consumer product safety. CPSC is an independent regulatory agency comprised of up to five commissioners, each appointed by the president for a seven-year term. CPSC's decision making is subject to a number of federal statutes that mandate procedural openness, including the "Government in the Sunshine Act" and the Administrative Procedures Act. One legal scholar has described the commission's deliberations as candid to the point of impeding rulemaking.[14]

The Consumer Product Safety Act authorizes CPSC either to issue a product standard or to ban a product.[15] The statute provides detailed guidance to CPSC concerning the basis for regulatory decisions. It also constrains the commission by specifying conditions that must be met before CPSC can issue regulations. For instance CPSC is only authorized to issue regulations if a voluntary standard is not feasible.[16] Regulations must be "reasonably necessary to prevent or reduce an unreasonable risk of injury," and must constitute the least burdensome way to adequately reduce the risk.[17] CPSC can only ban a product if no feasible product standard would adequately protect the public.[18] Finally, CPSC must demonstrate that the "benefits expected from [a] rule bear a reasonable relationship to its costs."[19] Overall the statute imposes a heavy burden of proof on the commission to justify any regulatory actions.

The act sets out an elaborate process for CPSC decision making, with full disclosure and opportunities for public comment at each step.[20] The commission must first publish an "advance notice of proposed rulemaking" inviting written comments and proposals for voluntary standards. If the commission then concludes that voluntary standards would not be adequate, it must publish a "notice of proposed rulemaking" and provide an opportunity for both written and oral submissions. Only then can the commission issue its final regulation. In contrast to the Canadian legislation, which allows only the affected industry to call for a board of review, any person affected by a CPSC decision can appeal it in court.[21] Thus in addition to industry challenges on the grounds that regulations are too stringent, U.S. regulatory advocates can challenge decisions that they perceive as insufficiently stringent, and even appeal CPSC decisions *not* to issue regulations.

Like the CGSB-CMHC process, there is a similar informal process for development of product standards in the U.S. The U.S. Department of Housing and Urban Development (HUD) insures about 15 to 20 percent of U.S. mortgages. Like CMHC, HUD "accepts" products that meet certain standards and requires use of only those materials in HUD-insured housing. With few exceptions, HUD product standards have been initiated by the industry in order to achieve a "level playing field."[22] HUD standards, like those of CGSB, are "consensus standards" usually developed by government- industry committees.

PRODUCT HISTORY IN CANADA

In 1970 the CMHC asked CGSB to develop a standard for urea-formaldehyde insulation. However CGSB did not actively seek to develop a standard for UFFI until 1975, by which time manufacturers had compiled research on their products and there was growing consumer demand for insulation.[23] The CGSB UFFI Committee had 24 members, including seven from the UFFI industry and six from the federal government.[24] No representatives of labour or competing industries were included. A single consumer representative was added to the committee in 1978, after a standard already had been developed.[25] No medical expertise was sought until late 1979.

Throughout the standard development process federal government representatives from the National Research Council, CMHC, and the Department of Energy, Mines, and Resources repeatedly expressed reservations about the product. However representatives of the latter, who were particularly critical of UFFI's performance, did not have a vote on the CGSB committee. There was almost no discussion at early committee meetings of the potential health effects of UFFI. Federal officials' concerns focused primarily on the product's poor performance as an insulation rather than its safety.[26]

Although CGSB develops so-called "consensus standards," consensus lies somewhere between unanimity and a simple majority. Comments by the secretary of the CGSB committee suggest that the required degree of consensus is ill-defined and relatively flexible.[27] Federal government committee members were in a relatively weak position because it was not clear that they had the capacity to veto an overly weak standard, and even if they could the departments represented did not have regulatory authority to issue more stringent standards. The federal members concluded that a standard imposing at least some restrictions would be better than no standard at all.[28]

The committee agreed on a provisional standard for UFFI in May 1977. They agreed at that time that the vote on a final standard would be delayed until the fall, pending completion of additional studies. However rumours of a planned federal program to subsidize home insulation provided the impetus to finalize the standard immediately. UFFI manufacturers on the committee knew that a CGSB standard would pave the way for CMHC acceptance and thus, presumably, for eligibility for government subsidies. At their request, the CGSB committee met again in July and approved the final standard, even though the awaited studies had yet to be completed.[29] The committee secretary later testified that "there was some industry pressure, as I have mentioned, saying they needed a CMHC acceptance number on the standard yesterday, and they were very concerned about getting a [CGSB] standard. That maybe influenced the rate of progress of the committee to the point that – squeaky wheels get oiled; if they are applying some pressure you respond, in some way, to satisfy that."[30]

The federal government committee members ultimately voted in favour of the CGSB standard, despite continuing reservations about the product's performance.[31] They supported the standard because they felt they had gained important concessions from the industry that would severely limit the market for the product. In particular, the committee gave UFFI a relatively low "R value," a measure of insulation performance. As one member put it, "By voting for the standard on that basis, the industry should have died, the material should have died, it no longer held a competitive place in the marketplace."[32]

Within weeks of the July meeting CMHC began to issue "acceptances" to UFFI manufacturers. Pressure from the industry to ensure eligibility for anticipated subsidies was again influential. The fact that

CMHC received the same letter from members of Parliament from all parties urging acceptance of UFFI,[33] indicates that the letter-writing campaign probably was orchestrated by the industry. The CMHC officer responsible for reviewing the UFFI applications stated, "You can imagine what industry, with the government dangling millions of dollars in front of their eyes, are going to do: they want their product accepted, and now. Any opposition is – well, you can imagine what it is like. But even though there was pressure, [CMHC] insisted on a limited acceptance."[34]

CMHC based its acceptance on the restrictive CGSB standard, adding conditions of its own, including a requirement that manufacturers advertise the low R value. According to one government official, "If the rules they had implemented were followed, very few homeowners would have accepted the material, because it meant telling the truth to the people about what a poor insulation it was."[35]

In retrospect it is evident that the informality of the process allowed the industry to work one agency against the other. CGSB committee members responded to industry pressure to issue a standard because it was needed to ensure CMHC acceptance. And CMHC felt compelled to accept the product because a CGSB standard already existed.[36]

As anticipated, in September 1977 the federal government launched the Canadian Home Insulation Program (CHIP), which offered subsidies of up to $500 to homeowners to install CMHC-accepted insulation. As a result of the program, most Canadian purchases of urea-formaldehyde home insulation were government subsidized. Of the estimated 55,000 to 60,000 Canadian homeowners that installed UFFI,[37] approximately 40,000 to 45,000 received CHIP subsidies.[38]

The limitations CGSB and CMHC imposed on the product might have averted many of the subsequent problems had they been enforced. Unlike the voluntary CGSB standard, CMHC's conditions of acceptance applied to all CHIP-subsidized purchases, the majority of UFFI installations. However enforcement was particularly difficult because of the decentralized nature of UFFI manufacture: its preparation at the site of application resulted in considerable variability in product quality. In any case there was no systematic investigation of the product's performance in the field. A former CMHC official explained that "The control [was] the integrity of the company."[39] Only later was it recognized that the companies' integrity left much to be desired. The National Research Council later concluded that the CGSB standard was never met by the foams installed in Canadian homes.[40]

One official within CMHC did monitor reports that UFFI manufacturers' product advertisements were claiming "R values" higher than the limit specified by CMHC.[41] With the approval of his supervisor, George Brewer notified all UFFI manufacturers on 29 May 1979 that CMHC was revoking their acceptance numbers and thus their eligibility for CHIP subsidies.[42] Two days later Brewer's supervisor met with representatives of the industry at the offices of their lawyers and agreed to reinstate acceptance.[43] Brewer left his job in anger when the acceptance numbers were restored. However his supervisor's testimony before a parliamentary committee implied that CMHC's action was intended all along to be temporary.[44] Whatever the original intent, it is clear that the manufacturers were once again taken at their word, despite their repeated failures to comply with the existing standard of acceptance.[45]

By this time health concerns were beginning to emerge, although that was not the reason for CMHC's shortlived withdrawal of acceptance. Complaints first emerged in the U.S., where the rate of UFFI installations peaked earlier than in Canada. As early as 1977 a U.S. report, which discussed irritation and odour problems associated with formaldehyde emissions from UFFI, was circulated to CGSB committee members.[46] In early 1978 Health and Welfare Canada established a working group on the toxicology of thermal insulation in response to U.S. reports of health effects associated with UFFI.[47] By that summer several Canadian government officials publicly expressed concerns about the toxicity of formaldehyde released into homes by UFFI.[48] A CBC news program on the growing U.S. concerns aired in November 1979, stimulating Canadian consumer complaints to the federal government. Before the CBC program aired, "there were more reports about UFOs than UFFI," according to one federal official.[49]

In 1979 the CGSB committee finally sought the advice of Health and Welfare Canada on a standard for formaldehyde in homes. The official who recommended a 0.1 ppm standard to the committee in November does not appear to have been aware of the preliminary results of animal carcinogenicity reported by U.S. researchers a month earlier.[50] The CGSB committee did not meet to discuss Health and Welfare's recommendation for five months, at which time it voted not to accept the proposed standard. The federal government representatives were the only committee members who voted in favour of the standard, and they were significantly outnumbered.[51] The incident illustrates the risk the federal government takes when it chooses to play the role of minority partner in a consensual decision-making process, rather than the more adversarial role of regulator.

In July 1980 Health and Welfare Canada met with representatives of the industry and warned them that if they did not accept the proposed 0.1 ppm voluntary standard, the federal government would examine its regulatory options under the Hazardous Products Act.[52] Government officials met again with manufacturers in October to discuss the fact that their products were continuing to fall short of the CMHC standards.[53] At that meeting the industry was also informed that the federal government had recently established an expert committee of five scientists to review UFFI's adverse health effects.

On 8 December 1980 the expert committee issued an interim report recommending a temporary moratorium on UFFI installation pending further studies of the health effects of formaldehyde.[54] Within days the federal government banned UFFI under the authority of the Hazardous Products Act. No opportunity for public comment was provided before promulgation of the ban. The federal government apparently took advantage of an emergency exemption in its policy requiring public consultation and socio-economic impact analysis. Although the ban was originally envisioned as a temporary measure,[55] it was finalized after the government received the expert committee's final report in April 1981.[56]

The Canadian ban was never contested in the courts. However, as required by the act, the minister of Consumer and Corporate Affairs did establish a Hazardous Products Board of Review in response to a request from a UFFI manufacturer. The board held 43 days of hearings and received testimony from 180 witnesses.[57] Its report, released in October 1982, concluded that no product standard could adequately protect residents of UFFI-insulated homes from the adverse health effects of formaldehyde, and in any case, "there appears to be no advantage to the use of urea-formaldehyde foam in its present quality as an insulation material for buildings."[58]

The economic impact of the ban was felt immediately, not only by UFFI manufacturers and installers but by homeowners who had already installed UFFI. Although residents of most UFFI homes had suffered no obvious ill effects from the product, resale values of most urea-formaldehyde insulated homes fell after the ban conveyed the impression that those homes were unsafe. Homeowners faced a minimum cost of several thousand dollars if they chose to remove the insulation.

The government was pressured to compensate UFFI homeowners for removal, largely because it had promoted UFFI installations in the first place through the CHIP subsidies. Moreover by that time, one of the two largest Canadian UFFI manufacturers was 40 percent government owned.[59] UFFI homeowner associations formed across the country to lobby the government. Their efforts were reinforced by media reports and the parliamentary opposition parties, which criticized the government's role in the UFFI story.

One year after UFFI was banned in Canada, the minister of Consumer and Corporate Affairs announced a compensation program for homeowners through which the government provided up to $5000 to allay the expenses of mitigation or removal of UFFI. Although compensation was initially offered only for homes with formaldehyde levels above 0.1 ppm,[60] eligibility soon was extended to all urea-formaldehyde insulated homes. The program ultimately cost the federal government more than $320 million.[61]

The federal compensation program typically did not cover the full costs of removing UFFI, and no compensation was provided for other costs incurred by residents of UFFI homes, including physical suffering and mental distress. One group of homeowners sought redress in the Quebec courts, claiming damages from UFFI manufacturers, installers, insurance underwriters, and both the federal government and the Quebec government, which also had provided subsidies for UFFI.[62] The fact that the Quebec government provided financial assistance to cover the group's considerable legal expenses explains why UFFI homeowners pursued civil remedies only in Quebec. Eight years and $26 million in legal costs after the case began, a Quebec Superior Court judge decisively dismissed the homeowners' claims on the grounds that they did not provide sufficient proof of either physical or economic harm.[63]

PRODUCT HISTORY IN THE UNITED STATES[64]

By the time the Department of Housing and Urban Development moved to issue a standard in 1977, at the request of the UFFI industry, U.S. installations had already reached a peak of 170,000 per year. On the recommendation of a joint government-industry committee, HUD issued a consensus standard in October 1977, which relied heavily on the CGSB standard issued earlier that year.[65]

As part of a national policy to encourage energy conservation adopted during the energy crisis of the 1970s, U.S. taxpayers were eligible for tax credits for expenditures on household energy conservation measures. Some U.S. consumers thus were eligible to deduct 15 percent of the cost of urea-formaldehyde foam installation.[66]

When UFFI consumers began to experience adverse health effects, they first registered their complaints with state and local agencies. As early as 1976 the Denver Consumer Affairs Office petitioned the CPSC to develop a standard for UFFI.[67] As the number of complaints accumulated, Massachusetts became the first state to ban the product in 1979. Several other states and municipalities followed suit.[68] When reports of health problems associated with the product were publicized, consumer demand rapidly fell to 10,000 installations per year by 1981.[69]

With the exception of a 1979 press release warning of possible health problems associated with UFFI, CPSC had taken no public action to respond to the 1976 petition when evidence emerged of formaldehyde's carcinogenicity. Ironically the Chemical Industry Institute of Toxicology (CIIT), an industry-sponsored research institute, first confirmed formaldehyde's carcinogenicity in laboratory animals. The Formaldehyde Institute, an industry trade association, informed the commission of CIIT's preliminary findings in October 1979.[70]

During the late 1970s the Consumer Product Safety Commission was redirecting its attention from product safety to chronic hazards.[71] Graham, Green, and Roberts concluded that "CPSC's initiative on formaldehyde can be viewed as an attempt by a troubled organization to justify its existence, particularly to potential congressional patrons."[72] Formaldehyde soon became a *cause célèbre* in the ongoing U.S. debate over cancer risk assessment. Meetings among senior regulatory officials in the Carter administration had culminated in the development of the Interagency Regulatory Liaison Group's cancer risk assessment policy, which CPSC supported.[73] Formaldehyde became a test case for application of the policy, with CPSC reviewing UFFI, the Environmental Protection Agency reviewing environmental releases of formaldehyde, and the Occupational Safety and Health Administration (OSHA) reviewing occupational exposure.

However when Reagan administration officials assumed office in early 1981, they challenged what they felt were overly cautious assumptions in risk assessment that would lead to unduly stringent regulation of business. Senior officials at EPA and OSHA reversed many of their predecessors' decisions on formaldehyde, drawing heavy criticism from Congress, interest groups, academics, and eventually the courts.[74] Although the second wave of Reagan appointees eventually reversed those policy decisions, regulatory action on formaldehyde was delayed in the interim.

In contrast to EPA and OSHA, CPSC, as an independent agency, was more insulated from Administration politics. President Reagan did not have an opportunity to replace any commissioners until after CPSC had already voted to propose a ban of UFFI. Moreover commissioners have greater autonomy than their counterparts in line departments. In fact the CPSC chair subsequently appointed by President Reagan actually voted in favour of the final UFFI ban in 1982.

After receiving the preliminary CIIT findings, CPSC convened a panel of 16 senior scientists from federal government agencies to review the evidence of formaldehyde's carcinogenicity. In November 1980 the panel concluded, "formaldehyde should be presumed to pose a carcinogenic risk to humans." The decision was based on clear evidence of carcinogenicity in rats, suggestive evidence in other animal species, and suggestive evidence from epidemiological studies of workers exposed to formaldehyde.[75] CPSC also contracted with the prestigious National Academy of Sciences (NAS) to review the acute effects of formaldehyde. On the basis of available data the NAS reported in March 1980 that "there is no population threshold for the irritant effects of formaldehyde in humans."[76]

CPSC held public hearings on UFFI in four cities between December 1979 and February 1980. The commission subsequently proposed a relatively weak labelling requirement for UFFI in June 1980.[77] After receiving the report of the federal panel, however, CPSC voted in January 1981 to propose a ban of UFFI. A request for public comments on the proposed action was published in February 1981.[78] One year later commissioners voted by a 4 to 1 margin to ban UFFI in homes and schools. Notice of the ban was published in April 1982, but it did not take effect until August.[79]

The CPSC decision was challenged in court from both sides. Public Citizen, an interest group affiliated with Ralph Nader, argued that the ban was not broad enough, while the industry, represented by the Formaldehyde Institute, argued that the ban was unnecessary because a product standard could adequately protect public health. A race to the courthouse ensued as both sides sought to have the case decided by a sympathetic court. The industry won (by a 10-second margin) and succeeded in having the case heard in the Fifth Circuit Court of Appeals in New Orleans, which had previously delivered decisions favourable to industry interests.[80]

The court overturned the CPSC ban in April 1983, ruling that the regulatory agency did not adequately demonstrate that the product presented an "unreasonable risk of injury," as required by the statute.[81] Although a majority of the CPSC commissioners voted to appeal the court's decision, federal appeals must be conducted by the solicitor general, a presidential appointee who refused to pursue the appeal on CPSC's behalf.[82]

In the absence of government grants for removal of UFFI, American consumers turned to the courts with greater frequency than their Canadian counterparts. Individual consumers, builders, and even installers seeking damages from UFFI manufacturers launched more than one hundred lawsuits. In an interesting contrast to the Canadian litigation, it appears that no American consumers sought damages from the U.S. government.[83]

HEALTH EFFECTS OF FORMALDEHYDE

A variety of acute and chronic health effects have been associated with exposure to formaldehyde, including eye, nose, and throat irritation, headaches, cough, shortness of breath, and asthmatic attacks.[84] Individuals' sensitivity to formaldehyde's irritant effects varies greatly. The U.S. National Academy of Science estimated that 10 to 20 percent of the population may be particularly sensitive to the gas.[85] In addition to potential problems associated with emissions of formaldehyde, the high water content of UFFI can lead to formation of molds in a building's walls, which can cause allergic reactions.[86]

The CIIT cancer study exposed groups of rats and mice to airborne concentrations of 14.3 ppm, 5.6 ppm, 2 ppm, and 0 ppm.[87] At the highest exposure level, about half the rats developed nasal cancer. Nasal cancers also were observed in the rats exposed to 5.6 ppm, but the number of tumours observed was not statistically significant. No malignant tumours were observed in either the group exposed to 2 ppm or the control group. Among the mice nasal cancers were observed only in the highest exposure group, but again the number of tumours did not reach statistical significance. Although the number of tumours among the rats at 5.6 ppm and mice at 14.3 ppm was not statistically significant at a 95 percent level of confidence, the fact that the same type of uncommon tumour was observed as in the rats exposed to 14.3 ppm led many scientists to conclude that the finding had "biological significance."[88] Researchers at New York University subsequently confirmed the CIIT findings of formaldehyde's carcinogenicity in rodents.[89]

In assessing the degree of cancer risk to humans, several familiar themes emerge. First, how should negative epidemiological studies be weighed against positive animal studies? At the time of the UFFI decisions there was no clear evidence from epidemiological studies that formaldehyde causes cancer in humans, but there was strong evidence of animal carcinogenicity. Second, how should human sensitivity be compared to that of animals? Mice were clearly less sensitive than rats. Should it be assumed that human sensitivity compares with that of rats or mice – or neither?

Finally, how should evidence at relatively high doses be extrapolated to lower doses? The experimental dose-response curve exhibited marked nonlinearity. When the dose was increased by a factor of 2.5 (from 5.6 to 14.3 ppm), the rate of tumours among rats increased by a factor of 50. The levels at which experimental animals developed nasal cancer were 10 to 100 times higher than typical levels measured in UFFI homes. Although that seems like a relatively small difference, particularly compared with the saccharin and Alar case studies, some scientists argued that the acute irritation experienced by the experimental animals at the higher doses may have played a role in the development of tumours.[90] They argued that evidence obtained at high levels of exposure therefore would have limited relevance to much lower levels in UFFI homes. Other scientists responded that many residents of UFFI homes do in fact experience acute irritant effects. Moreover they argued that formaldehyde is a known mutagen, albeit a weak one, and thus could be expected to initiate carcinogenesis even in the absence of a possible promotion effect associated with irritation.[91]

DISTRIBUTION OF THE COSTS AND BENEFITS OF A PRODUCT BAN

The decision to ban UFFI resulted in a redistribution of wealth between different industries and between different groups of consumers. While the ban was devastating to UFFI manufacturers and installers, it represented a benefit to manufacturers and installers of alternative insulation products.

The ban also imposed costs on future consumers, most of whom would not suffer any ill effects, by depriving them of a product they would otherwise buy in order to avoid harm to the minority of consumers who would experience problems.[92] This tradeoff among prospective consumers was not problematic, however, because one cannot identify in advance which consumers will fall in either group, both because it is difficult to predict what levels of formaldehyde will result from UFFI installation in a particular house and because it is not known in advance which residents will be sensitive to formaldehyde. Thus, given information on potential health effects, most consumers would rationally decline to purchase UFFI even in the absence of a ban. In fact, by the time CPSC voted to ban UFFI, U.S. consumers had already voted overwhelmingly with their pocketbooks, effectively banning the product from the marketplace.

The imposition of costs on those who had already installed UFFI presents a more serious concern, however. The prospective ban on sales of UFFI did nothing to mitigate any health risks faced by those who had already installed it. The ban did however have an immediate impact on the resale value of homes that contained UFFI, by alerting potential homebuyers to problems associated with the product. But it is important to recognize that it was primarily buyers' concerns about a faulty product, rather than the government's decision to ban the product per se, that devalued UFFI homes. If the Canadian government and CPSC had taken no regulatory action and simply publicized the health hazards associated with the product and its poor performance as a insulation, one would have anticipated similar consumer aversion to UFFI homes.[93]

RECONSTRUCTING THE CANADIAN DECISION

Assessing the Risks

The assessments of the health risks performed by both the expert committee and the board of review were much less formal and detailed than that prepared by the CPSC. In fact the expert committee's final report was only 20 pages long. The committee's conclusions were based primarily on a qualitative assessment of the risks. Canadian decision makers also placed much less emphasis on formaldehyde's potential carcinogenicity than did their U.S. counterparts.

In light of the fact that its findings ultimately led to the Canadian ban, the expert committee's relatively risk tolerant approach to cancer risk assessment is quite surprising. The committee simply refused to speculate about the carcinogenic risk to humans based only on an animal study, "particularly when account is taken of species differences in carcinogenic responses and the lack of precise data concerning levels of human exposure."[94] Interestingly the committee declined to adopt even the more traditional safety factor approach. As Graham, Green, and Roberts noted, reliance on a commonly used safety factor of 100 would have suggested an acceptable level of human exposure to formaldehyde of 0.02 ppm,[95] a level below that found in many UFFI and non-UFFI homes alike.

The report did offer a quantitative assessment of the risk *to rats*. The level of exposure corresponding to a cancer risk of one in a million was estimated to be between 0.004 ppm, based on a model that is linear at low doses, and 1 ppm, "based on other models that more closely fit the perceived mechanism of action of formaldehyde." The latter models were not specified, nor did the report offer any elaboration of "the perceived mechanism of action."[96]

By the time the subsequent board of review delivered its report, measurements of formaldehyde levels in UFFI homes had provided the "smoking gun" for irritant effects. The average level of formaldehyde in homes containing UFFI was significantly higher than that in non-UFFI homes. Average levels were even higher in urea-formaldehyde insulated homes in which residents had complained of adverse health effects.[97]

The board of review was less reticent than the expert committee to presume that formaldehyde is a human carcinogen. Its report stated, "It is apparent that there are sufficient data to demonstrate that formaldehyde is carcinogenic in animals. Although human epidemiological studies are not sufficient to assess the carcinogenic risk in humans, there is no evidence that sufficient difference exists in the manner in which formaldehyde is metabolized by animals and humans. Therefore, the available evidence does indicate that formaldehyde poses a cancer risk to humans."[98] Although the board cited CPSC's quantitative assessment of the cancer risk, it did not appear to rely heavily on quantitative risk assessment in drawing its conclusions. It is interesting that the board relied exclusively on U.S. scientists in its discussion of formaldehyde's potential carcinogenicity.

Weighing Costs and Benefits

The closed nature of the Canadian decision in this case makes it difficult to assess how the costs and benefits were weighed. When the Canadian federal government banned UFFI in December 1980, it did not publish a rationale for its decision. As Jasanoff noted, "The reasons for their actions ... were never completely articulated, so the decisions leave something to be desired in terms of intellectual rigour."[99] The Cabinet clearly relied on the expert committee, both in issuing the "temporary" ban in December within days of receiving the committee's interim report, and in deciding upon receipt of their final report that the ban would be considered permanent.

The fact that a ban was instituted on the recommendation of the expert committee is striking, since on closer examination it is evident that the formaldehyde industry had considerable influence on the committee's deliberations. Two of the five committee members were scientists affiliated with the industry.[100] In addition to reviewing government standards and scientific literature on formaldehyde, the committee received nine briefs from the industry. There was no input from labour, UFFI homeowners, or consumer groups. The only evidence of formaldehyde's carcinogenicity the committee considered was apparently provided by the two committee members affiliated with the industry, who testified as experts before their own committee.[101] Those factors help to explain the committee's marked reluctance to draw any conclusions about human carcinogenicity.

It is conceivable that events went further and faster than at least the industry committee members intended. When the committee's interim report recommended a temporary moratorium, one of the two industry representatives declined to endorse the report. The other withdrew his support when it became clear that the government would respond by instituting a full-fledged ban.[102] While the substance of the committee's final report implicitly supported a product ban, it is noteworthy that the report never explicitly endorsed the federal ban, although it did stress the possibility of future reinstatement of the product. It is also noteworthy that, although the report focused primarily on health effects of formaldehyde, the committee emphasized "that its deliberations were confined solely to the consideration of residential urea-formaldehyde foam insulation, and its findings should not be extended to other uses of urea-formaldehyde resins or indeed formaldehyde itself."[103] Though it was difficult to defend UFFI, the industry representatives may have attempted to shield the reputation of other formaldehyde-based products.

The Hazardous Products Act neither requires nor precludes the balancing of costs and benefits. It was not within the charge of the expert committee to consider the potential costs of a ban. The decision to ban UFFI was exempted from the government's policy of requiring a full socio-economic impact analysis, so there is no record of the anticipated costs and benefits. However deliberately the minister and Cabinet might have weighed the potential costs, health considerations clearly won out.

In making its decision to ban UFFI, the Canadian government apparently was well aware of events unfolding south of the border. One manufacturer who complained about the suddenness of the ban was told by a federal government official that a U.S. ban was expected within a matter of days.[104] Ministers and government officials later noted with pride that the Canadian ban preceded the U.S. action.[105]

RECONSTRUCTING THE U.S. DECISION

Assessing the Risks

The CPSC decision separately considered formaldehyde's irritant effects and potential carcinogenicity. With respect to irritation, the commission relied on the National Academy of Science's conclusion that there is no evidence of a population threshold. The NAS conclusion suggests that even at very low ambient levels of formaldehyde, some subset of the population could suffer adverse acute effects. CPSC did not estimate the fraction of residents of UFFI homes that would actually suffer such effects.

CPSC did however endeavour to quantify the cancer risk. Based on a number of conservative assumptions, including linearity of the dose-response function at low doses and human sensitivity comparable to that of the most sensitive animal species, the commission estimated an upper limit of 1.3 to 1.8 cases of cancer per 10,000 future UFFI installations.[106] In preparing its risk assessment, CPSC complied with the Interagency Regulatory Liaison Group's formal cancer policy.

In overturning CPSC's ban the court did not limit itself to consideration of procedural legal matters but delved into a number of highly technical questions, even drawing its own conclusions about the quality of CPSC's scientific analysis. The decision focused on CPSC's cancer risk assessment, and found it wanting in two respects: because CPSC relied primarily on measurements of formaldehyde levels in complainant homes rather than on a random survey of levels in UFFI homes, and because the cancer risk assessment relied exclusively on the CIIT study. The court argued that "it is not good science to rely on a single experiment, particularly one involving only 250 subjects, to make precise estimates of cancer risk."[107] The court's scientific and legal analysis has been criticized by a number of authors.[108]

Weighing the Costs and Benefits

CPSC was required by its statute to demonstrate that the benefits of a ban were at least comparable to the costs. By the time of the ban the UFFI industry was already in decline, presumably as a result of both consumer aversion and anticipation of regulatory action, so the number of jobs and revenues lost was less significant than it would otherwise have been.[109] In any case, the CPSC analysis assumed that the ban would have no *net* effect on manufacturing, since any loss to the UFFI industry would yield a corresponding gain to manufacturers of competing products. The only cost CPSC anticipated was the foregone energy savings for the 10 to 15 percent of homes for which there is no feasible alternative to UFFI. CPSC did not assess the cost to homeowners who would suffer reduced resale values, because it argued that the decline in homes' values was not a result of the ban itself, which was not retroactive, but of valid consumer concerns.[110]

The cost of foregone energy savings thus was the only factor compared to the estimated maximum number of cancer cases avoided by the ban. The cost arrived at was $164,000 to $292,000 per cancer prevented.[111] CPSC did not quantify the benefit of reduced irritant effects in weighing the costs and benefits.

INTEREST REPRESENTATION

The presence of identifiable victims distinguished the politics of urea-formaldehyde foam from the politics of many other suspected environmental carcinogens. Unlike the regulatory controversies discussed in other chapters, the UFFI case was generated by public complaints.[112] Even if formaldehyde is a human carcinogen, it would be difficult to identify UFFI's cancer victims. It was easier, however, to identify consumers who suffered from the irritant effects of the insulation.

Consumer complaints registered with government agencies in both countries were influential in leading to the ban in Canada and the attempted ban in the U.S. It is significant that injured consumers did not have to organize to be heard in either country, because bureaucracies were already in place to receive their individual complaints. In fact Canadian UFFI homeowners organized only after the product was banned.[113] Although only a minority of consumers were adversely affected by the product before the ban, virtually all were affected after the fact by reduced home values. Moreover homeowners harmed by reduced resale values represented a relatively affluent constituency. With the assistance of parliamentary opposition parties and the media, the network of local homeowner associations was influential in obtaining government compensation for removal of UFFI.

The involvement of U.S. consumer groups in the actual regulatory decision had no parallel in Canada. U.S. consumer groups seized opportunities to comment on CPSC's proposed rulemaking.[114] One group, Public Citizen, subsequently appealed the commission's final decision in court, although it was not successful in seeking a wider ban. (However a combination of unions and environmental groups was more successful in using the courts to force EPA and OSHA to reverse many of their early decisions on formaldehyde.)

Canadian consumer and other public interest groups became involved only after the decision was made to ban UFFI. Consumer representatives testified before the board of review and a parliamentary committee. Dissatisfied with the government's compensation package, angry consumers also went to court, though they were unsuccessful in seeking damages from CMHC and the federal government.

Three levels of private sector actors were involved in the UFFI case: formaldehyde manufacturers, manufacturers of the urea-formaldehyde foam product, and numerous independent contractors who prepared and installed UFFI under licensing arrangements with manufacturers. UFFI installers were almost invisible in the regulatory debate in both countries.[115] In any case, UFFI and formaldehyde manufacturers actively defended their own and installers' interests by strongly opposing product bans in both countries.

In Canada UFFI manufacturers were well represented in CGSB decision making. Their trade association, the Canadian Association of

Urea-Formaldehyde Manufacturers (CANUF), successfully lobbied for reversal of the shortlived CMHC withdrawal of eligibility for government subsidies. Formaldehyde manufacturers were represented in the expert committee's deliberations through both membership on the committee and written submissions. Representatives of the industry also testified before the board of review.

In the U.S., although CIIT discovered the original evidence of formaldehyde's carcinogenicity, the industry-sponsored research institute subsequently was an important source of scientific arguments supporting the industry's interests. CIIT scientists were among the leading proponents of theories that linked formaldehyde's carcinogenicity in rodents to irritant effects experienced only at relatively high doses.[116] Like consumer groups, representatives of the industry also participated in the U.S. notice and comment rulemaking. More important, the Formaldehyde Institute won the race to the courthouse and successfully appealed CPSC's final decision in court. Although the industry's arguments did not sway CPSC, they did find a receptive audience in the Fifth Circuit Court of Appeals.

EVALUATION

Stringency

Only Canada successfully banned UFFI. Unlike CPSC's ruling, the Cabinet decision was not vulnerable to lawsuits by interest groups. Even if the industry would have liked to appeal the decision, it could find little cause to sue given the discretionary language of the Hazardous Products Act. In contrast, the U.S. procedural obstacle course granted a veto to both the courts and in this case to the solicitor general. The UFFI case reveals the risk that the U.S. Congress takes in relying on the courts to police the Executive. Courts can blunt the actions of aggressive agencies and prod reluctant regulators with equal ease.

It is noteworthy that despite the absence of a formal U.S. ban, the final result was the same in both countries. As Weiner observed, "By the time of the final [CPSC] vote, it was mostly symbolic – the industry had evaporated."[117] In response to the adverse publicity surrounding the product, U.S. consumers effectively banned UFFI on their own. It is also ironic that, despite the fact that only Canada banned UFFI, formaldehyde's reputation escaped relatively unscathed in Canada. In the U.S., controversy over formaldehyde's carcinogenicity has abated little after a decade, with unions, environmental groups, and the industry continuing to contest EPA, OSHA, and CPSC decisions in court.

Timing

The Canadian government not only acted first to ban UFFI, but its decision took immediate effect. Cabinet banned the product within days of receiving the expert committee's interim report. In contrast, although CPSC first proposed to ban UFFI soon after the Canadian ban, it was 18 months and four *Federal Register* notices later before the U.S. ban took effect. And even then, the court overturned it a year later.

Canadian government decision makers could act with greater autonomy. Cabinet decided to ban UFFI based only on an unspecified number of homeowner complaints and a 20-page advisory committee report. Federal decision makers did not find it necessary to sponsor testing of UFFI homes or research on formaldehyde's health effects until after the ban took effect. In contrast U.S. regulators faced many constraints on their autonomy. The openness of the U.S. process mandated delays to allow time for hearings and written submissions at various stages in CPSC deliberations. CPSC also required time to sponsor studies and to construct a detailed justification for its proposed ban, which a critical court even then found wanting.

Although the Canadian government responded to consumer complaints sooner, one can question the promptness of either government's response. In Canada, the expert committee was not established until almost a year after CIIT's preliminary findings of formaldehyde's carcinogenicity became publicly available and more than two years after government officials publicly expressed concerns about the irritant effects of formaldehyde emissions from UFFI. CPSC did not finalize its ban until more than two years after it learned of the CIIT findings and after the commission first issued a press release warning consumers of the toxicity of formaldehyde gas released by UFFI.

Representativeness

It is striking that although on the face of it the Canadian process seemed more biased toward the industry – in the original CGSB and CMHC approvals of the product, in opportunities for participation on the expert committee, and in the opportunities for appeal afforded by the statute – in the end the industry's interests did not prevail. And in the U.S., where broader opportunities for participation were exercised by consumer groups and labour, and where CPSC based its decision on conservative scientific assumptions antithetical to the industry's interests, the formaldehyde industry ultimately succeeded in having the courts overturn the UFFI ban.

It is noteworthy that neither system protected consumers from the outset. Only after injured consumers alerted regulators to the product's hazards were steps taken to evaluate the safety of UFFI. There was no regulatory requirement for pre-market product testing in either country. In both Canada and the U.S. product standards were developed in a closed, informal process that provided ample opportunities for industry participation but neglected consumer and medical perspectives. It is noteworthy that a cooperative standard-setting process existed in the U.S. in parallel to the more adversarial and formal regime that is widely perceived as the American "national style of regulation."[118] The transformation of American administrative law and policy making in the early 1970s may have had a selective impact on certain policy areas, such as the environment and occupational health, while leaving pockets of the more cooperative New Deal regulatory regime intact in other policy areas.[119] This suggests that care should be taken not to characterize the U.S. regulatory style too broadly.

UFFI homeowners obtained compensation only in Canada, where the government was forced to offer compensation because it was widely perceived as having promoted the product through consumer subsidies. Although the U.S. government also subsidized UFFI installations through tax credits, it seems to have avoided a similar image of culpability.[120] The closed regulatory review and sudden announcement of the ban in Canada also made it easier for angry homeowners to blame the government for their losses. Home values dropped immediately after the ban, making the ban itself appear to be responsible, rather than the fact that prospective purchasers of homes were making a more informed choice.

Incorporation of Science

Both countries relied on the same body of scientific evidence of the health effects of formaldehyde, much of it American in origin. However the scientific basis for the regulatory decision was much more clearly and methodically argued in the U.S. Regulators in that country placed greater emphasis on formaldehyde's potential carcinogenicity, relying heavily on quantitative risk assessment. CPSC applied explicit risk assessment principles, which previously had been widely discussed, to the formaldehyde case. Not only did the science policy principles implicit in the expert committee's review of health effects sharply differ from CPSC's assumptions – for instance the Canadian committee was unwilling to extrapolate from animals to humans – they also were less clearly articulated.

Moreover the scientific basis for the ban received much closer scrutiny in the U.S. from consumer groups and industry. Even the court joined in the debate over CPSC's regulatory science. Though all participants in the U.S. debate seemed to accept the credibility of "science," their political differences gave rise to a debate over what constituted scientific consensus in the particular case at hand.

Risk/Benefit Balancing

The Canadian government did not offer an explicit rationale for its decision to ban UFFI. Thus one cannot know how heavily Canadian decision makers weighed the potential costs of a ban. However it is clear that health concerns prevailed. As required by the U.S. statute, CPSC offered a detailed analysis of the costs and benefits of a ban, including an estimate of the monetary cost per case of cancer avoided. CPSC also concluded that the health hazards posed by UFFI justified a ban. However in writing the Consumer Product Safety Act, the U.S. Congress placed a heavy burden of proof before CPSC, making it easier for a critical court to vacate the commission's decisions.

CONCLUSIONS

The UFFI case reveals similarities and interdependence between the Canadian and American regulatory decisions. For instance, in developing a product standard, U.S. decision makers in the Department of Housing and Urban Development relied heavily on the Canadian standard. The Canadian expert committee and board of review both relied heavily on U.S. science and scientists. Yet despite this interdependence, the two regulatory histories diverged in important respects. The product was banned only in Canada, and only the Canadian government compensated homeowners for removal of UFFI.

Although the Canadian regulatory process was generally more biased toward the UFFI industry than was the more open American regulatory process, the substance of the final decisions in both countries defied these procedural biases. The "politically insulated" Canadian process places the onus on government decision makers to represent the public interest and grants them the necessary capacity to do so. Cabinet not only has the authority to make difficult regulatory choices, even based on limited evidence, but its decisions are almost impervious to legal challenge. In contrast, the pluralistic U.S. regulatory process ensured that UFFI became "political insulation." With Congress writing explicit statutes, CPSC administering them, and interest groups and the courts reviewing them, opportunities arose for various actors to veto decisions. In particular, the unique role of the courts in U.S. regulation introduced an element of unpredictability in the politics of urea-formaldehyde insulation.

7 Acceptable Risks?
Regulating Asbestos in Canada
and the U.S.*

The case of asbestos demonstrates the harsh realities of exposure to hazardous substances in the workplace. A valuable industrial material, asbestos has been widely used during the twentieth century. Evidence of the devastating effects of asbestos on worker health emerged from studies of asbestos miners and others who worked with the product. As awareness of these effects produced efforts to control exposures, many of the worst operations were cleaned up or closed down. Asbestos still plays an important economic role, and as a result intense scientific and political conflicts remain over how stringently asbestos should be regulated.

Asbestos is a mineral that takes the form of extremely thin and flexible fibres, which are incombustable and virtually immune to corrosion and decay. These properties make asbestos an extraordinarily attractive substance for use in many industrial products, ranging from brake linings to building products. There are several types of commercially important asbestos, of which chrysotile is by far the most abundant.[1] Canada is the world's second largest producer of asbestos, virtually all of which is chrysotile from Quebec.[2]

The very properties that make asbestos such a valuable industrial product also make it a serious health risk. The innumerable fibres that make up its structure are so small that they are easily suspended in the ambient air. When inhaled these fibres bypass the protective hairs

---

* Co-authored with Gregory Hein

and mucous of the nasal passage and throat; once inside the body they remain as indestructible as they were outside. Epidemiological studies have linked asbestos to several diseases, including asbestosis, mesothelioma, and lung cancer.

This mix of industrial benefits and health costs makes the regulation of asbestos a particularly difficult task for policy makers. In both Canada and the United States governments have created a myriad of regulations to limit exposure to asbestos fibres. Regulations exist to protect miners and other workers producing asbestos-containing materials, consumers, occupants of buildings containing asbestos products, and the general population exposed to asbestos in the ambient environment.

Asbestos provides another clear case of policy divergence, u.s. regulations being significantly more stringent than Canadian regulations. Canadian regulators are strong proponents of the view that the risks posed by asbestos can be adequately managed through strict control measures, such as exposure limits, product labelling, and medical examination requirements. This "controlled use" philosophy has been widely accepted throughout the industrial world. However the u.s. approach to asbestos deviates sharply from this international pattern. The u.s. has shown far more concern with low-level exposures to asbestos, and has gone as far as instituting a ban of asbestos products, although parts of the ban recently have been overturned in court. The u.s. also has stricter regulations for occupational and environmental exposures to asbestos than many other countries, including Canada.

The asbestos case develops a number of prominent themes made throughout this book. First, the case vividly illustrates the two countries' divergent regulatory styles, with the u.s. style being more open and adversarial. For two decades in the u.s., asbestos has been the subject of a fractious conflict among not only various interest groups, such as labour, environmentalists, and business but also the different branches of the u.s. government. Asbestos regulations have repeatedly been challenged in court, and in the 1980s were the subject of one of the most intense regulatory conflicts between Congress and the executive branch in the era of modern social regulation. The case also illustrates markedly different mechanisms for interest representation, with the u.s. relying on interest group participation in formal regulatory proceedings, punctuated by court challenges, while Canada relies far more on indirect representation of interests by an elected executive, held accountable by the parliamentary opposition.

The asbestos case also offers yet another illustration of the often dramatically different ways in which the two countries interpret uncertain science. As in the cases of dioxin, radon, and Alar, the u.s. has shown far more concern with widespread, low-level risks. The asbestos case again illustrates how science can become intensely politicized when the knowledge base is uncertain and the economic stakes large. In fact the tremendous impact a u.s. ban would have on an economically signifi- cant Canadian industry led both the Canadian federal and Quebec pro- vincial governments to participate directly in the u.s. regulatory conflict. The two Canadian governments acted in much the same manner as u.s. interest groups, including challenging the EPA ban in court.

Several caveats are in order. Regulation of the hazards of asbestos is complicated by the varied uses of asbestos and the multiple sources of exposure – from occupational settings to consumer use and envi- ronmental contamination. Rather than address all forms of asbestos regulation, we focus on three areas that have been the most conten- tious and that are the most economically significant: regulation of workplace exposure, regulations concerning asbestos products, and standards concerning in-place asbestos in buildings. Much of Cana- dian asbestos regulation is done at the provincial level. Rather than survey all provinces the chapter focuses only on the two largest, Ontario and Quebec. Finally, the chapter does not address the excep- tionally complex questions involving compensation for those who have contracted diseases from exposure to asbestos.

REGULATORY FRAMEWORK

Because of the widespread use of asbestos products, the legal frame- work for regulating asbestos is extremely complicated. Our discussion here will be limited to asbestos regulation through workplace safety laws and general laws governing toxic substances. Although the regu- latory frameworks are similar in the authority that they grant to regulators to control asbestos, as in the case of the other toxic sub- stances discussed in this book, the two countries have quite different regulatory styles. In the u.s., regulators are more tightly constrained by Congress and the courts, while the Canadian system is characterized by ministerial discretion.

In laws governing occupational health and safety, the biggest differ- ence between the two countries is the degree of centralization. Worker safety is a federal responsibility in the u.s., carried out by the Depart- ment of Labor's Occupational Safety and Health Administration.[3] In Canada provincial governments are primarily responsible for work- place safety; the federal government only has responsibility for workers in its own facilities.[4]

Carolyn Tuohy has observed that in Canada, "rule-making authority regarding occupational health hazards rests with federal and provincial ministries and cabinets, and few procedural requirements are imposed by enabling statutes."[5] In Ontario workplace safety is governed by the Occupational Health and Safety Act, passed in 1978.[6] The statute authorizes Cabinet – in practice, the minister of labour – to regulate substances "likely to endanger the health of a worker." The normal mechanism for regulating a substance under the act is by listing it as a "designated substance," which has been done for 11 substances to date, including asbestos.[7] In order to designate a substance the minister must publish a regulatory proposal in the provincial *Gazette* and provide an opportunity for interested parties to comment. However the act grants the minister extremely broad discretion to control workplace hazards. Although Section 8 does require the consideration of such factors as the extent of exposure, the availability of substitute processes or substances, and data regarding the health effects of processes or agents, the statute does not constrain Cabinet's decision by specifying how those considerations should be weighed in devising a regulatory strategy.

Workplace safety is regulated somewhat differently in Quebec. Like the Ontario statute the Act Respecting Occupational Health and Safety authorizes the regulation of contaminants or dangerous substances which "constitute a danger to the health, safety, or physical well-being of a worker."[8] However instead of giving jurisdiction to the ministry of labour, the act delegates some of the responsibility for regulating the workplace to affected interests. The Commission de la santé et de la securité du travail (CSST) established by the statute is composed of an equal number of members from labour and industry, and is chaired by a government official. The commission has the authority to identify dangerous substances and to determine permissible exposure levels. The statute offers no guidance as to what factors the commission should consider in determining exposure levels. However draft regulations must be submitted to the Cabinet for approval, and while they are rare, there have been cases of the Cabinet's failing to approve regulations recommended by the commission.[9]

In the United States regulators are given far less discretion than their Canadian counterparts. The 1970 Occupational Safety and Health Act authorizes the Occupational Safety and Health Administration to regulate the workplace so that "no employee will suffer material impairment of health." The statute requires that OSHA consider the extent to which standards are "feasible ... reasonably necessary and appropriate," and that regulations must be based on "the best available evidence."[10] The language is only slightly more specific than that of comparable Canadian statutes, suggesting considerable discretion for u.s. regulators as well. However judicial interpretation has sharpened the meaning and significance of those phrases.

Two Supreme Court decisions have been particularly influential in establishing standards for osha's decision making. In a 1980 case involving osha's regulation on benzene, the Supreme Court ruled that the agency must demonstrate the existence of a "significant risk" before it can tighten an exposure standard.[11] The following year the court ruled that the agency did not have to go so far as justifying its regulations with cost-benefit analysis. The ruling stated that in using the phrase "to the extent feasible ... Congress itself defined the basic relationship between costs and benefits, by placing the benefit of worker health above all other considerations save those making attainment of this benefit unachieveable."[12] These decisions had the effect of limiting osha's discretion in two ways: first, although the agency does not have to support its rules with scientific certainty, it must demonstrate significant risk; and second, although osha does not have to undertake formal cost-benefit assessments, it must demonstrate that its standards are economically and technologically feasible.

The most important u.s. statute for the regulation of nonoccupational exposure to asbestos is the Toxic Substances Control Act (tsca).[13] Section 6 of the act authorizes the u.s. Environmental Protection Agency to regulate toxic substances if "there is a reasonable basis to conclude" that the substance "presents or will present an unreasonable risk of injury to human health or the environment." Pursuing regulatory action is cumbersome under tsca, however, because Section 9 requires epa to review other federal statutes, including laws administered by other agencies, to determine whether regulatory action under other statutes would be more appropriate.[14] tsca requires epa to consider the benefits of the substance's use, the availability of substitutes, and the economic consequences of regulation, but does not impose any requirement for formal cost-benefit analysis. Congress has amended tsca to force epa to pay greater attention to the issue of asbestos in schools, most recently through the Asbestos Hazard Emergency Response Act (ahera) of 1986 (see below).[15]

The Canadian equivalent of tsca is the the Canadian Environmental Protection Act (cepa). cepa authorizes regulation of substances that "may have an immediate or long-term effect on the environment" or "may constitute a danger in Canada to human life or health." However cepa has had little relevance to asbestos regulation thus far.

Regulators in both countries have been granted generous authority to regulate toxic substances, both in the workplace and in the general environment. Whether by virtue of statute or judicial review however, regulators in the u.s. tend to have less administrative discretion than their counterparts in Canada. The following section illustrates the significance of that fact in examining the evolution of asbestos regulation in the two countries.

CHRONOLOGY OF DECISIONS: U.S.

Asbestos has a long history of industrial use, and it has been linked to fatal diseases since the 1930s. However asbestos did not reach the regulatory agenda until the mid-1960s, when epidemiological studies by Dr Irving Selikoff of the Mount Sinai School of Medicine conclusively documented asbestos-related diseases among insulation workers.[16] In addition to Selikoff's scientific work, asbestos was forced onto the regulatory agenda in the u.s. as a result of the work of Paul Brodeur, an investigative journalist, who in the late 1960s and early 1970s published a series of articles in the *New Yorker* on asbestosis at a Pittsburgh-Corning plant in Texas.[17]

When the Occupational Safety and Health Administration was created in 1970, asbestos was the first hazardous substance it chose to regulate. OSHA tightened the existing 12 fibre per cubic centimetre (f/cc) occupational standard to 5 f/cc in 1972, and 2 f/cc in 1976. In response to a petition from a trade union, OSHA adopted an emergency standard of 0.5 f/cc in 1983, but it was struck down by the u.s. Court of Appeals.[18] Undeterred, in 1986 OSHA promulgated an even more stringent workplace standard of 0.2 f/cc. Labour criticized the standard for being too lenient, while industry argued that it was too stringent; both sides sued. This time a different circuit court ruled that the agency had failed to demonstrate that an even lower limit was not justified.[19] In response, OSHA proposed in 1990 to reduce the exposure standard to 0.1 f/cc.[20] A final rule is pending.

In terms of nonoccupational regulation, asbestos was one of the first substances investigated by the Environmental Protection Agency under the Toxic Substances Control Act. EPA issued a notice detailing its intentions to regulate asbestos under TSCA in 1979.[21] In 1982 EPA announced its intention to ban most asbestos products, but conflict between EPA and the Office of Management and Budget delayed any action for years. The battle between the two executive agencies was soon joined by Congress, labour, industry, and environmental groups. In 1985 a House subcommittee concluded that the Office of Management and Budget "unlawfully pressured EPA into halting plans to regulate asbestos," and that EPA deputy administrator James Barnes compromised the agency's integrity by caving in to OMB pressure.[22]

In July 1989 EPA finally promulgated its three-stage ban,[23] and in August the Asbestos Information Association (AIA), representing industry interests in both Canada and the U.S., filed a lawsuit asking the U.S. Court of Appeals to overturn the EPA rule. In October 1991 the court struck down a large part of EPA's ban.[24] While EPA requested that the ruling be appealed to the Supreme Court, the U.S. solicitor general decided against appealing the case. The agency is now considering whether to repromulgate all or parts of the rule to satisfy the court's objections.[25]

During the 1980s the issue of asbestos in schools became a prominent regulatory issue. In 1984 Congress passed the Asbestos School Hazard Abatement Act as an amendment to TSCA, authorizing EPA to provide aid to financially needy schools to abate asbestos problems that were emerging as a result of decay of insulation in aging buildings. The law was ineffective, however, both because of the scarcity of competent inspectors and because of the Reagan administration's funding cutbacks. Congress responded with the 1986 Asbestos Hazard Emergency Response Act, which strengthened the law dramatically. It called for EPA to issue regulations by October 1987 requiring schools to inspect for asbestos hazards and develop management plans to correct problems.[26]

As of March 1994 asbestos regulation is still a contentious issue in U.S. regulatory politics.[27] The decision by the Fifth Circuit Court of Appeals created considerable uncertainty about the fate of EPA's regulation. In addition the U.S. Congress allocated $6 million, to be matched by industry, for the Health Effects Institute to undertake an extensive research program on asbestos in buildings. The Institute's report, published in September 1991, provided support for those downplaying the concerns of asbestos exposure in schools, but failed to quell the scientific controversy over whether different types of asbestos should be regulated differently.[28]

CHRONOLOGY OF DECISIONS: CANADA

The Canadian regulatory agenda on asbestos also was strongly influenced by Selikoff's epidemiological studies. In 1974 the Quebec labour union Confédération des syndicats nationaux (CSN) publicized the findings of a study it had commissioned Selikoff to undertake. The study was designed to refute earlier epidemiological studies done at McGill University, which concluded that workers in the chrysotile mining industry had a lower mortality than the population of Quebec of the same age. In contrast Selikoff's study showed strong links between asbestos and lung cancer among Quebec asbestos workers, and that asbestos also had effects on the general population.[29] In Quebec the growing concern about the health effects of asbestos led to the appointment of the Beaudry Commission,[30] which in 1977 recommended an occupational standard of 2 f/cc.

Although concerns over the effects of asbestos were increasing, so too were concerns that stringent exposure standards would debilitate the profitable Quebec asbestos industry. A 1978 report prepared for the Quebec minister of natural resources concluded that stricter measures to protect the health of asbestos workers could jeopardize the profitability of an economically vital industry and that the government should work "to re-establish and protect as much as possible the reputation of asbestos."[31] The government opted for the less stringent standard of 5 f/cc, disregarding the recommendations of its Beaudry Commission.[32] In 1978, the Parti Québécois government took over the giant Asbestos Corp., thus giving the Quebec government a direct financial interest in the industry.[33]

Concern over the effects of asbestos intensified in the late 1970s with revelations of health problems among workers at the Johns-Manville plant at Scarborough, Ontario. In response the Ontario government appointed the Royal Commission on Matters of Health and Safety Arising from the Use of Asbestos in Ontario in April of 1980. The report of the royal commission, published in 1984, is without doubt the most important document in Canadian asbestos regulation.[34]

The Ontario labour minister was reportedly so concerned about the hazards of asbestos that he did not want to wait until the commission made its recommendations.[35] In 1982, two years before the royal commission reported its findings, the Ontario government reduced its occupational exposure limits from 2 f/cc to its present standards, which vary from 0.2 to 1.0 f/cc, depending on the type of asbestos.[36]

When the royal commission reported its findings, it supported the 1 f/cc chrysotile standard set in 1982, but called for a complete ban of crocidolite and amosite.[37] Although a ban was proposed by the Ontario government in 1987, three years after the commission made its recommendations, it has yet to be finalized by the Ministry of Labour.[38] Because OSHA's 1982 standard was rejected by the courts, Ontario's workplace regulations were more stringent than U.S. regulations until 1986, when OSHA promulgated its new rules.

In 1985 the ministry announced a regulation to reduce exposure to asbestos on construction sites and in building renovations and repair operations. The new regulation specified safety practices that must be followed in construction and other activities, such as brake repair.[39] In early 1990 the issue of asbestos in schools intensified in

Ontario. Although there are no separate regulations for schools, the Ministry of Labour issued an order requiring all schools to inspect for asbestos.[40]

In January 1990 the Quebec government significantly strengthened their workplace safety standards for asbestos, bringing them more in line with Ontario's. The Quebec regulations also ban (with some exceptions) the use of crocidolite and amosite asbestos, the two types of asbestos that, while used only rarely, are thought to be the most dangerous.[41]

So far asbestos policies in the two countries have been considered separately. In fact during the 1980s and early 1990s Canada was a significant actor in u.s. regulatory politics. When EPA proposed its asbestos ban in 1986, Canadian asbestos workers marched on the u.s. embassy in Ottawa.[42] In addition Canadian governments assumed the role of interest groups in lobbying u.s. officials. They invariably cited the fact that in 1986 the International Labour Conference's Committee on Asbestos called for a ban on crocidolite but concluded that other types of asbestos can be used safely under properly controlled conditions.[43] Canadian government officials even became embroiled in the bitter dispute between Congress and the OMB over EPA's asbestos regulations. A House subcommittee report criticized top OMB officials for "conspiring" with Canadian officials about the proposed regulations.[44] When EPA banned asbestos in 1989 the federal minister of mines, Marcel Masse, denounced the move as "rash, arbitrary, and irresponsible."[45] The Canadian federal government ultimately joined Quebec and the private asbestos industry in a successful challenge of the EPA ban in court.

Where do asbestos regulations stand now? The following section gives a capsule summary of the current state of regulation in the u.s. and in Canada's two largest provinces.

CURRENT REGULATIONS

There are a mind-numbing array of asbestos regulations to control the potential for exposure at various steps in the life cycle of asbestos, including regulations governing mining of the asbestos, workplace exposures, air pollution from industrial manufacturing, sale of asbestos-containing products, maintenance or removal of asbestos from buildings (particularly schools), and waste disposal. This overview will focus on three major categories: regulation of industrial workplaces, buildings, and asbestos products. Overall, u.s. asbestos regulations are more stringent than Canada's.

Workplace Standards

There are significant differences in the workplace standards of the three jurisdictions, most notably between the two Canadian provinces and the u.s. osha has established an occupational exposure standard of 0.2 f/cc, based on an 8-hour time-weighted average. The agency has made no distinction among different types of asbestos.[46] In contrast, both Ontario and Quebec's workplace exposure limits distinguish between different types of asbestos. The Ontario workplace limit of 0.2 f/cc in the case of crocidolite matches the osha limit, but standards for other types of asbestos are less stringent: 0.5 f/cc for amosite, and 1 f/cc for chrysotile and all other types of asbestos.[47] While Quebec has historically been less stringent, the issuance of new rules in 1990 made its workplace exposure standards similar to Ontario's.[48] Quebec's limit for crocidolite and amosite is 0.2 f/cc, and the limit for chrysotile and all other types of asbestos is 1.0 f/cc.[49] To put these figures in context, between 90 and 95 percent of asbestos used in North America is chrysotile,[50] the type for which there is the greatest divergence in standards. u.s. occupational standards for chrysotile are 5 times more stringent than those of either Canadian province.

Buildings

The u.s. has developed a relatively aggressive program for controlling asbestos in schools, although the program is based more on providing information than it is on regulating asbestos exposures. As required by the *Asbestos Hazard Emergency Response Act*, in 1987 EPA issued a final rule that requires local school boards to have an accredited person inspect all schools for friable and non-friable asbestos-containing materials. If friable asbestos is detected, school officials are required to inform school employees and parent-teacher associations. More important, school officials are required to develop management plans, including "response actions," that EPA requires depending on the condition of the asbestos-containing material. The rule explicitly does not always require removal, which in some cases can lead to higher asbestos exposures than other management options, such as containment.[51] EPA has not issued regulations covering buildings other than schools, although it has been under legal pressure to do so.[52]

Ontario has no specific regulations for schools; they are covered by the general regulations for buildings, which merely require inspection for friable asbestos if "demolition, alteration, or repair" is planned.

The regulations specify various inspection requirements, as well as measures to control dust during repairs.[53] Where friable asbestos is present, facilities are required to have an "asbestos management program." However because the requirements are less specific and not tied to particular required actions, Ontario's rules are less stringent than EPA's.[54]

General Manufacturing and Use

In addition to regulation of asbestos in workplaces and schools, there are also regulations concerning the manufacture and sale of products containing asbestos. It is in this area that one finds the widest divergence between the two countries. In 1989 EPA initiated a three-stage ban of virtually all asbestos products.[55] Although comprehensive in scope, there are some minor exceptions to the ban, such as high-grade electrical paper and missile liners, products that the agency concluded "do not have a reasonable substitute or do not pose a substantial risk to public health." Companies also can apply for specific exemptions to the ban. However the burden is placed on an applicant to show that it has made "demonstrable good faith efforts to develop substitutes for its products and that granting an exemption will not result in an unreasonable risk of injury to human health."[56]

The recent Fifth Circuit Court decision has created considerable confusion about the status of the EPA regulation. Only the ban on new uses now remains in effect. However EPA is considering re-promulgating all or parts of the EPA ban to satisfy the court's criticisms.

Rather than follow the U.S. lead of banning asbestos products, Canadian governments have sought to promote their "safe use." Indeed Canadian governments actively opposed EPA's ban and joined the lawsuit to overturn it in U.S. courts. In Quebec products containing crocidolite and amosite have been prohibited, "except where their replacement is not reasonable or practicable." It is noteworthy, however, that mention is made in the Quebec regulation neither of what constitutes "reasonable" or "practicable" nor of who will be responsible for defining those terms.[57] The Ontario government has proposed but not finalized a comparable ban on crocidolite and amosite. Both provinces permit the use of other types of asbestos, including chrysotile, with proper controls.

Thus in all three of these areas – workplaces, schools, and general products – U.S. regulations are more stringent than Canadian ones. While some provincial workplace standards match OSHA regulations, standards for the most common type of asbestos are five times less stringent. While the removal of in-place asbestos has occasionally attracted attention in Canada, the u.s. has put considerably more effort into controlling asbestos exposures in schools. Finally, more types of asbestos products have been banned in the u.s. than in Canada.

DECISION RECONSTRUCTION

How did Canada and the u.s. arrive at such different regulations for asbestos? This section analyzes how the different jurisdictions interpreted the scientific data on the health effects of asbestos, assessed the economic costs of controlling those risks, and balanced the benefits of reducing the risks with the control costs. As the analysis will show, there are differences in both risk assessments and cost estimates, but the most profound difference is in the way the two countries determined what risks are acceptable. For reasons of space and manageability, this section focuses only on workplace and general environmental exposures.

Asbestos causes four serious diseases: lung and gastrointestinal cancer, asbestosis (a disease involving the buildup of scar tissue in the lung that inhibits breathing), and mesothelioma (a type of cancer affecting the lining of the lung surface, inner chest wall, or the membrane around abdominal organs).[58] Unlike many other toxic substances of concern to regulators, there is solid epidemiological evidence linking asbestos to these diseases. According to the u.s. Occupational Safety and Health Administration, "osha is aware of no instance in which exposure to a toxic substance has more clearly demonstrated detrimental health effects on humans than has asbestos exposure."[59] Moreover there is substantial agreement among Canadian and u.s. officials on the presence or absence of thresholds for asbestos hazards. Asbestosis appears to be associated only with relatively high levels of exposure, whereas it is widely assumed that there is no threshold for either lung cancer or mesothelioma.

Despite the substantial degree of consensus concerning the hazards of asbestos, substantial remaining areas of uncertainty have provoked considerable scientific and political controversy in Canada and the United States. Two questions have provoked the most disagreement: how much do health effects differ by asbestos type, and how do the risks posed by asbestos substitutes compare with those of asbestos. Both questions have important implications for regulatory strategies to control asbestos hazards.

The u.s. Decision

Effects of Different Asbestos Types. There is intense scientific controversy about whether the type of asbestos influences health effects. Many scientists argue that the amphibole types of asbestos, notably crocidolite and amosite, are far more dangerous than chrysotile. Amphiboles are shaped like rods and thus can penetrate lung tissues with relative ease. Chrysotile fibres, in contrast, are curly and frequently occur in bundles, and for that reason are less likely to penetrate as far into the lung. Moreover amphibole fibres can more easily become airborne, creating a respirable cloud of asbestos dust. According to proponents of this view, the epidemiological studies showing asbestos to be a serious threat at relatively low levels of exposure are largely based on amphiboles, not the more widely used chrysotile.[60]

Scientific controversy over this issue has been widespread and highly publicized in the u.s. Conflict has been raging for several years between Irving Selikoff and his colleagues, who support the view that all fibre types should be considered dangerous, and Brooke Mossman, who is highly critical of Selikoff's work and the government regulations that have been justified with Selikoff's studies. The debate between Selikoff and Mossman has not been limited to questions of scientific interpretation; Selikoff has tried to cast doubt on the credibility of Mossman and her colleagues by alleging that most of them have been involved with the asbestos manufacturers as medical advisors or consultants.[61]

Both osha and epa addressed the issue of fibre type and firmly rejected the view that there are important differences in the health effects of various fibre types. With regard to lung cancer epa found evidence supporting the Canadian position to be "inconclusive and inconsistent." The agency gave more credence to the argument for mesothelioma, but found that "definitive conclusions concerning the relative potency of various types in inducing mesothelioma cannot be made on the basis of available epidemiological information." epa acknowledges that there is epidemiological evidence suggesting that amphiboles are more potent carcinogens than chrysotile, but noted a number of uncertainties in the studies, including the limited availability of exposure data and dose response information.[62] In addition epa highlighted animal studies which showed chrysotile to be at least as potent as other asbestos types. Given these uncertainties, the agency argued that it was "prudent and in the public interest to consider all types as having comparable carcinogenic potency in its quantitative assessment of mesothelioma risk."[63] epa adopted a regulatory science position that erred on the side of caution in the regulation of chrysotile.

Health Effects of Asbestos Substitutes. There is also considerable controversy about the safety of substitutes for asbestos. Many of the substitutes are also fibrous, raising concerns that they may present similar cancer risks. However far less is known about the health effects of asbestos substitutes, placing regulators in the unenviable position of having to choose to control known hazards at the risk of increasing exposure to unknown hazards.

In its analysis of this issue EPA concluded that there is not sufficient data on the health risks of asbestos substitutes from either epidemiological studies or animal experiments to perform quantitative risk assessments. The agency did, however, offer four reasons for its suspicions that the risks of substitutes would be less than the risks of asbestos: (1) some substitutes are known to be less harmful than asbestos, (2) the biological activity or pathogenicity of other substitute fibres appears to be less than that of asbestos, (3) a substantial fraction of the substitute fibres are non-respirable and thus not of concern, and (4) the design of future artificial substitutes for asbestos can be tailored to minimize health risks. Finally, and perhaps most important, EPA adopted an explicit regulatory science policy for choosing between known hazards and unknown hazards. The agency stated that "regulatory decisions about asbestos which poses well-recognized, serious risks should not be delayed until the risk of all replacement materials are fully quantified."[64] The agency supported this policy with a commitment to evaluate the risks of substitutes and regulate them accordingly. As in the case of the uncertainties about the different types of asbestos, EPA resolved the uncertainty in a way that supported the strict regulation of asbestos.

In its decision to overrule EPA's ban the Fifth Circuit Court rejected the EPA analysis of the safety of substitutes. The court held that EPA cannot demonstrate that its ban is reasonable "if it fails to consider the effects that alternate substitutes will pose after a ban." It denounced EPA's argument about substitutes as nothing more than an "educated guess," and criticized the agency for its failure to "say with any assurance that its regulation will increase workplace safety."[65] The decision has the effect of reversing the agency's regulatory science policy described above. The court effectively calls for postponing action on known risks until the hazards of the alternatives are better understood, a standard which makes regulatory action more difficult to justify.

Quantitative Risk Assessments. The quantitative risk estimates presented by OSHA and EPA in support of their regulations do not distinguish between different types of asbestos. OSHA estimated that at the pre-

1986 control limit of 2 f/cc, the cancer risk would be 64 in 1000 for those exposed for 45 years, 44 in 1000 for those exposed for 20 years, and 3 in 1000 for those exposed for 1 year. At a permissible exposure limit of 0.2 f/cc, OSHA estimated that the risks would be a factor of 10 smaller.[66] These estimates rank asbestos as the second most hazardous substance studied in this volume, next to radon.

EPA also provided a range of risk estimates for those in different exposure categories. The agency first considered those exposed to asbestos fibres by virtue of living near plants, construction sites or other occupational sources of fibres. EPA estimated that hundreds of thousands fall into this exposure category and incur lifetime risks of between 1 in 1000 and 1 in 10,000.[67] EPA also estimated that at least 40 million consumers face hazards as they install, use, repair, and dispose of asbestos-containing products, and that both consumers and members of the general population frequently incur individual lifetime cancer risks of 1 in 1 million or greater. While this level of risk is not usually cause for concern, EPA argued that even this relatively low level of risk is significant in light of the very large population exposed.[68] The agency estimated that its ban would result in between 148 and 202 fewer cancer deaths as a result of asbestos exposure.[69]

Cost-Benefit Balancing. In addition to assessing the risks posed by asbestos, policy makers also must consider the costs of reducing those risks. As stated earlier OSHA is required to assess the economic and technical feasibility of its standards, and under the Toxic Substances Control Act, EPA also is required to consider the economic consequences of its regulations. In its decision to tighten its asbestos standard, OSHA presented extensive information on the feasibility and cost of meeting the new standard. The agency concluded that the new standard would cost $453.5 million per year, and save 75 lives per year.[70] While OSHA did not make the explicit calculation, simple division shows these costs to be equivalent to, on average, $6 million per life saved.[71] In adopting the 0.2 f/cc standard, OSHA made it very clear that the permissable level of exposure was chosen not because it eliminated significant risk but because it was the lowest level feasible given current control technologies.[72]

OSHA's position on this matter was challenged by unions in the D.C. Circuit Court. Labour groups argued that OSHA's own data suggested that a lower level of 0.1 f/cc was feasible in industries employing 93 percent of all workers exposed to asbestos. The court accepted the union's argument and required OSHA to consider reducing its exposure limit further.[73] In July of 1990 OSHA proposed to do just that.[74]

TSCA requires EPA to consider the "reasonably ascertainable economic consequences" of regulations issued under the act. The agency provided relatively detailed estimates of the costs of its staged product ban, both in the aggregate and for specific product categories. The total costs were estimated to be between $460 and $810 million, depending upon assumptions about price changes of substitutes. The agency acknowledged that these costs were "significant," but outlined a number of reasons why its methodology overstated costs. EPA noted in addition (1) that the increasing availability of substitutes lessened the economic disruption resulting from the ban, and (2) that since these costs spread over 13 years (the period for analysis) and the entire U.S. population "the impact on most persons will be negligible."[75]

While EPA considered both the costs and benefits of its ban, it did not explicitly adopt a standard for deciding justified costs in the pursuit of risk reduction. Like OSHA, EPA chose not to calculate the cost effectiveness of its rule in terms of costs per life saved. Nonetheless the agency concluded that the rule was justified: "EPA, therefore, finds that, under the standards of section 6 of TSCA, the costs of the rule to be [sic] reasonable in light of the unreasonably large number of asbestos related deaths and serious illnesses that would occur if the actions in this rule were not taken."[76]

EPA did not get the last word on the reasonableness of the ban, however. In its decision striking down EPA's decision, the Fifth Circuit Court rejected the conclusion that the costs of the ban were justified. Unlike EPA the court did not hesitate to calculate the cost effectiveness of the regulation. Although the overall cost effectiveness of $2 to 6 million per life saved was consistent with regulatory precedents, and the least costly measure, a ban on asbestos replacement brake pads, was a relative bargain at $100,000 to $300,000 per life saved, the court questioned the higher costs of banning other products. For instance, the estimated cost of banning asbestos pipe was $43 to 76 million per life saved, the cost of banning asbestos shingles $72 to $106 million per life saved. The court held that "EPA, in its zeal to ban any and all asbestos products, basically ignored the cost side of the TSCA equation," and that the agency's willingness to require such costly life-saving measures "reveals that its economic review of its regulations, as required by TSCA, was meaningless."[77]

The Canadian Decision

Canadian regulations, based on a philosophy of "controlled use," offer a stark contrast to EPA's attempt to effectively eliminate asbestos from the market. In contrast to their American counterparts, Canadian regulators have concluded that certain types of asbestos are less hazardous than others. As a result Canadian risk estimates at relevant exposure levels are significantly lower.

It is easier to reconstruct the U.S. regulatory decisions because of the elaborate rationales provided in documents accompanying EPA's and OSHA's regulatory announcements. Canada's less formal regulatory style produces far less explicit discussion of the reasons for decisions. Nonetheless several crucial documents are available. Ontario's 1982 revision of its workplace safety standard was accompanied by a relatively detailed background paper. And much of Canadian asbestos policy relies on the comprehensive analysis of the Ontario Royal Commission on Asbestos.

The commission heard testimony from 53 expert witnesses, received about 150 written and oral submissions, and undertook 10 of its own research studies. It reported its findings in three volumes, totalling over 900 pages.[78] The report has dominated Canadian discourse on asbestos and is frequently used by others, including the U.S. industry, to support the "controlled use" philosophy. The discussion that follows will use the royal commission's analysis to represent the Canadian view where more directly relevant rationales are not available.

Health Effects of Different Asbestos Types. When the Ontario Ministry of Labour tightened its workplace asbestos standards in 1982, it was ambivalent on the issue of asbestos type. A supporting document noted that there were different views on the matter – the British Advisory Committee on Asbestos had concluded that it was appropriate to distinguish among fibre types, but a joint U.S. National Institute for Occupational Safety and Health/Occupational Safety and Health Administration Work Group argued that fibre types should not be distinguished for regulatory purposes. While acknowledging that the issue "remains controversial," Ontario adopted the British approach and set different workplace exposure limits for different fibre types.[79]

When the royal commission reported its findings two years later, it had little difficulty concluding that asbestos type made a crucial difference. According to the report, "There is strong evidence that crocidolite and amosite fibres tend to be more hazardous than chrysotile fibres."[80] The commission based this conclusion on a detailed analysis of epidemiological and laboratory studies. Different studies indicated different incidences of disease, and the commission related those differences to variations in exposure to particular types of asbestos.[81] It concluded, for instance, that mesothelioma "is generally associated with exposure to amosite or crocidolite, and rarely with exposure to chrysotile."[82] The commission also concluded that studies of lung cancer in humans suggest that chrysotile is less potent than other types of asbestos. It rejected animal studies that showed chrysotile to be at least as potent as the other fibre types, saying that exposure conditions in the laboratory were dramatically different from those encountered by humans.[83]

This approach contrasts sharply with that of EPA and OSHA. U.S. officials examined the same studies and concluded that it was not possible to draw these sorts of conclusions with any confidence, while officials in Canada and other countries considered these studies sufficiently reliable to draw conclusions about the health risks of different types of asbestos.[84] In the face of uncertainty Canadian officials drew conclusions implying less stringent regulation of chrysotile, while U.S. officials did just the opposite.

Health Effects of Asbestos Substitutes. Because Canadian jurisdictions have not moved to ban asbestos products, there has been less concern with the health effects of substitutes. The royal commission did examine the available data however, and concluded that there is a substantial amount of uncertainty. While substitutes "have not in general been proved to be carcinogenic or toxic," there are also "few cases where a substitute is available that has been proved safe."[85]

Quantitative Risk Assessments. Because of the quantity and quality of data on the health effects of asbestos, Canadian officials were less reluctant to perform quantitative risk estimates of asbestos hazards than in other cases in this book. The royal commission's risk assessments distinguished between both fibre type and industrial process, making comparisons with U.S. risk estimates difficult. However it is possible to generate some rough comparisons of risk estimates for similar exposure situations. For instance the royal commission estimated the risks of brake manufacturing to be 1.1 deaths per 1000 if workers are exposed to 1.0 f/cc for 25 years. The risks of textile manufacturing were estimated to be substantially higher, at 76 deaths per 1000.[86] In comparison, OSHA estimated that workers exposed to 1 f/cc for 20 years face a 22 in 1000 risk.[87] OSHA's risk estimates fall within the range of the royal commission estimates.

The commission also provided risk estimates for non-occupational exposure. Analyzing the risks of asbestos in buildings, particularly schools, it estimated that there might be 20 deaths if 1 million people were exposed to building insulation for 10 years at 0.001 f/cc.[88] No estimates were provided for exposures to asbestos in outdoor air, however. The commission merely concluded that since ambient outdoor exposures are likely to be lower than those in buildings, the risk is not significant and therefore not worth quantifying.[89]

It is interesting that the EPA rule on asbestos in schools did not provide quantitative risk estimates for asbestos in buildings.[90] However in support of its rule banning asbestos products, EPA estimated that most of the urban population is exposed to a risk of 1 in 1 million, but that hundreds of thousands of people living near asbestos mining, milling, and manufacturing facilities are exposed to significantly higher risks, ranging from 1 in 10,000 to 1 in 1000.

Cost-Benefit Balancing. Like EPA and OSHA, the Ontario royal commission estimated the costs for some of its recommendations. The report estimated the cost of moving from a 2 f/cc to 1 f/cc workplace standard for different industrial processes. The costs were estimated to range from $100,000 ($0.1 million) per life saved in the case of crocidolite asbestos-cement manufacturing to $68 million per life saved in the case of chrysotile manufacturing of friction products.[91] As noted earlier, OSHA's estimates suggest an average cost effectiveness of $6 million per life saved, and the cost effectiveness of EPA's regulatory measures ranged from $100,000 to $106 million per life saved, with an average of between $2 and $6 million per life saved. As in the case of quantitative risk estimates, the figures are difficult to compare, but they appear to be in a similar range.

The major differences in decisions on asbestos result not from different risk or cost estimates but from the way the different jurisdictions decided what level of risk was reasonable. In justifying its ban EPA did not articulate a standard for how to balance the costs and benefits of risk reduction, but its actions implicitly accept the objective of reducing risks to the extent technologically and economically feasible. OSHA was more explicit in arguing that it was obliged to reduce risks to the extent feasible. The Canadian approach has been fundamentally different. After reviewing a number of alternatives for determining acceptable risks, the royal commission decided the best way was to compare asbestos risks to other threats to health to help decide what sort of regulatory restrictions were justifiable.[92]

The commission assessed the acceptability of risks faced by workers exposed to asbestos by comparing them with other risks the same workers faced, principally the risks of accidents.[93] For instance the commission concluded that the risks faced by workers in asbestos mines and general asbestos manufacturing at the 1 f/cc 1982 standard were acceptable because they were far below the industrial accident rate. Since workers in textile manufacturing face risks higher than the industrial accident rate, however, the commission recommended that regulatory measures be undertaken.[94] In assessing the acceptability of risks to occupants in asbestos-insulated buildings, the commission compared the risks from asbestos with the greater risk of being killed

in an automobile accident going to and from the building, and concluded that the risks posed by asbestos in buildings were acceptable.[95]

It must be noted that the royal commission articulated this approach
to risk management, but that the Ministry of Labour did not use it
when it adopted its standards in 1982. Indeed the rationale provided
at that time was remarkably tentative:

The exposure limits proposed in this regulation are those recommended in
the Report of the British Advisory Committee. These are *admittedly as arbitrary
as any others one might care to propose* and cannot be considered the last word
on the subject. Asbestos-related disease is the subject of ongoing research
worldwide and developments will be monitored continually. As new information becomes available, the Ontario exposure limit will be re-assessed and
modified as appropriate.[96]

It is striking that the Ministry of Labour's report failed to address the
recommendations by its own scientists. In a study included as an
appendix to the report, Murray Finkelstein recommended that no
distinctions be made among fibre types, and that the standard should
"be set no higher than 0.5 fibres/cc."[97] The report not only failed to
explain why the ministry rejected Dr Finkelstein's recommendation,
but did not even acknowledge it.

The royal commission's more thoughtful approach provided an
effective post hoc rationale for the 1982 standards. In the case of
asbestos, the relative risk approach led to conclusions substantially
different from those produced by the U.S. approach of reducing risks
to the maximum extent feasible. It was the different assessments of
the acceptability of risks, far more than different estimates of the
magnitude of either the risks or costs of control, that drove the
divergence between Canadian and U.S. asbestos regulations.

INTEREST REPRESENTATION

Asbestos regulation has been intensely politicized. In both Canada and
the U.S. it pits workers against manufacturers of asbestos-containing
materials, and environmental groups against government and industry. In Canada, however, the lines are more difficult to judge because
there is a blurring of government and private interests. First, the
Quebec government has a direct financial interest in the asbestos
mining industry. Second, the principal forum for the presentation of
the scientific and policy viewpoint of the Canadian industry, the Asbestos Institute, is funded not only by the asbestos industry, but by the
Quebec and Canadian federal governments as well.[98] This industry-

government coalition has proved a formidable adversary for advocates of more stringent regulation of asbestos.

More unique to the case of asbestos, however, is the international character of the political conflict. The Canadian asbestos industry, Quebec asbestos workers, and the federal and Quebec governments are pitted against the U.S. EPA, U.S. environmental and labour interests, and OSHA. The political rhetoric, particularly from the Canadian side, has been intense. For example, in 1986 the federal mines minister Robert Layton denounced EPA's proposal to ban asbestos as "unfair and based on emotion rather than scientific evidence,"[99] and his Quebec counterpart summed up the policy divergence between the U.S. and Canada as "a battle between the irrational and rational."[100] Even the Canadian media has got into the act; Canada's "national newspaper" denounced EPA's ban as "eco-zealotry."[101]

Despite international pressures the regulation of asbestos in both countries has been driven largely by domestic politics. Both the U.S. and Canadian regulatory processes offer channels for regulatory advocates and opponents and mechanisms for the resolution of conflict. However while the U.S. regulatory process is open, formal, adversarial, and legalistic, the Canadian process tends to be more closed, informal, cooperative, and discretionary. There also are differences between the Quebec and Ontario approaches, but it is the U.S. system that stands out as the most distinct (see below).

The United States: Legalism in Action

In many ways asbestos is a textbook case of American legalism. The interests of workers and environmentalists have been represented through formal petitions requesting agency action, participation in formal agency deliberations, and petitions for judicial review of agency actions. Each of these mechanisms of participation is guaranteed by law. For instance TSCA requires the agency to respond to citizen petitions within 90 days. While the Occupational Safety and Health Act does not have a similar petition provision, a general right to petition administrative agencies is provided by the Administrative Procedures Act, and the courts have intervened to force agencies to respond in a timely and sincere manner.[102]

OSHA asbestos regulations have been caught in a never-ending cycle of petition, agency action, and judicial review. Shortly after OSHA was created, the AFL-CIO petitioned the agency to lower its asbestos exposure limit from 12 f/cc to 2 f/cc. The agency responded in 1972 by adopting a 5 f/cc standard immediately and a 2 f/cc to take effect in 1976. The union sued OSHA for not going far enough fast enough, and the court upheld most of the agency's rule.[103] In 1983 labour petitioned OSHA to tighten its standard to 0.1 f/cc. In response the agency issued an "emergency temporary standard" of 0.5 f/cc. Industry sued the agency – the court ruled that the agency had improperly relied on its emergency powers and struck the new standard down.[104]

In response to further labour pressure OSHA adopted the 0.2 f/cc standard in 1986, prompting both labour and industry to sue. In its 1988 decision the DC Circuit Court claimed that "when called upon to review technical determinations on matters to which the agency lays claim to special expertise, the courts are at their most deferential."[105] The court nonetheless struck down the agency's determination that the 0.2 f/cc standard was the lowest feasible and rejected its failure to issue a short-term exposure limit. In response OSHA has issued a short-term limit and proposed to reduce the limit to 0.1 f/cc. No doubt the court will have another opportunity to consider the issue.

While it does not have as lengthy a history, EPA's asbestos policies have been subject to the same dynamic.[106] Environmentalists pressured the agency, occasionally through formal petition, to ban asbestos products.[107] Once the agency's ban was announced, industry interests immediately challenged it in court. The Fifth Circuit Court, while declaiming more than once that "we do not sit as a regulatory agency ourselves," acted like one nevertheless, challenging EPA risk assessments and its regulatory science policies in deciding to overturn the ban.[108] This record demonstrates that the courts have clearly played the role of "partner" in the regulation of asbestos.[109]

Interests also are represented in the U.S. by White House agencies and the Congress. The Office of Management and Budget played a central role in the asbestos dispute, particularly regarding the EPA ban. While earlier presidents sought to use OMB to exercise control over regulatory agencies, its own role was expanded dramatically by the Reagan administration.[110] OMB's principal concern is the cost-effectiveness of regulations, and it has sought to force agencies to give greater attention to economic considerations in their decision making. OMB intervened directly in EPA's decision making on asbestos, holding up the decision for a number of years and ultimately pushing the agency to use the deferral provision in TSCA to leave asbestos regulation to OSHA and the Consumer Product Safety Commission.

EPA's action set off a firestorm of protest in Congress. The formidable chair of the House Energy and Commerce Committee, John Dingell (D-MI), launched an investigation, which concluded that the OMB had acted as a conduit for industry and Canadian government pressure on the agency and had illegally interfered with EPA decision making.[111] Aggressive oversight by Congress was effective at counteracting OMB pressure on EPA, which proposed the asbestos ban within months of the release of the Congressional report.[112]

The White House has got the last word, for a time at least. EPA found the appeals court's rejection of its ban disconcerting because it seemed to undermine the regulatory capacity embodied in TSCA, so it tried to appeal the ruling to the Supreme Court. But the appeal has to go through the solicitor general, who in the midst of a pre-election, anti-regulation mood within the Bush White House, refused EPA's request. This same dynamic occurred in the UFFI case described in chapter 6 when the regulatory agency and the White House had different ideas of what legal course to pursue.

In the U.S. system, interest representation is highly formalized, whether through petition, hearings, or judicial review. The nature of the system forces regulatory agencies to consider carefully the interests and arguments of both regulatory advocates and opponents.

Canada: Ministerial Discretion and Corporatism

The systems of interest representation in Canada differ fundamentally from those in the U.S., but there also is a significant amount of variation within the Canadian jurisdictions analyzed here. The traditional system in Ontario was characterized by ministerial discretion.[113] The statute provides for the establishment of an advisory council representing important sectoral interests and requires that regulatory proposals be published in the Ontario Gazette and allow at least 60 days for comment. But there is no requirement for agency response to petitions or for public hearings, and government actions are virtually insulated from judicial review.

Interest representation has occurred largely through two mechanisms.[114] First, while not required by law, the minister routinely consults interested groups as part of the regulatory process.[115] In the case of asbestos the Ministry of Labour announced proposed regulations for asbestos as part of a package of seven designated substances in August 1980. The ministry received comments from 54 respondents on the asbestos proposal, 39 from industry, three from labour, and 12 others. In its 1982 report explaining the basis for the 1982 standards, the ministry reviewed those comments and responded to them. This consultation process does not differ significantly from that used by OSHA in the development of its regulations. The important difference is that the Ontario Ministry of Labour is not subject to the petition mechanism that forces OSHA to consider labour's demands for tighter regulations. Nor is it subject to routine judicial scrutiny.

The Ministry of Labour is hardly insulated from demands for action by labour interests, however. The second principal mechanism for interest representation is pressures on the government through opposition parties in the legislature. Indeed the major impetus for action on asbestos in the workplace was pressures from the labour-supported New Democratic Party (NDP) in the Ontario legislature. During March and April of 1980 the NDP persistently attacked the Conservative government on the issue of asbestos in the workplace and in schools.[116] This incessant opposition pressure was an important factor that led to the appointment of the royal commission on Asbestos on 29 April 1980.[117] There also is evidence that NDP pressure in the legislature forced the government to adopt new workplace regulations in 1982, before the royal commission had time to complete its work.[118]

In the parliamentary system ministerial discretion is accompanied by ministerial accountability, and on occasion opposition demands can force the government to act. As the case of the EPA asbestos ban shows, the U.S. legislature can also be an effective vehicle of interest representation. But regulatory advocates in the U.S. also have opportunities to influence the regulatory agenda through petitions and to influence regulatory outcomes through judicial review.

Interestingly the legitimacy of the system of ministerial discretion in Ontario was challenged after the promulgation of the general chemical hazard regulation in 1986.[119] Both labour and industry were concerned that the minister had not consulted them. As a result a new process has been created, the centrepiece of which is a bipartite committee comprised of an equal number of labour and employer representatives, which is charged with making recommendations concerning the regulation of hazardous substances.[120] Although the committee was established in 1987, it is too early to guage its impact, as the committee had proposed no new regulations as of November 1991.

The new system in Ontario comes closer to the Quebec model, which is quite different from the traditional model of ministerial discretion. It is based on a European-style model of corporatism, where there is a more direct relationship between affected interests and regulators.[121] The principal regulatory body in Quebec is the Commission de la santé et de la sécurité du travail (CSST). The governing board of the commission is made up of equal numbers of labour and management representatives appointed by the government in consultation with major employer and labour federations.[122] Rather than merely offering a forum for consultation, the function of CSST is to actually draft regulations for approval by Cabinet. Because affected interests participate directly in the decision-making process, this system has the potential to deliver outcomes that will be perceived as legitimate by both sides in the regulatory debate. However Tuohy has reported that the first eight years of the commission were characterized by political contention and instability. Moreover despite a strong labour presence, Quebec's permissible exposure levels lag behind those of Sweden, West Germany, and the United States.[123] Certainly this is the case for asbestos. Quebec's workplace standards for asbestos were less stringent than Ontario's until 1990 and are still less stringent than those in the u.s.

CONCLUSION

The asbestos case reveals the operation of strikingly different regulatory styles, which result in significantly different regulatory outcomes. This concluding section assesses the case using our five evaluative criteria: stringency, timing, incorporation of science, balancing of risks and benefits, and interest representation.

Stringency

The recent Fifth Circuit Court decision striking down EPA's ban on asbestos creates considerable uncertainty about the state of u.s. regulations. It is likely that EPA will respond by merely reducing the scope of its ban rather than withdrawing from asbestos regulation altogether. Nonetheless we still can conclude that u.s. asbestos regulations are substantially more stringent than the comparable Canadian standards. For the amphibole types of asbestos, OSHA, Ontario, and Quebec have similar workplace standards. But for chrysotile, which accounts for about 95 percent of the asbestos used in North America, u.s. standards are five times more stringent than those in Canada. While the chapter has only touched on policies concerning asbestos in schools and other buildings, the u.s. actions in these areas also have been much more aggressive.

Timing

Issues of timing in asbestos regulation are more complex. Regulation of asbestos in the workplace has been a high priority for OSHA since 1971, whereas the issue did not emerge on the Canadian regulatory agenda until the late 1970s. However OSHA did not reduce its 1976 standard to below 2 f/cc until 1986, four years after Ontario had set more stringent limits.

In some circumstances the legalistic and formalistic nature of the
U.S. process promotes rapid decision making because regulators are
forced to respond to the initiatives of regulatory advocates. In other
cases, however, the fragmentation of authority and constraints on
agency discretion can prove cumbersome, producing significant delays
in decision making. For instance the courts thwarted OSHA's attempt
to tighten its exposure standard in 1983, postponing the promulgation of a new standard until 1986. EPA first announced its intentions
to regulate asbestos under TSCA in 1979, but did not reach a final
decision until 1989 – and even then its decision was remanded by the
courts.

The greater discretion granted to Canadian regulators allows them
to act more decisively when they have the desire to do so. This
flexibility allowed the Ontario labour minister to issue stronger asbestos regulations in 1982 without waiting for the results of the royal
commission. But flexibility also permits Canadian regulators to avoid
action. Ontario has yet to implement several important recommendations of the royal commission, such as requiring certification of asbestos workers, while Quebec successfully avoided any significant action
on asbestos until 1990.

Incorporation of Science

As in other case studies in this book there are substantial differences
in the way the two jurisdictions made regulatory decisions in the face
of uncertain science. U.S. regulators relied on more elaborate and
detailed scientific justifications for their decisions. For instance the
Federal Register notices issued by EPA and OSHA offer a far richer
discussion of scientific issues than the 1982 background document for
the Ontario workplace regulation. The quantity of documentation is
a function of the political system in which the agencies operate.[124]
Both EPA and OSHA must offer detailed justifications for their decisions in anticipation of legal challenges. Had OSHA offered the
Ontario Ministry of Labour's 1982 support document as the rationale
for its regulations, the admission that the adopted standards were
arbitrary and the failure to explain why the agency was rejecting the
advice of its own scientists could not possibly have survived the fine-
toothed comb of the U.S. courts.

In addition the incorporation of science in the U.S. is far more
pluralistic. Unions and environmentalists support their petitions with
extensive scientific rationales, and the scientific basis of agency decisions has been probingly scrutinized by the Office of Management
and Budget, Congressional committees, and the courts. The scientific

basis for Canadian decisions, in contrast, has been less explicit – and far less controversial.

The asbestos case demonstrates the potential significance of scientific uncertainty for regulatory outcomes. In a number of cases U.S. regulators resolved scientific uncertainties in a manner that led to greater concern for the health effects of asbestos and thus to stronger rationales for more stringent regulation. The most significant example of this is the decision by U.S. officials to treat all asbestos fibres alike. In contrast Canadian decision makers invariably resolved uncertainties in a manner which led them to take the potential risks of the most abundant form of asbestos, chrysotile, less seriously.

Risk-Benefit Balancing

Even with these differences in risk assessments, however, what is striking about the asbestos case is not the differences in the assessments of health effects or of the costs of controlling health risks. Regulatory standards in the two countries differ primarily because regulators established different standards for the acceptability of risks.

Given the extensive scientific justifications U.S. regulatory agencies provided for their decisions, it is striking how little explicit discussion is given to the question of how to decide what risks are acceptable. In the case of OSHA a rough standard has emerged as a result of judicial interpretation of the language of the statute: the agency must reduce significant risks to the extent feasible. Because the concepts of both significance and feasibility are vague, however, the courts have provided only limited guidance to regulators as to what risks are acceptable. EPA's standard is even less well defined. With virtually no discussion, the agency adopted a rationale similar to OSHA's (which the court found wanting). In the end both U.S. agencies adopted standards for acceptable risks that produced very stringent regulation. Both sought to reduce significant risks to the extent technologically and economically feasible.

In contrast to the U.S. agencies the Ontario royal commission provided an admirably clear explanation for its approach to judging the acceptability of risks. (It should be noted, however, that when the Ontario government adopted its 1982 standards, it did not rely on any such rationale, and ended up admitting that their new standards were "admittedly as arbitrary as any others one might care to propose."[125]) The commission set its standard for acceptability not at the minimum level of risk technically or economically feasible but at the level of risk currently faced by workers and the public. On one hand the strength of this "relative risk" approach is that, if applied consistently, it would lead to greater regulatory attention to only the most significant risks. On the other hand the commission can be criticized for adopting a Panglossian approach to risk management, which implicitly assumes that all current risks are acceptable. It is noteworthy that the industrial accident rate in Canada, on which the commission relies heavily as a point of comparison to judge the acceptability of asbestos risks to workers, is in fact one of the highest in the western world.[126]

Interest Representation

The asbestos case also reveals two different systems of interest representation in action. The u.s. system is far more open, formal, and legalistic. Regulatory advocates can force reluctant agencies to at least consider taking action on a substance through petitions. The American system of administrative law forces agencies to offer detailed, written responses to the arguments of various interests. The Office of Management and Budget has attempted to ensure that agencies carefully consider economic interests. In the asbestos case, Congressional pressure tipped the balance of pressures in the direction of more stringent regulation. Any interest aggrieved by agency decisions has the right to judicial review, and the asbestos case demontrates both that u.s. interest groups do not hesitate to exploit that right, and that courts have not been reluctant to challenge agency decisions.

Canadian regulators are granted greater autonomy from their political environment. Until recently Ontario's system was characterized by ministerial discretion. Because ministers are accountable to the legislature (and ultimately to the electorate), opposition parties can serve as an effective vehicle for the interests of regulatory advocates. But such political checks on ministers seem to be episodic. Given the complexity of regulatory issues, the limited time, resources, and expertise of opposition members prevents them from serving as vigilant watchdogs. Moroever regulatory advocates do not have a legal petition device to force agencies to take their interests seriously, and neither side can use the courts to constrain goverment actions. This greater autonomy gives regulators more freedom to respond to whichever interests they choose. In Canada the power of the asbestos industry, and the close ties between the industry and the Quebec and Canadian governments, has created formidable obstacles to those favouring more stringent asbestos regulations.

The open style of the u.s. system has, interestingly, given even Canadian interests multiple avenues of representation in the u.s. policy process. More than any other case described in this book the asbestos case reveals the interdependence of regulatory policy in the two countries. While it is not clear that decisions would have been any different without Canadian input, Canadian private and governmental interests have played a significant role in U.S. regulatory disputes by commenting on regulatory proposals, working through the sympathetic OMB, and joining successful judicial challenges to EPA's ban.

The asbestos story is hardly over. Ontario's regulatory proposals have yet to be finalized, and OSHA has proposed new standards to tighten occupational exposure limits by a factor of two. Recent court actions against EPA's ban have rendered the future of the agency's regulation highly uncertain, since it is likely that EPA will repromulgate some form of the ban, and the legal battle will begin anew. However while there is a great deal of uncertainty about the future of asbestos regulations in the both countries, the extent of divergence between them is sufficiently great that it is unlikely that Canada and the United States will arrive at comparable regulatory standards for asbestos in the forseeable future.

8 The Perils of Paternalism: Controlling Radon Exposure in Canadian and U.S. Homes

Hope: "It's this house Michael. We didn't know this house. We fell in love with it, we bought it. We thought it would all be perfect, and it's not."
Michael: "Okay. So that is life, so we do something about it."
Hope: "Radon, Michael. Lung cancer. Disease. Death."
Michael: "Wait a minute, Hope, the number's 175 to 183, it's just numbers, we take precautions, that's all. We'll get an estimate right away."
Hope: "Will you call now?"

thirtysomething, 1989

"As we say, you can't tame nature; you just have to live with it."

Roger Eaton
Health and Welfare Canada, 1987

Radon is another clear case of policy divergence. Radon has been a much higher priority in the United States than in Canada, and the issue even found its way into popular culture, as the scene from *thirtysomething* demonstrates. While the u.s. approach has been to publicize the hazards of radon so that homeowners can decide what actions to take, the Canadian government has downplayed the hazard and adopted a more paternalistic approach of deciding, on the home-owners' behalf, that the risks of radon do not warrant the costs of mitigation.

The case of indoor radon is unique because it occurs naturally. Radon is a colourless, odourless radioactive gas that is a product of the natural decay of uranium. Because uranium is a common trace element in the earth's crust, radon in very small concentrations is a natural component of air. In some areas, however, radon concentrations in the earth can be relatively high. Radon can seep into homes through cracks in the foundation and can accumulate to dangerous concentrations, especially if the house is not well ventilated.

Radon is a concern because it causes lung cancer. Unlike many other regulatory controversies where regulators have relied exclusively on toxicological studies of laboratory animals, there is strong evidence linking radon gas to lung cancer in humans. This evidence comes from epidemiological studies of uranium miners, which show a strong correlation between levels of radon exposure and the incidence of lung cancer.[1] However miners tend to be exposed to much higher levels of radon than those present in most homes, so there is still uncertainty concerning the risks posed by low levels of radon.

Neither the Canadian nor the u.s. government has taken a regulatory approach to radon, in part because it occurs naturally but also because exposure occurs largely in private homes. Nonetheless it is clear that the u.s. government has taken a far more aggressive approach to the problem than is the case in Canada. The u.s. Environmental Protection Agency launched an aggressive public information campaign designed to alert citizens to the danger and how to avoid it. The Canadian government, in contrast, has pursued an approach of performing more research rather than taking action to alert the public.[2]

The radon case highlights two central themes in this book. First, it illustrates the different way the two countries interpret science in the regulatory process. As in other cases u.s. officials have spent considerable effort developing quantitative assessments of risks to the public, while Canadian officials have been extremely reluctant to do so. Second, the radon case reveals dramatic differences in the way the governments communicate risks to the public. u.s. officials have concentrated on informing the public and overcoming complacency, while the Canadian government has been reluctant to publicize radon risks for fear of public overreaction.

REGULATORY FRAMEWORK

The problem of radon contamination in homes was first detected in uranium mining towns in the 1970s. Despite the localized nature of the problem, the federal governments of both countries got involved because of their jurisdiction over uranium mining. As the problem was discovered to be much more widespread, however, jurisdiction shifted. In the u.s. the Environmental Protection Agency, under Congressional pressure after its initial reluctance, asserted primary jurisdiction over radon at the federal level, although a great deal of supporting research has been performed by the Department of Energy. Health agencies at the state level are also active. In Canada the Department of Health and Welfare has played a key role, particularly in research. Jurisdiction over ambient radiation rests with the provinces. The federal government, especially Health and Welfare Canada, plays an important role through the establishment of guidelines in cooperation with the Federal/Provincial Advisory Committee on Radiation Surveillance.

Indoor pollutants have received far less regulatory attention than more traditional pollutants. Among indoor air contaminants, radon poses particularly vexing problems because it occurs naturally, making the justification for government intervention more tenuous. Since neither country has adopted a regulatory approach to address radon hazards, there is no need for an elaborate discussion of the standards and procedures underlying regulatory authority in the two countries.

CHRONOLOGY OF EVENTS: UNITED STATES

The dramatic story of one individual's exposure catalyzed public concern over radon in the United States. In late 1984 Stanley Watras, an employee at a nuclear power plant near Philadelphia, repeatedly triggered radiation alarms on his way out of the plant. After weeks of frustration, Watras discovered that he also could set off the alarm on his way into the plant, demonstrating that he was being exposed to radiation outside the plant. Testing of his home revealed extraordinarily high levels of radon. It has been estimated that radon levels in his home presented a lung cancer risk equivalent to smoking up to 135 packs of cigarettes per day.[3]

Radon reached the public agenda in May 1985, when the *New York Times* ran a front-page story on the issue. The story focused on unexpectedly high levels of radon found in homes in the "Reading Prong" area of Pennsylvania, New Jersey, and New York. Shocked by the "Watras incident," the Pennsylvania Department of Environmental Resources surveyed more than 2000 homes, finding about half of them to have what the state considered unacceptably high levels of radon.[4] It was the results of this survey that prompted the *New York Times* story, which triggered a surge in media interest on the issue.

Several members of the u.s. Congress took up the radon issue. For years the Reagan administration had been under pressure from certain Congressional committees for inadequate attention to indoor air pollution.[5] The growing awareness of radon gave this campaign focus, and a coalition of members of Congress from the high radon states of Pennsylvania, New York, New Jersey, Rhode Island, and Maine held hearings into radon and pushed for legislative amendments to spur EPA research on the subject.

By October 1985 EPA had developed a strategy for radon, focusing mainly on monitoring of radon levels throughout the country and developing technical assistance for states to aid in mitigation.[6] While radon surveys were being undertaken, EPA issued a document entitled

A Citizen's Guide To Radon in August 1986.[7] The document described
the risks from radon, methods for radon detection, and how homeowners could reduce radon contamination in their homes. The most
important part of the document was the issuance of so-called "action
levels." EPA advised homeowners that if radon concentrations
exceeded 0.02 Working Levels (WL), (equivalent to 4 picocuries per
litre, or pCi/l), action should be taken to reduce exposure. There was
significant controversy concerning this level. EPA estimated that exposure to this level of radon over a lifetime results in a lung cancer risk
of between 1 and 5 out of 100. Although some scientists argued that
this estimate was "outlandishly high," environmental groups criticized
EPA for accepting such high risks.[8] The agency also published a
supplementary guide for homeowners concerned about reducing
radon levels in their homes.[9]

The first results of EPA's survey were reported in August
1987.[10] One in five homes in the ten-state survey was found to have
radon levels exceeding the EPA action level. More extensive testing
was performed, and EPA officials became sufficiently alarmed by September 1988 that they issued a "national public health advisory"
urging that most homes be tested for radon.[11] The health advisory was
given substantial media attention.

Congress maintained pressure to ensure that the agency continued
to consider radon a high priority. In 1988 Congress enacted a measure
that increased EPA's radon budget, and required the agency to adopt
model construction standards for new homes and to publish a more
aggressive public information booklet. Congress was particularly concerned that "the public [be] made aware of the risks that remain at
levels below 4 picocuries per litre," the action level used in the 1986
citizen's guide.[12] The legislation went as far as establishing a "national
long-term goal" for radon policy "that the air in buildings in the
United States should be as free of radon as the ambient air outside
the buildings."[13]

In October 1989 further results from EPA's national survey of radon
levels were published, confirming earlier findings.[14] In May 1992 EPA
issued the second edition of its citizen's guide. Despite occasional
criticism in the conservative media for exaggerating risk levels,[15] the
4 pCi/l action level was retained, and the document placed more
emphasis on risks below that level, claiming that "radon levels less than
4 pCi/l still pose a risk, and in many cases may be reduced."[16] The
citizen's guide was accompanied by a technical support document
which explained EPA's rationale for the action level in great detail.
The technical support document noted that the previous citizen's

guide "resulted in apathy, not panic." It surveyed recent research in risk communication in an effort to redesign the guide to get the public to take radon risks seriously.[17] In April 1993 EPA proposed voluntary guidelines for the construction of new homes in areas known to be high in radon.[18]

CHRONOLOGY OF EVENTS: CANADA

Canadian governments, both federal and provincial, have been much less aggressive in communicating the hazards of radon to the public. Ironically the Canadian government was well ahead of the U.S. in its research efforts. Alarmed about high levels of radon in uranium mining towns, the federal government launched a survey of 14,000 homes in 19 Canadian cities in 1977.[19] Despite the completion of the survey in 1980, evidence of disturbingly high levels of radon in Winnipeg was not released until an exposé by the *Fifth Estate* in October 1984. Even with this revelation the rest of the national media did not pick up the radon issue. At the time the government sought to downplay the concerns.[20]

Somewhat surprisingly the surge in concern over radon in the U.S. following the May 1985 *New York Times* story did not spill over into Canada. In fact the *Canadian Newspaper Index* reveals no entries on radon for the entire year. Media interest in radon did not increase until 1987, when both the *Montreal Gazette* and Toronto *Globe and Mail* ran feature-length investigative stories on radon, the latter in a high-profile five day series.[21] Both stories were alarmist in tone, proclaiming that radon "kills hundreds of Canadians each year."[22]

Rather than initiate an aggressive public information campaign, however, the Canadian federal government made a concerted effort to dismiss the significance of the hazard. Dr Roger Eaton, a spokesperson for Health and Welfare Canada, argued that "until everybody stops smoking, there's not much point in spending money on ... techniques to reduce radon in homes." In a startling statement from a government health official, Eaton went on to say, "As we say, you can't tame nature; you just have to live with it."[23]

The federal government did develop guidelines for radon exposure in homes. The level was set at 0.1 Working Levels, or the equivalent of 20 pCi/l, the Canadian exposure standard for uranium miners, five times higher than EPA's action level. Canadian officials estimate that this level of exposure carries a risk of 1 in 1000 lung cancer deaths per year,[24] equivalent to smoking between one and two packs of cigarettes a day. In contrast to EPA's action level, the Canadian guideline has not been widely publicized. It was announced in a Health Protection Branch "Issues" release in January 1989, two and one-half years after the release of EPA's *Citizen Guide*. The official guideline states:

It is recommended that remedial measures be taken where the level of radon in a home is found to exceed 800 Bq/m3 [20 pCi/l] as the annual average concentration in the normal living area. Because there is some risk at any level of radon exposure, homeowners may wish to reduce levels of radon as low as practicable.

A year later Health and Welfare Canada issued a more elaborate pamphlet presenting the guideline and additional information on mitigation, but in contrast to the U.S. it was not accompanied by any significant public information campaign.[25]

The Canadian government's response to EPA's national health advisory in September 1988 most clearly demonstrated the different national approaches to radon. Canadian officials responded that they believed EPA overestimated the magnitude of the problem, and decided against following EPA's strategy of recommending that all homeowners perform tests.[26] Health and Welfare Canada made a conscious decision not to elevate radon to a higher priority, despite the escalating concern in the U.S.

While the Canadian federal government has been slow to adopt radon as a priority issue, several provincial governments have been more aggressive. Health and Welfare Canada's cross-national survey in the late 1970s revealed that the highest urban radon levels were found in Winnipeg, Manitoba, and that province has taken the most aggressive response to radon. In September 1989 Manitoba issued a citizens' guide much like the one EPA issued in August 1986.[27] However the guide adopted the Canadian action level of 20 pCi/l, recommending that remedial action be taken within 12 months to "reduce levels as low as practical." If tests show concentrations below this level, the guide suggests that "remedial work be considered at these levels at [the homeowners'] discretion."

With the issuance of this guide, the province of Manitoba reached the same level of concern and action as the U.S. EPA had more than three years earlier. Even then, Manitoba's action levels were significantly greater than EPA's. Saskatchewan also has taken some action. In 1980 it initiated a survey of homes and published the results in 1985.[28] That province has also recently issued a public information pamphlet adopting the federal Canadian guideline as a suggested action level.[29]

DECISION RECONSTRUCTION: U.S.

The evidence that radon causes lung cancer comes from studies of miners who have been exposed to relatively high levels of radon over long periods of time. The link between radon exposure and elevated levels of lung cancer in miners was made as early as the 1920s, but was not confirmed until the 1960s. It has since been confirmed by at least 11 separate studies of miners.[30] The presence of solid epidemiological evidence on radon obviates the problem of extrapolation from laboratory animals to humans. Instead the regulatory science problem is extrapolation from relatively high exposure levels in mines to the lower exposure levels typically found in homes, and it is on this issue that Canadian and u.s. officials disagree.

The extrapolation problem is not so great as it might be, however, because there is some overlap between indoor exposure and carcinogenic effects observable in the miner studies. The lowest cumulative exposure level causing statistically significant elevated lung cancers is 40 to 80 working level months (wlm), whereas exposure in homes ranges from 1 to over 10,000 wlm, with the average between 10 and 20 wlm.[31]

In the u.s. epidemiological studies have been used to develop a dose-response curve to estimate health risks from routine exposure to radon in homes. On the basis of such analyses epa estimates that annual lung cancer deaths in the u.s. due to radon exposure are between 7000 and 30,000, with a central estimate of 14,000.[32] Given the approximately 130,000 annual lung cancer deaths in the u.s., these figures suggest radon may be responsible for between 5 and 23 percent of lung cancer deaths, with a central estimate of 11 percent. This suggests that radon is by far the largest environmental health problem in North America, dominating health threats from any of the other contaminants evaluated in this book. In its survey of priorities among environmental problems, epa listed radon as tied for first with worker exposure to chemicals as the most significant population cancer risks.[33]

epa has been very explicit in its strategy of communicating radon risks to the public. In its 1986 citizen's guide epa graphically displayed the probabilistic risk estimates at various levels of radon exposure, shown in figure 2. epa estimates that its action level is equivalent to a lifetime risk of between 1 and 5 out of 100. The agency compares these risks to other risks with which the public may be more familiar, such as chest x-rays and smoking (figure 3). In the 1992 revised citizen's guide, the strategy for communicating risks was altered somewhat. Far more attention was given to the differences in risk faced by

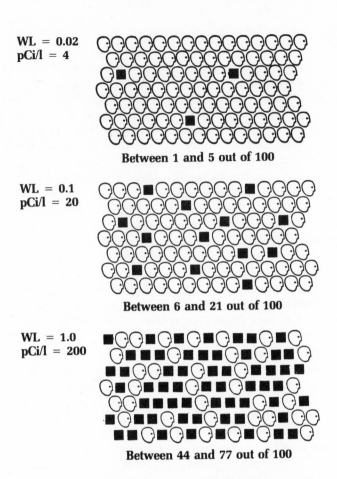

WL = 0.02
pCi/l = 4

Between 1 and 5 out of 100

WL = 0.1
pCi/l = 20

Between 6 and 21 out of 100

WL = 1.0
pCi/l = 200

Between 44 and 77 out of 100

If these same 100 individuals had lived only 10 years (instead of 70) in houses with radon levels of about 1.0 WL, the number of lung cancer deaths expected would be:

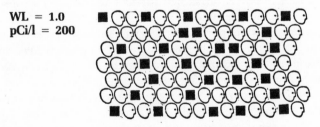

WL = 1.0
pCi/l = 200

Between 14 and 42 out of 100

Fig. 2 Lung Cancer Deaths Associated with Exposure to Various Radon Levels over 70 Years

Source: EPA, *A Citizen's Guide to Radon*, August 1986, p. 9.

pCi/l	WL	Estimated number of lung cancer deaths due to radon exposure (out of 1000)	Comparable exposure levels		Comparable risk
200	1	440—770	1000 times average outdoor level		More than 60 times non-smoker risk
					4 pack-a-day smoker
100	0.5	270—630	100 times average indoor level		
					20,000 chest x-rays per year
40	0.2	120—380			
20	0.1	60—210	100 times average outdoor level		2 pack-a-day smoker
					1 pack-a-day smoker
10	0.05	30—120	10 times average indoor level		
					5 times non-smoker risk
4	0.02	13—50			
2	0.01	7—30	10 times average outdoor level		200 chest x-rays per year
					Non-smoker risk of dying from lung cancer
1	0.005	3—13	Average indoor level		
0.2	0.001	1—3	Average outdoor level		20 chest x-rays per year

Fig. 3   Radon Risk Evaluation Chart

Source: EPA, *A Citizen's Guide to Radon,* August 1986, p. 10.

smokers and non-smokers, and the risk comparison to smoking and X-rays was replaced by a comparison to being killed in different types of accidents.[34]

DECISION RECONSTRUCTION: CANADA

While Canadian governments have lagged behind U.S. efforts to reduce radon hazards, Canada has given the issue a great deal of research attention. In addition to the survey of exposure levels mentioned above, Health and Welfare Canada has performed a somewhat crude epidemiological study of the relationship between the average levels of radon in various urban areas and deaths from lung cancer. That study was unable to detect any statistical relationship between average radon levels and lung cancer. However the relatively small number of cities considered (14) made detection of a such a relationship very difficult. In fact the study could not even detect any relationship between smoking and lung cancer among women.[35] That study is not cited in government officials' survey of the relevant scientific knowledge on the subject.[36]

A new, more refined epidemiological study had just recently been completed by scientists at Health and Welfare Canada.[37] The study involves a case-control analysis of the potential link between lung cancer and radon exposure in Winnipeg homes. The study failed to detect any link between residential radon exposure and lung cancer, and as a result has been welcomed by Canadian officials as support for the more conservative approach to the radon issue taken in Canada. Because the study has yet to appear in print, it is too early to gauge its impact on U.S. radon policy or the more general controversy over radon. It should also be noted that other recently published studies have produced quite different results. A new Swedish study, similar in design to the Canadian study, found that exposure to radon in homes is linked to elevated rates of lung cancer.[38]

Canada's regulatory science concerning the health effects of radon differs significantly from that of the U.S. EPA. Canadian officials state that radon may cause between zero and 5 percent of lung cancer deaths, a figure significantly smaller than EPA's. The most important difference between the U.S. and Canadian risk estimates is the reliance on fundamentally different methods of calculating radon's health effects. Rather than use the miner studies to extrapolate to indoor concentrations, Health and Welfare Canada has relied on a much more informal and indirect method of estimating risks. Health and Welfare officials assumed that 90 percent of lung cancer deaths are caused by smoking and that 5 percent of lung cancer deaths occur "spontaneously," leaving a residual of up to 5 percent which could possibly be attributed to radon exposure.[39]

Government scientists disagree with their U.S. counterparts on the applicability of the miner studies to radon exposure in homes. Their concern is not with thresholds; in fact, the government's guideline makes it clear that "there is some risk at any level of radon exposure."[40] Rather, Canadian officials emphasize the difference between mine and home conditions of exposure, including age, sex, and breathing patterns.[41] For example miners breathe at higher rates due to physical exertion, so they inhale more radon gas. EPA documents have considered the differences between exposure conditions in the mine and in the home and arrived at a quite different conclusion. EPA argues that while miners do breathe at a higher rate, radon is likely to be attached to larger particles in a mine than in a home, and the larger the particle the less deeply radon would penetrate into the lung, and the less damage it would cause. In addition the presence of the young and infirm in homes broadens exposure of more vulnerable groups in the population. For the purpose of calculating risk estimates EPA assumes that the risk from a given unit of radon exposure was 30 percent less in homes than it is in mines.[42]

Canadian officials are sufficiently troubled by the uncertainties surrounding extrapolation from the workplace to homes that they prefer to wait for additional epidemiological evidence.[43] In one publication, however, Heath and Welfare Canada's Dr Roger Eaton did state that exposure at Canada's guideline carries a risk of 1 in 1000 lung cancer deaths *per year* (or approximately 1 in 100 for a 70 year lifetime).[44] While he did not document the basis for the figure, it is comparable to the risk estimates set out in EPA's citizen's guide, and according to that guide equivalent to smoking between one and two packs of cigarettes a day.[45]

Because of Canada's reticence to use quantitative risk estimates, its public information documents do not give citizens information about the risk levels associated with various indoor exposure levels. The only information on risk levels provided by Health and Welfare Canada in its 1989 pamphlet is the following explanation of how its guideline was chosen:

This level was chosen as we know that the risk at this level, including the uncertainties of the risk, is significant for occupants of houses. Home-owners should also recognize that there is risk at any level of radon exposure and as a consequence they may wish to reduce the concentration of radon to a level that is as low as practical.[46]

This statement contrasts sharply with EPA's risk communication strategy discussed above, and could lead citizens to discount the magnitude of radon hazards. It is one thing merely to tell someone that a risk is "significant," and another to tell them that it is equivalent to smoking between one and two packs of cigarettes per day, or 100 times the risk of drowning. Unlike EPA's explicit attempt to "personalize risks" by drawing analogies to risk more familiar to homeowners, Health and Welfare Canada presents no comparative risk information.

COST-BENEFIT BALANCING

Unlike all the other case studies in this volume, radon is not the result of an activity that produces any economic benefits. For that reason, the relevant economic issue is not balancing risks with benefits, but rather balancing reduced health risks with the costs of radon mitigation. Another source of divergence in radon policies is the different assumptions the two governments have made about whether the risks of radon exposure warrant the costs of reducing those exposures, and about who should make that decision.

The United States' public information campaign alerts citizens to the risks of radon and the costs of mitigating those risks, but leaves the decision of whether to do so up to the homeowner. EPA has performed extensive cost-effectiveness analyses and determined that the cost per life saved of reducing exposures to the action level is in the same range as comparable expenditures for the reduction of other environmental risks as required by law. EPA estimates that the average cost per life saved through radon reduction is $700,000. The agency reports that this estimate is superior or comparable to programs for medical screening, highway safety, air transportation safety, and occupational safety.[47]

In contrast Canadian government officials performed their own internal assessments of the costs and benefits of exposure mitigation, and concluded on behalf of those exposed that expenditures of their resources to mitigate the risk are not warranted. The government originally estimated that it would cost $1.85 million for every lung cancer avoided.[48] This figure is clearly an overestimate, as the analysis assumed that remediation would cost $7500 per home (1985 Canadian dollars), when better supported U.S. estimates of mitigation costs range from $50 to $5000, with an average of $1200 (1989 U.S. dollars).[49]

An updated assessment used more reasonable costs of remediation and derived much lower estimates of the cost per life saved. In the scenario most similar to the EPA approach, Health and Welfare Canada estimates an average cost-effectiveness nationally of $57,000 per lung cancer death avoided, ranging from a low of $23,000 per life saved in Winnipeg to $5.8 million in Vancouver. Despite these exceptionally low cost-per-life-saved estimates, the report concludes that "it is clear that any comprehensive programme to reduce the levels of radon gas in Canadian homes will be extremely expensive.[50] In emphasizing the overall costs of the program rather than the relatively low cost per life saved, the report departs significantly from the approach taken in the U.S.[51] To place these numbers in context, the Ontario Royal Commission on Asbestos, discussed in chapter 7, argued that a ban on the use of asbestos in textile manufacturing was justified at a cost of $660,000 per life saved.

Canadian officials have used this cost-effectiveness argument to justify their lack of a more aggressive policy toward radon. In doing so they compare the risk from radon to the risk from smoking. For instance, as noted earlier, one Health and Welfare Canada official stated that because 90 percent of lung cancer deaths are caused by cigarette smoking, spending money on reducing radon is not justified "until everybody stops smoking."[52] While it is undoubtedly true that the most effective way to reduce lung cancers is to reduce smoking, the public policy problems of smoking and radon are quite different. Smokers voluntarily assume an elevated risk of lung cancer, whereas radon exposures are involuntary, at least up to the point where home-owners are made aware of the risks.

When asked why the Canadian government did not follow the U.S. strategy of communicating the risks and then leaving the decision up to the consumer, a Health and Welfare official responded that the government concluded that it would not be worth "disturbing" the public with the information given that the risk is "such a small one."[53] In light of the strikingly low figures for the costs per life saved, and given that 5 percent of lung cancer deaths is equivalent to 570 deaths per year in Canada, an extraordinarily high risk for environmental contaminants, the Canadian approach to radon seems surprisingly cavalier. As a point of comparison this Canadian upper bound figure of 5 percent of lung cancer deaths is equivalent to a lifetime risk of 1 in 100. Canada banned the pesticide alachlor in 1988, when excess lifetime cancer risk was projected to between 1 in 1000 and 1 in 10,000, with much less widespread exposure (see chapter 4).

INTEREST REPRESENTATION

One of the remarkable features of the radon issue is the lack of interest group involvement. Since no industry is threatened by regulatory restrictions, business groups have shown little interest in the issue. More surprisingly, especially given the magnitude of the health risks at stake, environmental and consumer groups have played little role in either country. There was some early involvement of groups in the U.S., where it was the activism of a Pennsylvania citizens' group, People Against Radon, and the Environmental Defense Fund that brought the Watras story to the attention of the *New York Times* environment reporter. EDF also testified at hearings on the 1988 U.S. legislation.[54] But environmental group interest in the issue has not been nearly so intense as it has on a number of other issues.

In Canada there has been even less group activity. In the past Energy Probe has been active on the issue of radiation in uranium mining towns, but it has not translated that expertise into activism on indoor radon from natural sources. Energy Probe's Norm Rubin admits that radon may have fallen between the cracks when Energy Probe split from Pollution Probe over nuclear issues in 1981, creating problems in representation on issues of pollution from radiation not associated with the nuclear fuel cycle.[55]

The lack of group activity appears to result from the fact that environmental groups see few political incentives in picking up the issue, in part because there are no corporate actors to blame.[56] A prominent Canadian environmentalist expressed a great deal of scepticism about the radon issue, suggesting it was merely a way for governments to deflect concern from environmental pollutants, such as pulp mill dioxins.[57]

While environmental groups in both countries have played a limited role, one of the most important reasons for the divergent approaches taken by the two governments has been the level of activity of legislators. In the mid-1980s the issue was adopted by members of Congress from areas with high radon levels, whose persistent pressure on the reluctant Reagan administration eventually bore fruit.[58] Congress kept up this pressure with the 1988 legislation.

The Canadian Parliament, in contrast, has been virtually silent on the issue. There have been no Parliamentary committee hearings on the subject, and the radon issue has only emerged once in question period. The day that EPA issued its "national health advisory," Lloyd Axworthy, a Liberal member of the opposition from Winnipeg, a city noted for its high radon levels, challenged the health minister Jake Epp on the issue. Epp responded that he was not convinced by the U.S. results, and the issue was not raised again.[59] Axworthy had a clear incentive to publicize the radon problem and the government's failure to respond to it, but at the time was distracted by his role as trade critic in the midst of the 1988 election campaign. Staff members for both Axworthy and Liberal environment critic Charles Caccia claim that they did not press the issue further because of a lack of public concern.[60]

CONCLUSION

Stringency

While neither government has adopted regulations to control radon exposures in homes, there is no question that the U.S. approach to radon is far more aggressive. The U.S. has issued a national health advisory recommending testing for most homes, and its action level is five times more stringent than Canada's. Moreover its public information campaign has been far more aggressive. This difference in part reflects substantial departures in risk assessments. EPA's central estimate is that radon causes 11 percent of lung cancer deaths, whereas Health and Welfare Canada estimates that radon causes from 0 to 5 percent. But the difference also reflects different ways of balancing benefits and communication risks to the public, as discussed below.

Incorporation of Science

The two countries have exhibited different approaches both in the way the science of radon risks has been interpreted and the way information about risks has been communicated to the public. While the u.s. epa has developed extensive quantitative estimates of radon risks, Canadian officials have been extremely reluctant to do so. The Canadian approach reveals a highly "risk tolerant" approach to the interpretation of uncertain science. Along with asbestos radon is the only case analyzed in this book where there is solid epidemiological evidence linking the substance to cancer in humans. In fact in the case of radon the problem of extrapolating demonstrated hazards to policy-relevant exposure levels is much less significant than in the case of asbestos, because exposure levels that have been associated with elevated lung cancer rates in miners actually overlap with exposure levels in some homes.

Nonetheless Canadian officials have been extremely hesitant to take the problem of radon exposure in homes seriously. They have placed greater emphasis on negative epidemiological studies than their counterparts in the u.s. In addition they have adopted assumptions regarding the difference between conditions of exposure in mines and homes that err on the side of risk tolerance rather than risk aversion.

u.s. and Canadian officials have also adopted different points of reference for assessing the severity of the risks posed by radon. epa has compared radon risks to risks from other environmental contaminants and concluded that the risks are quite substantial and that an aggressive campaign to inform the public is justified. In contrast Canadian officials routinely compare radon risks to the risks from smoking. Because smoking clearly overwhelms all environmental health risks, this comparison can be used to downplay the significance of almost any health threat. The Canadian approach also represents a conspicuous departure from the consensus of risk analysts, who emphasize the importance of distinguishing risks that are assumed voluntarily, like smoking or sky diving, from involuntarily assumed ones.[61] Smoking is only a relevant comparison to radon if the amount of information individuals have about each risk is equivalent. Clearly this is not the case, particularly given the Canadian risk communication strategy.

The most profound divergence between Canadian and u.s. radon policies lies in the strategies adopted for communicating risk information to the public. The epa citizen's guide provides readers with probabalistic risk estimates for various levels of radon exposure and relates them to other risks more familiar to the public – chest x-rays, smoking, and accidental deaths. Readers learn that exposure to 20 pCi/l (the Canadian guideline) presents a health risk estimated to be equivalent to smoking between one and two packs of cigarettes per day. The Canadian pamphlet, on the other hand, merely informs readers that the risk of exposure to the Canadian guideline is "significant."

The u.s. approach relies on providing the individual with relevant information to make choices about testing and mitigation, costs that will be borne by the homeowner, not the government. Canadian officials are unwilling to be more specific not only because they are skeptical of quantitative estimates but also because they are concerned about creating undue public alarm. The u.s. strategy risks provoking public alarm. In fact EPA officials have been frustrated by the relatively apathetic public response, and with Congressional prodding developed a new citizen's guide designed to overcome this apathy. Thus far the response does not appear to be much different from that to the earlier version.

This u.s. approach is predicated on a classically liberal view of limited government, in which government's only role is to provide information to enable citizens to make their own choices. Ironically the Canadian response reflects a philosophy of the government assuming a greater role in the protection of citizens. Yet in their paternalism, Canadian officials seem so preoccupied with avoiding undue alarm that they have taken a far less active role on the issue, with the potential effect of denying the Canadian public the necessary information to make informed choices about radon.

Benefit Balancing

From the start u.s. officials were more concerned about getting information about radon to the public than about justifying the cost-effectiveness of the program. Extensive economic analyses have been performed, beginning in 1990, which reassured EPA that the cost-effectiveness of radon mitigation measures were comparable – in many cases superior – to other measures that had been required by law.

In Canada the federal government seems to have been inordinately concerned with the costs of mitigation – at the expense of minimizing public awareness about risks. Although a recent study derived much lower estimates of costs per life saved, in fact far lower than EPA's estimates, Canadian officials have not altered their position that radon mitigation strategies are not justified. In rejecting even those relatively low costs, Canadian officials have been willing to tolerate levels of risk from radon that are quite high in comparison to other environmental health risks.

Interest Representation

The radon issue has attracted remarkably little attention from interest groups. The lack of environmental or consumer group involvement is particularly striking, given that the evidence suggests that radon is by far the most serious health threat of the substances analyzed here. While U.S. environmental groups have been quite passive on the issue, the interest of protection from radon exposures has been taken up more actively by members of Congress who have sought political mileage from an issue where there were opportunities to blame the administration for insufficient action. As a result radon has remained on the regulatory agenda despite widespread public apathy and environmental group indifference. In contrast Canadian legislators have been inactive on the issue, despite the fact that the government's approach to the problem seems ripe for opposition criticism.

This analysis of radon supports two of the major themes of this book. First, in its decisions about "regulatory science," the U.S. tends to adopt more risk averse assumptions than Canada does. Second, the U.S. approach is more liberal, in the sense that it stresses giving information to individual citizens but leaving them with the decision and the costs. Ironically the more paternalistic Canadian approach – the philosophy typically associated with more active governmental role – in this case ends up being the less protective one.

9 Conclusion:
Risk, Science, and
Public Policy

The cases presented in this volume clearly reveal two different regulatory styles in action. In each case there was more open conflict over risks in the United States than in Canada, with interest groups, the media, legislators, and the courts playing a much more important role south of the border. The regulatory process in Canada tended to be closed, informal, and consensual, in comparison with the open, legalistic, and adversarial style of the u.s.

Despite the striking contrast in regulatory styles, perhaps the most important conclusion of this book is that there is no simple and direct relationship between regulatory processes and their outcomes. In some of the cases studied the adversarial u.s. process led to more stringent outcomes, while in others the quiet Canadian approach was more aggressive. In the u.s. the multiplicity of actors and complexity of the process can lead to unpredictable outcomes, with different actors prevailing in different circumstances. In Canada the executive has a greater degree of discretion, which it can use to regulate either stringently or loosely.

COMPARATIVE EVALUATION

The seven case studies analyzed here allow some generalizations about the impacts of regulatory style. Before proceeding with that analysis, however, we must offer a caveat that the case studies were not randomly selected. Although we attempted to cover a broad range of toxic substance problems, from pesticide residues in food to occupational health risks, we also chose these particular cases in part because each generated controversy in at least one of the countries and thus offered sufficient documentation to permit detailed analysis. While we cannot predict with great confidence how the observed patterns would change if the sample of cases was larger and more representative, we do believe that the sample is biased in one important way: it probably overstates the extent of divergence in regulatory outcomes between the two countries. Other studies have suggested that while the patterns of outcomes are quite complex, there is a substantial degree of convergence in environmental regulation between the two countries, reflecting the influence of a high degree of social and economic integration.[1]

Stringency

In the case of stringency, the results are mixed. The outcome of the dioxin case is uncertain at this point. The Canadian government has taken relatively aggressive regulatory actions to control dioxins in pulp mill effluents. Final u.s. national effluent standards are not expected until 1995. However a u.s. regulatory proposal published in 1993 promises stricter regulations than those adopted at the federal level in Canada. Moreover, in the meantime EPA's more cautious risk assessment has prompted several states to require tighter controls than those demanded by the Canadian federal government.

In the case of asbestos, the u.s. clearly has developed more stringent regulations than Canada. Although the courts recently reversed EPA's ban of asbestos products, u.s. workplace regulations are still more stringent than those in Ontario and Quebec. u.s. regulators also were more aggressive with respect to Alar and radon. Although Alar was withdrawn voluntarily by the manufacturer in both countries, u.s. regulators were close to banning it while Canadian regulators continued to express support for the product. In the case of radon, while neither country has adopted formal regulatory standards, u.s. guidelines are significantly more stringent.

Saccharin and urea-formaldehyde foam insulation are both cases of greater Canadian stringency. Canada banned both products, and while u.s. regulatory agencies originally did the same, they were overruled by institutional sovereigns – Congress in the case of saccharin, the courts in the case of UFFI. Canada also banned alachlor, while the u.s. elected to keep it on the market.

Thus of the six cases in which there were clear regulatory outcomes, Canadian standards were more stringent on three (alachlor, saccharin, and UFFI), and the u.s. was more stringent on three (asbestos, Alar, and radon). It bears emphasis that there is no evidence of a direct relationship between the sharply divergent regulatory styles of the two countries and the most important indicator of policy outcomes – how stringently toxic substances are regulated.

Timeliness

Our second criterion for regulatory effectiveness is timeliness. In the case of dioxin both countries became aware of the presence of dioxins in pulp mill effluents at about the same time. Only the Canadian federal government has to date finalized national effluent regulations, some three years in advance of anticipated U.S. regulations. However it was an extensive and costly U.S. monitoring program that discovered the problem in the first place.

Canadian decisions were more timely in the cases of saccharin and UFFI. The FDA proposed to ban saccharin the same day that Canada announced its ban, but the decision was delayed and ultimately reversed by the intervention of Congress. The U.S. did not finalize its ban of UFFI until 18 months after the Canadian ban went into effect, and even then it was subsequently overruled by the courts.

EPA acted first in the cases of Alar and radon. EPA developed its radon strategy several years before Canada; it also initiated its review of Alar first, although regulators in both countries were overwhelmed by the furor of public concern once the story hit *60 Minutes*.

The comparison is more difficult in other cases. The U.S. acted to reduce workplace exposure to asbestos before Canada did, but Canada revised its regulations more quickly when new evidence arose in the 1980s. In the case of alachlor the Canadian decision-making process was extended over a five-year period, as opposed to three years in the United States. However Canada began its review process earlier, and alachlor remained off the market while the industry appealed the government's decision to ban the product.

As in the case of stringency there is no simple relationship between regulatory style and timeliness. In some cases the U.S. acted more quickly in response to new risk perceptions, in others Canada did. This is a particularly important conclusion, because one of the most frequent criticisms of the U.S. regulatory process is that cumbersome procedures delay regulatory action.[2] These case studies reveal that while the greater discretion granted Canadian regulators gives them the *capacity* to act decisively, they do not always exercise it. While there are numerous instances of extraordinary delays in the U.S. regulatory process, the record here suggests that the U.S. fares no worse than countries with less adversarial regulatory styles.

Incorporation of Science

Despite the fact that the policy problem in each case was similar in Canada and the u.s., the policies the two countries adopted often differed substantially. An important question is whether that divergence resulted from different assessments of the magnitude of risk or whether it was the result of different evaluations of the acceptability of the risk.

The case studies clearly reveal the operation not only of two different styles of regulation but also different styles of regulatory science. Not only do the political processes and policy decisions differ between Canada and the u.s., but the way that government scientists answer questions of fact also can differ in important ways. In the face of scientific uncertainty scientific judgment and value-based decisions are inevitably intertwined, and the way they are combined in each country reflects the political environment in which its regulatory scientists operate.

Publication of detailed scientific rationales for regulatory decisions, reliance on generic regulatory science principles, and open debate over the inherent value judgments characterize the u.s. style of regulatory science. The case studies reveal Canadian regulatory science to be exemplified by closed scientific decision making, case-by-case review of toxic substances, and emphasis on the scientific aspects of regulatory science.

In every case in this volume the u.s. provided much more extensive documentation of the scientific and policy bases for its decisions. Typically, Canadian regulators merely stated broad, qualitative conclusions about the nature and acceptability of the risks in question, while their American counterparts offered extensive discussions of the methodology behind each assessment, including responses to criticisms received during the public comment period. This observation conforms to the arguments made by others that the adversarial, legalistic style of u.s. regulatory politics creates incentives for regulators to provide more detailed scientific justifications for their decisions than regulators who operate in a more cooperative and informal environment.[3] The political context of risk assessment also helps explain the greater affinity in the u.s. for the use of mathematical models in risk assessment: such models provide regulators with a veneer of objectivity that they can use to justify their positions in a hostile political environment.

In performing risk assessments in these cases u.s. regulatory scientists relied on generic cancer policies, which had been extensively debated both within the scientific community and the attentive public.

Canada has established no comparable inference guidelines. Decisions about regulatory science are made on a case- by-case basis, based heavily on the professional judgment of government scientists.

Reliance on generic principles has tended to produce more cautious regulatory science in the u.s. At each of the inference junctures described in chapter 2, the u.s. adopted a risk averse position. For instance, as a matter of policy u.s. regulatory agencies typically do not accept negative epidemiological evidence as proof that a substance is "safe." In contrast Health and Welfare Canada initially used a crude epidemiological analysis to downplay the risks of exposure to low levels of radon. More recently they have relied on a more sophisticated study yielding negative evidence to justify their risk tolerant approach, despite the existence of well-designed epidemiological studies showing positive results. u.s. agencies also rely extensively on models based on a risk averse assumption of a linear dose-response relationship at very low doses;[4] Canadian officials often rely on safety factors to estimate acceptable levels of exposure, a methodology consistent with the threshold assumption.

The tendency toward greater caution in u.s. risk assessments did not prevail in every case, however. The ad hoc Canadian approach produced more cautious assumptions in the saccharin, uffi, and alachlor cases. In two of these cases, saccharin and uffi, u.s. regulators adopted risk assessments that were at least as risk averse as the Canadian assessments, but Congress and the courts overruled them. The case of alachlor is an interesting exception, where extremely risk averse exposure assumptions – resulting from the influence of one government scientist – produced a more cautious Canadian risk estimate.

Salter among others has emphasized that regulatory science seeks to satisfy two different standards – truth and justice.[5] Inasmuch as regulatory science attempts to answer questions of fact, the standard of truth that guides research science seems most relevant. However since value judgments are unavoidable when science cannot provide reassurances of truth, the democratic standard of justice is also relevant. In the case studies examined in this volume Canadian officials tended to place greater emphasis on the scientific or "truth-seeking" character of regulatory science, while the u.s. process placed greater emphasis on the value-laden policy components of regulatory science.

Because of the tremendous scientific uncertainty about the link between chemicals and cancer risks, it is impossible for us to say which country's approach is more scientifically valid. What we can say is that in none of the cases did regulators adopt assumptions that were clearly "bad science." In every case there was substantial support within the scientific community for the regulatory science position adopted by regulators, even in cases like asbestos and radon, where the assumptions adopted by the two countries diverged widely. The regulatory science positions adopted by non-scientists, particularly by the u.s. Congress in the saccharin case, are more vulnerable to criticism, however.

The Canadian approach relies heavily on government scientists' professional judgment in weighing the available evidence. In relying instead on generic cancer policies, the u.s. runs the risk of "freezing science." u.s. regulatory scientists may be forced to rely on policy-based rules that they do not consider most appropriate to the case at hand. In addition the Canadian approach has the flexibility to adapt quickly to changes in science. According to Jasanoff, "Scientific change is most easily accommodated in policy systems where risk decisions are made incrementally."[6]

As EPA discovered in attempting to revise its dioxin risk assessment, it can be especially difficult to revise risk estimates downward in the face of intensive public scrutiny. Yet that is just the direction the agency often will have to move. The public health philosophy that has guided the American approach to date has meant that at virtually every inference juncture, the u.s. has adopted risk averse assumptions. u.s. regulatory agencies consciously adopted risk estimates at the outer bounds of uncertainty. It follows that as new information leads to greater precision of risk estimates, thus reducing the extent of uncertainty, it often will be necessary to revise original risk estimates downward.[7] However because such revisions tend to undermine the rationale for restrictive regulations, they are vulnerable to challenge by regulatory advocates, who can argue that revised risk estimates inevitably will lead to a weakening of existing regulations and thus, ultimately, increased public exposure to risks.

Indeed, in the dioxin case u.s. environmentalists depicted EPA's proposed revision of its risk assessment as a politically motivated attempt to evade responsibility for clean-up of toxic waste dumps. The regulatory implications of revising risk estimates downward thus place government officials in the politically difficult position of explaining that relaxation of regulations may be needed because the government originally erred and provided the public with a higher degree of protection than it had intended.

While the u.s. approach runs the risk of rigidity, the ad hoc Canadian approach runs the risk of inconsistency – or at least the appearance thereof. In some cases Canadian regulators relied on threshold assumptions, and in others they did not. There may have been sound scientific reasons for their choice of approach, but it is frequently extremely difficult to tell from the public record.[8] Unless Canadian regulators provide greater elaboration of the scientific basis for their decisions, the appearance of inconsistency may undermine both the scientific credibility and the political legitimacy of their actions.

One Canadian official we interviewed spoke of being "grateful that our hands are not tied" like those of u.s. counterparts, who must respond to "emotion and political pressure."[9] In stressing only the scientific characteristics of regulatory science, however, Canadian regulators fail to acknowledge that their professional decisions are not devoid of value judgments. Canadian officials' pride that their scientific integrity has not been compromised by emotion and politics may be misplaced.

The Canadian approach also risks loss of accountability. Without offering more explicit rationales for regulatory decisions, it is easier for Canadian decision makers to hide political judgments behind science – or to appear to be doing so. For instance government officials have routinely depicted the Canadian standard for dioxin in fish as a purely scientific assessment of "safety," even though there is evidence that factors other than health risks were taken into account in setting the standard. However in the absence of a "paper trail" documenting the logic of the standard, it is not easy to challenge the government's statements.

There are many critics of EPA's efforts to separate risk assessment from risk management, but one need not adopt the false view that risk assessment is pure science to prefer a more explicit discussion of the ingredients going into a particular decision. More explicit rationales may actually illuminate the policy choices made at both stages. We will return to the link between regulatory style and political accountability in the final section.

Risk-Benefit Balancing

In addition to different assessments of the magnitude of risks, regulatory divergence can also result from different evaluations of the benefits of the substance causing the risk. Although only Canada has issued final standards for dioxins in pulp mills effluents to date, it is possible to compare Canadian and u.s. tolerances for dioxin in fish. Both countries weighed potential health risks against the adverse economic impacts on consumers and the Great Lakes' commercial fishery. Comparable standards, which happened to impose little economic hardship on either consumers or business, were developed jointly by Canada and the u.s.

The benefits of Alar played almost no role in the heated debate over the chemical. The controversy centred exclusively on whether or not the product was a cancer risk to humans. In the case of asbestos, although there were differences in the estimates of health risks, what drove the decision was not risk assessments but judgments about what risks were acceptable. The technical feasibility standard used in the u.s. produced much more stringent regulation than the "relative risk" approach used in Canada. As a primary producer of asbestos Canada has much to lose from stringent regulation in either country. u.s. asbestos-dependent industries and their allies in the Office of Management and Budget used arguments about the benefits of asbestos to postpone the EPA ban and then have it overturned in an appeals court ruling. However despite those successes industry and OMB influence did not compare to that of their counterparts in Canada, where the industry worked with allies in the Quebec and federal governments to enshrine the "safe use" philosophy in Canadian regulatory policy.

In the alachlor case the two countries evaluated benefits differently and thus came to different conclusions about the magnitude of benefits. Canada's estimates of alachlor's benefits were lower than EPA's. However risk estimates were also higher in Canada, so it is impossible to ascribe the divergence in the decisions to risk-benefit balancing alone.

There also were differences in both the risk and benefit assessments in the radon case. The biggest difference between the two countries lay not in their own assessments of the acceptability of risks but in their positions with respect to who should decide whether the risks of radon exposure warrant the costs of mitigation. The United States adopted a public information campaign to alert citizens to the risks of radon and to provide information on techniques for mitigating those risks, ultimately leaving the decision up to the homeowner. In contrast, the Canadian government performed its own assessment of the costs and benefits of mitigation and concluded on behalf of those at risk (on the basis of some questionable assumptions) that committing greater resources to addressing the problem was not justified.

Regulatory agencies in the two countries agreed that the risks of cancer from saccharin consumption outweighed the benefits of availability of the sweetener. However in overturning FDA's proposed ban the u.s. Congress both rejected FDA's risk assessment and placed greater weight on the benefits of saccharin availability to dieters and diabetics.

In the case of UFFI the fact that Canada did not offer an explicit rationale for its decision to ban the insulation makes it difficult to discern how heavily decision makers weighed the potential costs of a ban. What is clear is that health concerns prevailed. As required by the u.s. statute, cpsc offered a detailed analysis of the costs and benefits of a ban, including an estimate of the monetary cost per case of cancer avoided. Like its Canadian counterpart, the agency also concluded that the health hazards posed by uffi justified a ban. The court overruled the cpsc ban, but did so by criticizing the agency's risk assessment, not its evaluation of benefits or its risk/benefit balancing.

With many of these cases it is difficult to compare the relative importance of differences in risk estimates from differences in assessments of the relative costs and benefits or of the acceptability of risks. In only one case, asbestos, did different standards of acceptability clearly overwhelm differences in risk estimates as the driving force behind the divergent policy outcomes. With Alar, standards of acceptability of the risks appeared irrelevant, presumably because of a strong societal consensus in both countries concerning risks to children.

In most of these cases there was a relationship between risk estimates and assessments of the acceptability of risks. In the alachlor, radon, and saccharin cases, the country that considered the risks to be highest also viewed the costs of control to be least significant. In the dioxin case fda and Health and Welfare Canada both appear to have assessed the magnitude of risks and their acceptability at the same time. With the possible exception of the uffi case, which is difficult to interpret, in no case did one agency arrive at both a low estimate of risks and a low estimate of the costs of control (or a high estimate of risks and a high estimate of costs).

This observation casts doubt on the effort to separate the risk assessment and risk management components of regulatory decisions. While we find it an analytically useful device and a worthy ideal, it appears that in the minds of regulators these questions concerning the magnitude and acceptability of risks are not easily separated. Whether because the same officials are responsible for making both decisions or because a disturbing risk estimate by certain officials inspires their colleagues to dig deeper to find an economic rationale for stringent regulations, it appears that regulators either allow their a priori ideas about the magnitude of risks to colour their assessments of the costs of control – or vice versa.

Interest Representation

One of the most fundamental differences between the Canadian and American regulatory styles is the manner of interest representation in the regulatory process. The u.s. system is open and highly fractious. Regulatory decisions are the subject of intense conflicts between regulated industries and regulatory advocates, including environmentalists, consumers, and unions. Each of these interest groups takes full advantage of the multiple veto points within the American system of government to pursue their interests. The Canadian regulatory system seems closed and quiet in comparison. There is simply much less interest group or partisan conflict over regulation, although there are signs that that is beginning to change.

There are three fundamental differences in interest representation in the two countries. First, with important exceptions the u.s. system is more formal. As outlined in the discussion of regulatory frameworks in chapter 1, and as revealed in each of the case studies, there are strict rules concerning administrative procedures in the u.s. Interest group participation occurs through open Congressional hearings, formal notice and comment procedures, and litigation. In Canada group participation has historically occurred through informal consultations between regulatory officials and those directly affected. The major exception is occupational health and safety in Quebec, where the affected interests – industry and labour – are themselves the regulators. A similar system appears to be emerging in Ontario occupational health and safety regulation as well.

Second, the multiple points of access within the u.s. system give interest groups more avenues of expression, heightening the level of conflict within the system. In Canada executive departments dominate toxic substance regulation. When a minister and/or cabinet makes a regulatory decision, that is typically the end of the matter. In two cases studied here, uffi and alachlor, industry pursued administrative appeals of government decisions, but under Canadian law the minister or Cabinet still retained the final say. In the uffi case the board of review supported the government's ban, while in the alachlor case, the minister of agriculture maintained the ban despite a highly critical report from the Alachlor Review Board. The only case where legal action followed a decision in Canada was alachlor, where the federal court easily dismissed the manufacturer's suit with a bow to ministerial discretion.[10]

Legislatures also have played a relatively deferential role in Canadian risk regulation. There are instances of significant legislative influence – opposition parties in Ontario were instrumental in forcing action on workplace standards on asbestos, and federal opposition parties were influential in forcing the government to establish a program to compensate homeowners affected by uffi. But for the most part Parliament and the provincial legislatures lack the expertise, time, or incentive to play a significant role in the technically complex matter of toxic substance regulation. Mechanisms do exist for legislative supervision, such as standing parliamentary committees like Agriculture, Environment, and Health and Welfare, and in particular the Standing Joint Committee for the Scrutiny of Regulations. According to Sharon Sutherland, however, "With the qualified exception of the Standing Committee on Finance it is fair to say that no House standing committee 1986–90 has to date had a serious impact on policy."[11]

In comparison with the finality of Canadian regulatory decisions, agency action in the U.S. is frequently merely an interim stage in the battle. Losers in the regulatory arena typically appeal to the agency's sovereigns, whether legislative or judicial. In the saccharin case industry launched an effective campaign to get Congress to overrule the FDA ban. In the cases of both UFFI and asbestos industry succeeded in convincing the courts to strike down agency decisions.

Intervention by other branches does not occur only after regulatory decisions are made. U.S. regulatory advocates used the courts to force issues onto the regulatory agenda in a number of cases. In the cases of dioxin and Alar environmentalists' lawsuits forced EPA to initiate regulatory action. In the asbestos case, the U.S. Congress was strongly critical of intervention by the Office of Management and Budget, spurring EPA to resist OMB pressure and proceed with a ban. Regulatory advocates succeeded largely because Congressional statutes contain very specific requirements and thus provide enforceable claims to agency action. With the exception of the field of environmental impact assessment, such detailed statutory requirements simply do not exist in Canada. The influence of Canadian regulatory advocates is further undermined by the fact that, unlike the regulated industry, they have no right to appeal via boards of review under most regulatory statutes.

Third, only in the U.S. does interest group conflict typically penetrate beyond risk management to regulatory science. Although U.S. officials have attempted to depoliticize regulatory decisions by offering detailed scientific rationales, the adversarial nature of U.S. politics tends to spill over into discussions of regulatory science. This point was most clearly illustrated by the dioxin case, where U.S. environmentalists and their allies in Congress and the media subjected EPA risk assessments to intense scrutiny. While Canadian environmentalists have conducted aggressive political campaigns on the issue of dioxins in pulp mill effluents, they have played only a peripheral role in the regulatory science debate about health risks. Whether this is because they are content to leave risk assessment to government scientists or whether they do not have the resources to muster an effective challenge, the effect is the same. Alar offers an even more extreme example, where U.S. environmentalists published their own risk assessment, inciting the public alarm that engulfed Canada as well as the u.s. Their greater resources and expertise have enabled u.s. environmentalists to maintain a presence in policy-relevant science, while in Canada regulatory science has remained insulated from political conflict and thus from public scrutiny of the policy decisions embedded in "scientific" statements.

TECHNOCRACY VS DEMOCRACY

The comparison of cases here reveals the operation of two competing models of the relation between scientific experts and regulators on the one hand, and the public, interest groups, and the media on the other.[12] The u.s. approach is more pluralistic in relying upon interest group participation in risk management and even risk assessment. The Canadian approach is more paternalistic, entrusting the task of risk regulation to politicians and government experts with far less input from the public.

These different models are clearly revealed in the two countries' approaches to risk communication. The Canadian government generally assumes a greater role in assessing the acceptability of risks, whereas the u.s. gives a greater responsibility to individuals. In the case of radon, for example, the u.s. agency left the decision about whether the risks warrant the costs of mitigation to individual home-owners, while the Canadian government effectively made the decision on their behalf.

The greater paternalism in Canada does not always produce less aggressive action on risks, however. In the saccharin case Congress decided that as long as citizens were given a health warning, it should be up to them to decide whether to use the product. Canadian regulators were highly skeptical about the efficacy of warning labels, particularly for one high-risk group, children, and thus banned the product. It is also noteworthy that despite EPA's greater concern about radon, the agency's strategy is primarily directed toward homeowners, with little attention to renters or others who cannot afford mitigation measures.

Government discussions of low-level risks also reflect these different approaches. Canadian regulators are more likely to assure the public that exposures to low level or uncertain risks are "safe." u.s. regulators are more willing to concede the possibility of residual risks, even when making the additional claim that those risks are acceptable. The Canadian approach risks being disingenuous; even when experts disagree about the risks at low doses Canadian officials often offer reassurances of absolute safety in order to avoid public alarm. In contrast,

U.S. regulators err on the side of openness at the risk of occasionally provoking public alarm.

Alar provides a classic case of this pattern. When EPA announced its decisions to accelerate its cancellation process, it stated that new studies "raise serious concern about the safety of continued, long term exposure."[13] When an environmental group published its own study several weeks later, EPA lost control over the messages the public was receiving. In the midst of what it considered to be overreaction by the public, the agency found it difficult to provide sufficient reassurances when it had already acknowledged the existence of a risk sufficient to warrant regulatory action in its own publications.

REGULATORY STYLE AND REGULATORY SUBSTANCE

What is striking about these different models of the public's role in regulation, as well as the other differences in the regulatory style of the two countries, is that there is no direct relationship between regulatory style and regulatory substance. In some cases the U.S. regulated more stringently, in others Canada did. This is indeed surprising because two essential characteristics of the U.S. style would seem to bias the system toward aggressive regulation. First, because the public is easily alarmed by cancer risks – whether from pesticides in food or asbestos in schools – the more open regulatory style in the U.S. might be expected to produce more stringent regulations. Second, because of its risk averse assumptions, the U.S. approach to risk assessment also would seem to be biased toward aggressive regulation.

Under certain circumstances, however, aspects of regulatory institutions in the two countries can counteract these more protective tendencies in the U.S. The UFFI, saccharin, and asbestos cases demonstrate that the protective tendencies of U.S. regulatory agencies can be overruled by Congress or the courts. The saccharin case also reveals that public alarm is not a foregone conclusion. In that case the U.S. public perceived that the artificial sweetener offered significant benefits, and Congress intervened to overrule the protective tendency of the regulatory agency.

While Congressional pressure on regulatory agencies tended to coincide with public alarm, or the lack of it in the saccharin case, notice and comment rulemaking and subsequent litigation rely primarily on participation by organized interest groups. Different groups were able to work the complex regulatory system to their advantage in different cases. The UFFI and asbestos cases, in particular, reveal that judges – particularly those on the Fifth Circuit Court of Appeals – are not always as alarmed as the public.

Finally, as the alachlor case illustrates, the ad hoc Canadian approach does not preclude adoption of extremely risk averse decisions. The greater insulation of Canadian decision makers gives them the formal *capacity* to act on their own policy preferences. Moreover the parliamentary tradition of responsible government places the *responsibility* on the minister to defend the public interest. In cases like asbestos and radon this produced less aggressive action; in others, like saccharin and UFFI, it produced more stringent regulation.

Thus uncertainty and unpredictability in the relationship between regulatory style and outcome exists in both countries, but for different reasons. In the U.S. the complex system of multiple veto points – giving aggrieved parties opportunities to reverse the decisions of regulatory agencies – produces the uncertainty. In Canada ministerial discretion produces the uncertainty.

The results of our comparison support the conclusions of other recent studies on the impact of state institutions on policy making. Rather than playing a determinative role in policy outcomes, the effects of institutions are contingent on a number of other variables that influence policy, such as the balance of power between competing interest groups and the interests of the party in power.[14] We do not argue that institutions have no impact, but that they interact with other variables in influencing policy outcomes. Because these non-institutional factors vary from case to case, the links between regulatory style and outcome are complex and uncertain.

Several important non-institutional variables influenced the outcomes of the cases we examined in this book. The role of economic interests was instrumental in several cases. For instance the power of the asbestos industry in Canada, and its close ties to provincial and federal governments, can be credited with Canada's resistance to the more aggressive regulatory policies found in the U.S. In the case of alachlor the fact that the agricultural sector most dependent on the herbicide – corn growers – is far more important to the U.S. economy than it is to Canada's magnifies the disincentives of U.S. regulators to ban the product.[15]

It is important to re-emphasize that our cases do not constitute a representative sample of toxic substance regulations in the two countries and that we have strong reasons to suspect that these cases overstate the extent of regulatory divergence in the two countries. Nonetheless one of the most striking features of this comparison is that seemingly powerful forces for convergent outcomes failed to overwhelm decision makers in these cases. The fact that regulators in both countries based their decisions on the same scientific data had surprisingly little impact. Scientific uncertainties were sufficiently large that regulatory scientists in the two countries were able to adopt different estimates of risks, contributing to different outcomes. Moreover the significant degree of social, cultural, and economic integration between the two countries – clearly evident in many of the cases presented here – in general failed to overwhelm forces for divergence. In only one case, Alar, did such integration have an overpowering effect.

CONCLUSION: THE POLITICS OF UNCERTAINTY

If as our analysis suggests, the consequences of the two regulatory styles are uncertain and unpredictable, which is preferable? The choice of regulatory approach has much in common with the nature of the risk management dilemma itself. As we explained in the first two chapters, the pervasive scientific uncertainties confront regulators with a vexing dilemma: they must balance the possibility of incorrectly assuming that a substance is harmless, with potentially tragic consequences, against the possibility of falsely assuming that a substance is harmful, at substantial unnecessary cost to business, consumers, and workers. Risk averse scientific assumptions can lead to over-regulation, while risk tolerant assumption can result in under-regulation. The choice of approach depends on the extent to which different outcomes are valued – on which side would you prefer to err?

The choice of regulatory style offers a similar dilemma. Both the Canadian and u.s. regulatory styles offer uncertain risks and benefits; the key question is how the risks compare to the benefits, and which consequences we value the most. The benefit of the Canadian system is that it avoids the intense conflict of the American system, and for that reason it has the potential both to conserve the time and resources that would be spent on legal battles and to reflect more accurately scientific expertise. The Canadian system also places both the responsibility and the capacity to serve the public interest in the hands of democratically elected officials.

The risk is loss of accountability. With no effort to explore the boundary between science and policy, it is easier for the Canadian system to deliver political decisions cloaked in scientific arguments. In the cases presented here there was little examination of the value judgments government scientists routinely made. At the same time the tendency to depict standards as purely scientific assessments of "safety" made it difficult to scrutinize politicians' policy judgments. Finally, there is reason to doubt the effectiveness of traditional mechanisms of democratic accountability – bureaucrats to ministers, ministers to Cabinet, Cabinet to Parliament, and Parliament to the people – in the case of technically complex and often obscure questions of toxic substance regulation. Opposition parties and Parliamentary committees simply do not have the resources or expertise to perform their oversight function aggressively. Furthermore with limited public dissemination of information, voters have little basis to evaluate the performance of their elected representatives.

The benefit of the American system is that it promotes openness, allowing a diversity of views to be presented on both science and policy choices. At the same time openness fosters examination of the blurred boundary between science and politics. Interest groups, the courts, the media, and Congress routinely scrutinize the scientific and policy bases of regulatory officials' decisions. The risks are that the u.s. system provokes conflict and provides an inexpert public (interest groups, consumers, and the media) as well as inexpert government institutions (Congress and the courts) a much larger role in scientifically complex decisions.

The choice between this mix of risks and benefits ultimately depends on one's belief about what values are most important in the policy process. We acknowledge a preference for the openness of the American style, despite the risks. Openness is important not only because it reinforces political accountability, but also for the positive role it plays in ensuring a sound scientific basis for decision making. As Sheila Jasanoff has argued, "Honesty, rationality, and full disclosure are virtues of paramount importance to science as well as public policy."[16]

Admittedly there are times when the participation of nonexperts produces scientifically questionable results, as in the case of the apparent congressional misunderstanding of the scientific arguments in favour of a saccharin ban, or the u.s. environmentalists' campaign against Alar, which most analysts believe provoked unwarranted public alarm. However that is a risk we would willingly take. Some time ago, Thomas Jefferson wrote: "I know of no safe deposition of the ultimate powers of society but the people themselves; and if we think them not enlightened enough to exercise their control with a wholesome discretion, the remedy is not to take it away from them, but to enlighten their discretion."[17] Rather than try to insulate risk assessment and management from public scrutiny, greater emphasis should be placed on more effective dialogue between citizens and regulators about both the magnitude and acceptability of risks.

Unfortunately neither of these two systems seems to contain the optimal mix of desired qualities. It would be preferable if we could take the desirable elements of one system and combine them with the attractive features of the other – for instance the openness of the American style with the flexibility and cooperativeness of the Canadian style. The problem is that regulatory styles tend to come in packages, and these styles themselves depend upon the background macro-political context in which they are situated.

It is perhaps not surprising that each country has displayed interest in elements of the other's approach. In the u.s. frustrations with the conflictual and lengthy regulatory process have led to experiments with "regulatory negotiation," as we saw in the asbestos case study. At the same time Canada has moved to open its regulatory process to more public scrutiny. Pushed both by businesses concerned about the economic justifications for regulation as well as by environmentalists demanding a more open process, regulators have begun to provide broader opportunities for consultation and to justify their actions in greater detail.

While it is unclear how far the u.s. can or will depart from its pattern of adversarial legalism, it seems inevitable that the Canadian system will face growing demands for openness. Pressures will increase to formalize the process, and Canadian regulators will confront a more hostile and challenging political environment than they have in the past. No doubt this change is uncomfortable for many, but there is little choice but to embrace it. Indeed Canada has a unique opportunity to forge an alternative regulatory style – one that is open and accountable, but avoids the adversarial legalism so prevalent in the United States.

Notes

CHAPTER ONE

1 Talbot Page, "A Generic View of Toxic Chemicals and Similar Risks," *Ecology Law Quarterly* 7 (1978):207–44.
2 David Vogel, *National Styles of Regulation* (Ithaca: Cornell University Press, 1986).
3 National Cancer Institute of Canada, *Canadian Cancer Statistics 1990* (Toronto: National Cancer Institute of Canada, 1990), 42. The comparable figure for the u.s. was 22 percent in 1984. See American Cancer Society, *Cancer Statistics, 1987* (New York: American Cancer Society, 1987), 6.
4 For different views in the debate, see Samuel S. Epstein, *The Politics of Cancer* (San Francisco: Sierra Club Books, 1978), and Edith Efron, *The Apocalyptics: Cancer and the Big Lie* (New York: Simon and Shuster, 1984). The debate is reviewed in Mark E. Rushefsky, *Making Cancer Policy* (Albany, NY: State University of New York, 1986), chapter 7.
5 A. Weinberg, "Science and Trans-Science," *Minerva* 10 (1972):209–22.
6 See Nicholas A. Ashford, C. William Ryan, Charles C. Caldart, "A Hard Look at Federal Regulation of Formaldehyde: A Departure from Reasoned Decisionmaking," *Harvard Environmental Law Review* 7 (1983):297–370; Thomas O. McGarity, "Substantive and Procedural Discretion in Administrative Resolution of Science Policy Questions: Regulating Carcinogens in EPA and OSHA," *Georgetown Law Journal* 67 (1979):729–809; Liora Salter, *Mandated Science: Science and Scientists in the Making of Standards* (Boston: Kluwer Academic Publishers, 1988);

Sheila Jasanoff, *The Fifth Branch: Science Advisors as Policymakers* (Cambridge, MA: Harvard University Press, 1990). On underlying value distinctions in the choice of names for "science policy," see Sheila S. Jasanoff, "Contested Boundaries in Policy-Relevant Science," *Social Studies of Science* 17 (1987):195–230.

7 Salter, *Mandated Science*. This distinction originated with John Thibault and Laurens Walker, "A Theory of Procedure," *California Law Review* 66 (1978):541–66.

8 Harvey M. Sapolsky, ed., *Consuming Fears: The Politics of Product Risks* (New York: Basic Books, 1986); John D. Graham, Laura C. Green, Marc J. Roberts, *In Search of Safety: Chemicals and Cancer Risks* (Cambridge, MA: Harvard University Press, 1988), 8; Dorothy Nelkin, *Controversy: The Politics of Technical Decisions* (Beverly Hills, CA: Sage Publications, 1979); Allan Mazur, "Disputes Between Experts," *Minerva* 11 (1973):243–62.

9 Frances M. Lynn, "The Interplay of Science and Values in Assessing and Regulating Environmental Risks," *Science, Technology, and Human Values* 11 (1986):40–50. See also Thomas Dietz and Robert Rycroft, *The Risk Professionals* (New York: Russell Sage Foundation, 1987).

10 Graham, Green, and Roberts, *In Search of Safety*, 190–8.

11 National Research Council, *Risk Assessment in the Federal Government: Managing the Process* (Washington, DC: National Academy Press, 1983), 18.

12 The following is based on Health and Welfare Canada, *Health Risk Determination: The Challenge of Health Protection* (Ottawa: Supply and Services Canada, 1990).

13 See for instance William Leiss and Daniel Krewski, "Risk Communication: Theory and Practice," in William Leiss, ed., *Prospects and Problems in Risk Communication* (Waterloo, Ont: University of Waterloo Press, 1989).

14 William W. Lowrance, *Of Acceptable Risk: Science and the Determination of Safety,* (Los Altos, CA: William Kaufman, 1976).

15 There are subtle differences in where Canadian and American agencies draw the line between risk assessment and risk management. In the conceptual model presented above, U.S. agencies define steps 1 and 2 as risk assessment and subsequent steps as risk management. Health and Welfare Canada includes the third step in its definition of risk assessment. See Health and Welfare Canada, *Health Risk Determination*. For a review of risk assessment in the U.S. government, see U.S. Congress, Office of Technology Assessment, *Identifying and Regulating Carcinogens*, OTA-BP-H-42 (Washington, DC: U.S. Government Printing Office, 1987).

16 See, for instance, William D. Ruckelshaus, "Science, Risk, and Public Policy," *Science* 221 (1983):1026–8.

17 National Research Council, *Risk Assessment in the Federal Government: Managing the Process* (Washington, DC: National Academy Press, 1983).

18 The foregoing suggests that values are inevitably engaged in efforts to answer questions of fact, both in the process of framing the questions and in responding to them in the face of uncertainty. A similar point is made by Conrad G. Brunk, Lawrence Haworth and Brenda Lee, who distinguish between "inherently normative" questions, which consider which questions of fact should be addressed, and "conditionally normative" questions, which unavoidably arise in light of scientific uncertainty. See *Value Assumptions in Risk Assessment: A Case Study of the Alachlor Controversy* (Waterloo, Ont: Wilfred Laurier University Press, 1991), 28–32.

19 See, for instance, Mary Douglas and Aaron Wildavsky, *Risk and Culture* (Berkeley: University of California Press, 1982). For a review of the debate between the social constructivist and "naïve positivist" views of risk assessment, see K.S. Schrader-Frechette, *Risk and Rationality* (Berkeley: University of California Press, 1991).

20 The term was coined by Graham, Green, and Roberts, *In Search of Safety*, 218. For other "neo-separationist" perspectives, see also William D. Ruckelshaus, "Risk, Science, and Democracy," *Issues in Science and Technology* 1 (1985):19–38; and Lester B. Lave, "Introduction," in Lester B. Lave, ed., *Quantitative Risk Assessment in Regulation* (Washington, DC: The Brookings Institution, 1982).

21 Sheila Jasanoff, "Norms for Evaluating Regulatory Science," *Risk Analysis* 9 (1989):271–3.

22 Vogel, *National Styles of Regulation*; Joseph Badaracco, *Loading the Dice: A Five Country Case Study of Vinyl Chloride Regulation*, (Cambridge, MA: Harvard University Business School Press, 1985); Ronald Brickman, Sheila Jasanoff, Thomas Ilgen, *Controlling Chemicals: The Politics of Regulation in Europe and the United States* (Ithaca: Cornell University Press, 1985); and Vincent T. Covello, Kazuhiko Kawamura, et al., "Cooperation Versus Confrontation: A Comparison of Approaches to Environmental Risk Management in Japan and the United States," *Risk Analysis* 8 (1988):247–60.

23 Brickman, Jasanoff, and Ilgen, *Controlling Chemicals*.

24 Sheila Jasanoff, *Risk Management and Political Culture* (New York: Russell Sage Foundation, 1986); Thomas Ilgen, "Between Europe and America, Ottawa and the Provinces: Regulating Toxic Substances in Canada," *Canadian Public Policy* 11 (1985):578–90; George Hoberg, "Risk, Science and Politics: Alachlor Regulation in Canada and the United States," *Canadian Journal of Political Science* 23 (1990):257–79; and Liora Salter, "Science and Peer Review: The Canadian Standard-Setting Experience," *Science, Technology, and Human Values* 10 (1985):37–46.

25 The burgeoning interest in consensually negotiated rulemaking is reflected in the collection of documents and articles contained in David Pritzker and Deborah Dalton, *Negotiated Rulemaking Sourcebook* (Washington, DC: Administrative Conference of the United States, 1990).

26 George Hoberg, "Environmental Policy: Alternative Styles," in Michael Atkinson, ed., *Governing Canada: State Institutions and Public Policy* (Toronto: HBJ-Holt Canada, 1993).

27 For a review of the environmental provisions in NAFTA and GATT, see Steve Charnovitz, "NAFTA: An Analysis of its Environmental Provisions," *Environmental Law Reporter–News and Analysis* 23 (February 1993):10067–73.

28 This conclusion is consistent with the survey of social regulatory statutes in the two countries presented in Peter Nemetz, W.T. Stanbury, and Fred Thompson, "Social Regulation in Canada: An Overview and Comparison with the US Model," *Policy Studies Journal* 14 (1986):580–603.

29 The U.S. figure comes from the Lawyers edition of the U.S. Code Service, which includes various annotations to cases and thus exaggerates the length. But this bias is probably offset by the fact that the R.S.C. is bilingual, doubling the length of the Canadian federal statutes.

30 These initiatives are described in John M. Evans, H.N. Janisch, D.J. Mullan, and R.C.B. Risk, *Administrative Law: Cases, Text, Materials*, 3rd ed. (Toronto: Emond Montgomery, 1989), 233–7.

31 Richard B. Stewart, "The Reformation of American Administrative Law," *Harvard Law Review* 88 (1975):1667–813.

32 William D. Ruckelshaus, "Environmental Protection: A Brief History of the Environmental Movement in America and the Implications Abroad," *Environmental Law* 15 (1985):455–69, at 463.

33 The courts also played a central role in clarifying the meaning of the standard in FIFRA. See Angus MacIntyre, "A Court Quietly Rewrote the Pesticide Statute: How Prevalent is Judicial Statutory Revision?" *Law and Policy* 7 (1985):249–79.

34 See Brickman, Jasanoff, and Ilgen, *Controlling Chemicals*, for an effort to apply this approach to toxic chemical regulation. An initial attempt to apply it to a comparison of environmental policies in Canada and the United States can be found in George Hoberg, "Governing the Commons: Environmental Policy in Canada and the United States," prepared for delivery at symposium for Canada-U.S. Project, Queen's University, 1–2 November 1991, to be published in Keith Banting, George Hoberg, and Richard Simeon, eds., *Canada and the United States in a Changing World*, (forthcoming).

CHAPTER TWO

1 Lester B. Lave, "Methods of Risk Assessment," in Lester B. Lave, *Quantitative Risk Assessment in Regulation* (Washington, DC: The Brookings Institution, 1982).

2 There are two possible approaches. One can compare a group of people with a particular type of cancer with an otherwise similar control group to ascertain whether differences in exposure might explain the different rates of disease (the case-control method). Alternatively one can compare a group exposed to the substance with an otherwise comparable control group to investigate whether their rates of cancer differ (a cohort study).

3 International Agency for Research on Cancer, *Overall Evaluations of Carcinogenicity: An Updating of IARC Monographs Volumes 1 to 42* (Lyons: IARC, 1987).

4 For an overview of bioassay protocols, see U.S. Congress, Office of Technology Assessment, *Assessment of Technologies for Determining Cancer Risks from the Environment* (Washington, DC: U.S. Government Printing Office, 1981).

5 Office of Science and Technology Policy, "Chemical Carcinogens: A Review of the Science and its Associated Principles," *Environmental Health Perspectives* 67 (1986):201–82, at 209.

6 Ibid., 234.

7 Bruce C. Allen, Kenny S. Crump, Annette M. Shipp, "Correlation Between Carcinogenic Potency of Chemicals in Animals and Humans," *Risk Analysis* 8 (1988):531–44.

8 For a discussion of treatment of false positives and false negatives in toxic substance regulation, see Talbot Page, "A Generic View of Toxic Chemicals and Similar Risks," *Ecology Law Quarterly* 7 (1978):207–44; and K.S. Shrader-Frechette, *Risk and Rationality* (Berkeley: University of California Press, 1991), chapter 9.

9 Conrad G. Brunk, Lawrence Haworth, Brenda Lee, *Value Assumptions in Risk Assessment: A Case Study of the Alachlor Controversy* (Waterloo, Ont: Wilfred Laurier University Press, 1991), 38; and Shrader-Frechette, *Risk and Rationality*, 134–5.

10 L.S. Gold, C.B. Sawyer, et al., "A Carcinogenic Potency Database of the Standardized Results of Bioassays," *Environmental Health Perspectives* 58 (1984):9–319.

11 John H. Weisburger, Gary M Williams, "Carcinogen Testing: Current Problems and New Approaches," *Science* 214 (1981):401–7; Lester B. Lave, Arthur C. Upton, "Regulating Toxic Chemicals in the Environment," in Lester B. Lave, Arthur C. Upton, eds., *Toxic Chemicals, Health, and the Environment* (Baltimore: Johns Hopkins University Press, 1987).

12 Office of Technology Assessment, *Technologies for Determining Cancer Risks,* 164.

13 Ibid., 123.

14 Ibid., 161. More recent work suggests that the possibility of supralinearity should not be dismissed out of hand. See John C. Bailar III, Edmund A.C. Crouch, Rashid Shaikh, Donna Spiegelman, "One-Hit Models of Carcinogenesis: Conservative or Not," *Risk Analysis* 8 (1988):485–97.

15 R. Stephen McColl, *Biological Safety Factors in Toxicological Risk Assessment* (Ottawa: Department of National Health and Welfare, 1990).

16 Health and Welfare Canada uses the term "tolerable daily intake" in referring to chemical or microbial contaminants.

17 Another problem with the approach is that exclusive reliance on the NOAEL does not take into consideration experimental evidence of the shape of the dose-response curve. See Daniel Krewski, Charles Brown, Duncan Murdoch, "Determining 'Safe' Levels of Exposure: Safety Factors or Mathematical Models," *Fundamentals of Applied Toxicology* 4 (1984):S383–94.

18 Although the body has natural defenses against cancer, such as DNA repair, a finite risk would still exist even at very low doses, since DNA repair could be neither instantaneous nor 100 percent effective. See Charles C. Brown, Thomas R. Fears, et al., Charles McGaughey, Kenny Crump, Jerzy Neyman, E. Scherer and P. Emmelot, "Letters to the Editor," in *Science* 202 (1978):1105–7. See also Dale Hattis and John Smith, Jr, "What's Wrong with Quantitative Risk Assessment?" in Robert F. Almeder and James M. Humber, eds., *Biomedical Ethics Review 1986* (Clifton, NJ: Humana Press, 1986).

19 McColl, *Biological Safety Factors,* chapter 4.

20 Other models have been based on assumptions about the tolerance distribution within the human population and the length of time it takes for tumours to develop. Office of Science and Technology Policy, "Chemical Carcinogens," 255–6.

21 Curtis C. Travis, Samantha Richter, et al., "Cancer risk management: A review of 132 federal regulatory decisions," *Environmental Science and Technology* 21 (1987):415–20.

22 The choice of a virtually safe dose is a function of the population exposed because both individual and population risks are relevant. Although a risk of one in a million is diminishingly small for an individual, the consequences could be unacceptable if many millions of people face that level of risk. On the other hand, a cancer risk of one in a hundred may appear quite high for an individual, but if only a handful of people face that level of risk, the chances of any one of them contracting cancer are very small.

23 It is conceivable that the safety factor approach could lead to the lower estimates of acceptable exposure, particularly if very large safety factors are used. However in the early 1980s the U.S. Environmental Protection Agency proposed to use a relatively large safety factor of 1000 to assess the risks from a number of waterborne carcinogens. Even then the resulting standards would have been 100 to 1000 times less stringent than those based on a linear model. See Frederica P. Perera, "The Genotoxic/Epigenetic Distinction: Relevance to Cancer Policy," *Environmental Research* 34 (1984):175–91; and Eliot Marshall, "EPA's High-Risk Carcinogen Policy," *Science* 218 (1982):975–8.

24 Weisburger and Williams, "Carcinogen Testing," 406.

25 Office of Science and Technology Policy, "Chemical Carcinogens," 223.

26 See Perera, "The Genotoxic/Epigenetic Distinction"; and I. Bernard Weinstein, "Letter to the Editor," *Science* 219 (1983):794–6.

27 It has been mathematically demonstrated that the assumption of additivity necessitates linearity at low doses. K.S. Crump, D.G. Hoel, C.H. Langley, R. Peto, "Fundamental Carcinogenic Processes and their Implications for Low Dose Risk Assessment," *Cancer Research* 36 (1976):2973–79. See also, Hattis and Smith, "What's Wrong with Quantitative Risk Assessment?" 69.

28 It has also been argued that available tests cannot distinguish well between initiators and promoters, and that there is evidence that some promoters in fact do interact with DNA or chromosomes.

29 Bruce N. Ames, Lois Swirsky Gold, "Too Many Rodent Carcinogens: Mitogenesis Increases Mutagenesis," *Science* 249 (1990):970–1.

30 Office of Science and Technology Policy, "Chemical Carcinogens."

31 The distribution of exposure over time also may be important. Exposure to 1 part per million of a substance in the air 24 hours a day would not be equivalent to exposure to 24 parts per million for one hour if the dose-response function for that substance is non-linear.

32 Adam M. Finkel, "Is Risk Assessment Really too Conservative?: Revising the Revisionists," *Columbia Journal of Environmental Law,* 14 (1989): 427–67; and Dale Hattis, "The Promise of Molecular Epidemiology for Quantitative Risk Assessment," *Risk Analysis* 6 (1986):181–93, at 185.

33 See, for instance, Finkel, "Is Risk Assessment Really too Conservative?"

34 Hattis, "The Promise of Molecular Epidemiology," 190.

35 Ibid.; McColl, *Biological Safety Factors*, 34.

36 A.M. Finkel, *Confronting Uncertainty in Risk Management: A Guide for Decision-Makers* (Washington, DC: Resources for the Future, 1990).

37 This is not meant to suggest that the boundary of "science" is a bright line. As Jasanoff has argued, regulatory science debates often revolve around "boundary work," with scientists attempting to stake out their jurisdiction and interest groups emphasizing the policy components

implicit in regulatory scientists judgments. See Sheila S. Jasanoff, "Contested Boundaries in Policy-Relevant Science," *Social Studies of Science* 17 (1987):195–230, and *The Fifth Branch* (Cambridge, MA: Harvard University Press, 1990.)

38 U.S. Environmental Protection Agency, "Guidelines for Carcinogen Risk Assessment," 51 *Federal Register* (FR) (24 September 1986): 33992.

39 See, for instance, Edith Efron, *The Apocalyptics* (New York: Simon and Schuster, 1984); Aaron Wildavsky, *Searching for Safety*, (New Brunswick, NJ: Transaction Publishers, 1988).

40 See John Graham, Laura Green, and Marc Roberts, *In Search of Safety: Chemicals and Cancer Risk*, (Cambridge, MA: Harvard University Press, 1988); Lave, *Quantitative Risk Assessment in Regulation.*

41 Aaron Wildavsky, *Searching for Safety.*

42 See Dennis J. Paustenbach, "Health Risk Assessments: Opportunities and Pitfalls," *Columbia Journal of Environmental Law* 14 (1989):379–410; and Elizabeth O. Anderson, "Scientific Developments in Risk Assessment: Legal Implications," *Columbia Journal of Environmental Law* 14 (1989):411–25.

43 See Finkel, "Is Risk Assessment Really too Conservative?"

44 National Research Council, *Risk Assessment in the Federal Government* (Washington, DC: National Academy Press, 1983), 4.

45 Thomas O. McGarity, "Substantive and Procedural Discretion in Administrative Resolution of Science Policy Questions: Regulating Carcinogens in EPA and OSHA," *Georgetown Law Journal* 67 (1979): 729–810, at 756.

46 Hattis and Smith, "What's Wrong with Risk Assessment?"

47 Graham, Green, and Roberts, *In Search of Safety*, 210; Adam M. Finkel, "Is Risk Assessment Really too Conservative?"

48 See Rushevsky, *Making Cancer Policy* (Albany: State University of New York Press, 1986).

49 For a discussion of the failure of attempted reforms by early Reagan appointees, see Rushevsky, *Making Cancer Policy*, and Marshall, "EPA's High-Risk Cancer Policy."

50 Graham, Green, and Roberts, *In Search of Safety*, 76.

51 Office of Technology Assessment, *Identifying and Regulating Carcinogens*, 5.

52 Bernard D. Goldstein, "Risk Assessment and the Interface Between Science and Law," *Columbia Journal of Environmental Law* 14 (1989):343–55, at 353.

CHAPTER THREE

1 This chapter is based on a previously published article. See Kathryn Harrison, "Between Science and Politics: Assessing the Risks of Dioxins in Canada and the United States," *Policy Sciences* 24 (1991):367–88.

2 A technical discussion of risk assessments for dioxins in different countries is provided by H.P. Shu, D.J. Paustenbach, F.J. Murray, "A Critical Evaluation of the Use of Mutagenesis, Carcinogenesis, and Tumor Promotion Data in a Cancer Risk Assessment of 2,3,7,8-Tetrachlorodibenzo-p-dioxin," *Regulatory Toxicology and Pharmacology* 7 (1987):57–88.

3 The term was coined by David Vogel, *National Styles of Regulation* (Ithaca: Cornell University Press, 1986).

4 33 U.S.C.S. 1251–376.

5 R.S.C. 1985, C. 27.

6 21 U.S.C.S. 331.

7 21 U.S.C.S. 346.

8 21 U.S.C.S. 348(c)(3)(A).

9 Richard A. Merrill, "Regulating Carcinogens in Food: A Legislator's Guide to the Food Safety Provisions of the Federal Food, Drug, and Cosmetic Act," *Michigan Law Review* 77 (1978):171–250, at 191.

10 21 U.S.C.S. 346.

11 Statement by Sanford A. Miller before the Subcommittee on Natural Resources, Agriculture Research and Environment, Committee on Science and Technology, U.S. House of Representatives, 30 June 1983.

12 A.B. Morrison, "Dioxins in Canada–Deciding the Public Health Risk," in M. Kamrin, P. Rodgers, eds., *Dioxins in the Environment* (New York: Hemisphere, 1985), 39.

13 M.J. Boddington, V.M. Douglas, et al., "Dioxins in Canada," *Chemosphere* 1 (1983), 477; Robert Scheuplein, "Proposed Food and Drug Administration Approach to Tolerance-Setting for Dioxins in Foods," in W. Lowrance, ed., *Public Health Risks of the Dioxins* (Los Altos: William Kaufmann, 1984), 367.

14 Food and Drug Regulations, B.01.046.

15 Ibid., B.01.047.

16 For a review of the emergence of the issue on the political agenda, see Kathryn Harrison and George Hoberg, "Setting the Environmental Agenda in Canada and the United States: The Cases of Dioxin and Radon," *Canadian Journal of Political Science* 24 (1991):3–27.

17 Environment Canada, Health and Welfare Canada, *Priority Substances List Assessment Report No. 1: Polychlorinated Dibenzodioxins and Polychlorinated Dibenzofurans* (Ottawa: Minister of Supply and Services Canada, 1990).

18 B. Birmingham, A. Gilman, et al., "PCDD/PCDF Multimedia Exposure Analysis for the Canadian Population: Detailed Exposure Estimation," *Chemosphere* 19 (1989):637–42.

19 Bev Houston, quoted in Mary Lynn Young, "High dioxin found in mothers' breast milk," *Vancouver Sun*, 29 October 1990, B2. As of March 1993 the department had drafted a new standard, but had yet to publish it for public comment.

20 Environment Canada, Health and Welfare Canada, *Priority Substances List Assessment Report No. 1.*

21 Government of Canada, "Pulp and Paper Mill Chlorinated Dioxins and Furans Regulations," SOR/92–267, *Canada Gazette Part II* 126 (1992):1940–54. Other federal dioxin standards for foods and pesticides are summarized in Environment Canada, Health and Welfare Canada, *Priority Substances List Assessment Report No. 1*, 37.

22 The 20 ppq figure is from Environment Canada, "Reference Method for Determination of Polychlorinated Dibenzo-para-dioxins (PCDDs) and Polychlorinated Dibenzofurans (PCDFs) in Pulp and Paper Mill Effluents," EPS 1/RM/19, 1991, 48. This so-called "limit of quantitation" is considerably higher than the actual analytical detection limit, which is less than 10 ppq for many laboratories, since measurements at or near the detection limit tend to be highly variable, and thus would be easier to challenge in court.

23 Personal communication with Environment Canada official.

24 At a public meeting in Toronto on 5 May 1990, an Environment Canada official stated, "We will only do amendments to allow people to do tests better – not to get a tighter number ... *We promise!!*" (emphasis in original). Environment Canada, "Report on Public Meetings in Eastern Canada on Proposed Regulations for the Pulp and Paper Industry. April 28 through May 10, 1990," June 1990.

25 Alberta was the first province to take action, when it announced in December 1988 that "leading edge" technology would be required on all pulp mills in the province. Although the implications vary from mill to mill, in practice all mills in Alberta are expected to meet AOX standards of 1.5 kg/ADt or less. In March 1992 British Columbia established an AOX limit of 1.5 kg/air-dried tonnes (ADt) in pulp mill effluents to be met by the end of 1995, with zero discharge of AOX required by 2002. Quebec regulations requiring AOX discharges of less than 2.0 by the end of 1995 and 0.8 by 2000 were finalized in October 1992. Ontario adopted an interim AOX requirement of 2.5 kg/ADt by the end of 1991, and subsequently adopted more stringent final standards of 1.5 kg/ADt by the end of 1995, and 0.8 kg/ADt by the end of 1999, with a non-mandatory "target" of zero discharge by 2002.

26 Although the federal dioxin regulations do not expressly limit AOX discharges, they are considered equivalent to an AOX limit of roughly 2.5 kg/ADt.

27 *Food Drug and Cosmetic Law Reporter,* 8 September 1981, 41602.

28 Letter from Joseph P. Hile to Dr Sidney Wolfe, Health Research Group, 14 August 1985.

29 Statement by Sanford A. Miller before the Subcommittee on Natural Resources, Agriculture Research and Environment.

30 U.S. Environmental Protection Agency, "Ambient Water Quality Criteria for 2,3,7,8-TCDD," EPA 440/5-84-007 (Washington, DC: EPA, 1984).

31 *Natural Resources Defense Council, et al. v. Train*, 8 Environmental Reporter Cases (ERC) 2120 (District Court of Columbia [DDC] 1976), modified, 12 ERC 1833 (DDC 1979).

32 It is difficult to comprehend such a small number. One EPA official has offered the analogy that it would take McDonalds one billion years to make one quintillion burgers.

33 U.S. Environmental Protection Agency, "A Cancer Risk-Specific Dose for 2,3,7,8-TCDD," Review Draft, EPA/600/6–88/007Aa, June 1988.

34 "No Scientific Basis to Lower Estimate of 2,3,7,8-TCDD Cancer Risk, SAB Panel Says," *Chemical Regulation Reporter*, 12 December 1988, 1315.

35 "EPA Agrees in Consent Decree with Groups to Tackle Regulation of Releases of Dioxins," *Environment Reporter*, 29 July 1988, 427.

36 U.S. Environmental Protection Agency, "Environmental News: EPA to Regulate Dioxin in Paper Industry," 30 April 1990.

37 56 *Federal Register* (FR) 21802 10 May 1991. Further regulatory action on pulp mill sludge is on hold, however, pending a regulatory proposal to address air and water discharges of dioxins from pulp mills.

38 "First-Ever Multimedia Rules Proposed by EPA to Control Emissions from Pulp, Paper Mills," *Environment Reporter*, 5 November 1993, 1227–8; and Gary Lee, "Tougher EPA Rules Sought for Paper Mills," *Washington Post*, 2 November 1993, A5. A *Federal Register* notice had not yet been published at the end of November 1993.

39 See "Environmentalists Criticize EPA's Approval of Maryland Dioxin Standard," *Environment Reporter*, 21 September 1990, 1043; "Virginia Dioxin Limit For Paper Mills Approved by EPA in Sequel to Maryland Action," *Environment Reporter*, 8 March 1991, 1989.

40 "Decision on Maryland's Dioxin Standard Expected to have Impact on Other States," *Environment Reporter*, 22 June 1990, 360.

41 Personal communication, EPA official, September 1991.

42 "First-Ever Multimedia Rules," *Environment Reporter*, 1227.

43 EPA, "Environmental News: EPA To Regulate Dioxin In Paper Industry"; "EPA Refers Food Packaging Regulation to FDA; FDA Official Says Action May Not Be Required," *Chemical Regulation Reporter*, 4 January 1991, 1395.

44 However, new techniques to estimate individuals' past exposure based on current levels of dioxins in blood and body fat offer promise as a way to address this problem.

45 For reviews of the evidence on human health effects of dioxins, see U.S. Environmental Protection Agency, "Health Assessment Document for Polychlorinated Dibenzo-p-Dioxins," EPA/600/8–84/014F, 1985;

and Environment Canada, Health and Welfare Canada, *Priority Substances List Assessment Report No. 1*.

46 The evidence from epidemiological studies is reviewed in Environment Canada, Health and Welfare Canada, *Priority Substances List Assessment Report No. 1*; and David L. Bayliss, "Epidemiologic Cancer Studies on Polychlorinated Dibenzo-p-Dioxins, Particularly 2,3,7,8-TCDD," U.S. EPA, *A Cancer Risk-Specific Dose Estimate for 2,3,7,8-TCDD*, Review Draft, Appendix B, June 1988.

47 The political controversy surrounding these studies is discussed in Salter, *Mandated Science: Science and Scientists in the Making of Standards* (Boston: Kluwer Academic Publishers, 1988), chapter 6.

48 Carol Van Strum, Paul Merrell, "Fraud Alleged in key Dioxin Human Health Studies," *Journal of Pesticide Reform* 10 (1990):8–12.

49 Marilyn A Fingerhut, William E. Halperin, et al., "Cancer Mortality in Workers Exposed to 2,3,7,8-Tetrachlorodibenzo-p-dioxin," *New England Journal of Medicine* 324 (1991):212–18.

50 The study relied upon in most regulatory assessments is R.J. Kociba, D.G. Keyes, et al., "Results of a Two-year Chronic Toxicity and Oncogenicity Study of 2,3,7,8-TCDD in Rats", *Toxicology and Applied Pharmacology* 46 (1978):279–303.

51 Environment Canada, Health and Welfare Canada, *Priority Substances List Assessment Report No. 1*, 21.

52 Many scientists argue that because TCDD has not demonstrated genotoxicity in a battery of tests, it is probably not a complete carcinogen. See, for instance, Shu, Paustenbach, et al., "Critical Evaluation." This controversy is reviewed in U.S. Environmental Protection Agency, "A Cancer Risk-Specific Dose Estimate for 2,3,7,8-TCDD," EPA/600/6-88/007Aa, 1988.

53 See Jon R. Luoma, "Scientists Are Unlocking Secrets of Dioxin's Devastating Power," *New York Times*, 15 May 1990, B7.

54 An overview of the "promoter" vs "initiator" controversy, as applied to TCDD, is provided by Adam M. Finkel, "Dioxin: Are we Safer now than before?" *Risk Analysis* 8 (1988):161–5.

55 I.C. Munro, D.R. Krewski, "Risk Assessment and Regulatory Decision Making," *Food and Cosmetics Toxicology* 19 (1981):549–60.

56 The model is known as the "linear multistage model." It is compared to alternatives in Munro and Krewski, "Risk Assessment and Regulatory Decision Making."

57 Michael Gough in "Science Policy Choices and the Estimation of Cancer Risk Associated with Exposure to TCDD," *Risk Analysis* 8 (1988):337–42.

58 Interdepartmental Committee on Toxic Chemicals, "Dioxins in Canada: The Federal Approach" (Hull: Interdepartmental Committee on

Toxic Chemicals, 1983), 12. One can reconstruct Health and Welfare Canada's rationale as follows: if a 70 kg adult consumes 16 g/day of fish (the Canadian average rate of consumption) contaminated with 20 ppt TCDD, and if contaminated fish is the only source of exposure to dioxins, he or she would be exposed to 1/218th of the dose at which there was no observed increase in the rate of tumours in rats.

59 Environment Canada, Health and Welfare Canada, *Priority Substances List Assessment Report No. 1.*

60 Environment Canada, Health and Welfare Canada, *Priority Substances List Assessment Report No. 1*, 43.

61 Environment Ontario, "Scientific Criteria Document for Standard Development No. 4–84: Polychlorinated Dibenzo-p-dioxins (PCDDs) and Polychlorinated Dibenzofurans (PCDFs)" (Toronto: Environment Ontario, September 1985).

62 National Research Council of Canada, *Polychlorinated Dibenzo-p-dioxins: Criteria for their effects on man and his environment*, Publication 18574 of the Environmental Secretariat (Ottawa: National Research Council, 1981).

63 The committee concluded that, at Health and Welfare's standard of 20 ppt TCDD, Canadians should only consume fish between once every 1.3 to 44 months. "Report of the Joint Health and Welfare Canada/Environment Canada Expert Advisory Committee on Dioxins" (Ottawa: Health and Welfare Canada, 1983).

64 Robert Scheuplein, "Proposed Food and Drug Administration Approach to Tolerance-Setting for Dioxins in Foods," in W. Lowrance, ed., *Public Health Risks of the Dioxins* (Los Altos, CA: William Kaufman, 1984); Sanford Miller, Testimony before the Subcommittee on Natural Resources, Agriculture Research and Environment. These authors do not actually claim that FDA chose the 25 ppt advisory level *because* it was equivalent to a risk of 3 in a million. However, since no other rationale is presented, that is the impression left by both authors.

65 FDA assumed that 15.7 g/day of fish is consumed (the upper 90th percentile of fish consumption in Great Lakes states), that only 10 percent of fish in the Great Lakes were contaminated, that if the standard was set at 25 ppt, the actual resulting average level of contamination would be lower, at about 8 ppt, and that a typical adult weighs 80 kg. This series of assumptions suggests several questions. First, why was the 90th percentile of fish consumption chosen? It is noteworthy that the 90th percentile figure of 15.7 g/day is markedly similar to the 16 g/day *average* reportedly used by Health and Welfare Canada. One might also question the basis for assuming that 10 percent of fish would be contaminated, or that 8 ppt would be a typical level of contamination.

66 F. Cordle, "The use of epidemiology in the regulation of dioxins in the food supply," *Regulatory Toxicology and Pharmacology* 1 (1981):379–87.

67 Letter from Joseph P. Hile to Dr Sidney Wolfe, Health Research Group, 14 August 1985.

68 "2 EPA Studies Confirm Threat to Fish of Dioxin from Paper Plants," *New York Times*, 14 March 1989, C4.

69 For a comparison of U.S. agencies' estimates, see U.S. Environmental Protection Agency, "A Cancer Risk-Specific Dose", Appendix A, 30.

70 U.S. Environmental Protection Agency, "A Cancer Risk-Specific Dose," 40–1.

71 U.S. Environmental Protection Agency, "A Cancer Risk-Specific Dose," 1.

72 See, for instance, Finkel, "Dioxin: Are we Safer?"

73 *Chemical Regulation Reporter*, 1 July 1988, 484.

74 U.S. Environmental Protection Agency Science Advisory Board Ad Hoc Dioxin Panel, "Review of Draft Documents 'A Cancer Risk-Specific Dose Estimate for 2,3,7,8-TCDD' and 'Estimating Exposure to 2,3,7,8-TCDD'" Mimeo.

75 *Chemical Regulation Reporter*, 17 November 1989, 1100.

76 Michael Gough, "Dioxin: Perceptions, Estimates, and Measures," Center for Risk Management, Resources for the Future, Mimeo, 49.

77 Although initial reports after the conference suggest that there was consensus on the threshold theory as well, later reports suggest that that was an overstatement. See Jeff Bailey, "Dueling Studies: How Two Industries Created A fresh Spin on the Dioxin Debate," *Wall Street Journal*, 20 February 1992, A1; and "Scientists Say Potential Risks May Exceed 1991 Estimates That Prompted EPA Reassessment," *Chemical Regulation Reporter*, 12 June 1992, 576. On disagreements among scientists about whether a receptor-mediated mechanism necessarily implies a threshold, see Leslie Roberts, "More Pieces in the Dioxin Puzzle," *Science* 254 (1991):377.

78 "EPA Position on Toxicity to be Reassessed, Reilly Says," *Chemical Regulation Reporter*, 12 April 1991, 32.

79 "EPA Reassessment's Early Findings Say Substances Still Pose Major Threat," *Chemical Regulation Reporter*, 2 October 1992, 1196.

80 *Food, Drug and Cosmetic Law Reporter*, 8 September 1981, 41602.

81 Boddington, Douglas, et al., "Dioxins in Canada," 479.

82 Scheuplein, "Proposed Food and Drug Administration Approach," 369.

83 Cordle, "The Use of Epidemiology in the Regulation of Dioxins," 385.

84 Scheuplein, "Proposed Food and Drug Administration Approach," 372.

85 Greenpeace, "Dioxins, Furans and PCBs: The True Story" (Vancouver: Greenpeace, n.d.).

86 Early in the Reagan administration, a senior EPA official resigned under Congressional pressure over allegations that he had applied pressure on agency staff to revise a report on TCDD to reflect Dow Chemical's suggestions. (Janice R. Long, David J. Hanson, "Dioxin Issue Focuses on Three Major Controversies in U.S.," *Chemical and Engineering News* 61 [6 June 1983], 23–6.) More recently, Greenpeace has argued that EPA's proposal to revise its TCDD risk assessment was motivated by a desire to avoid responsibility for costly regulatory actions. (Carol Van Strum, Paul Merrell, "No Margin of Safety: A Preliminary Report on Dioxin Pollution and the Need for Emergency Action in the Pulp and Paper Industry," [Tidewater, OR: Greenpeace USA, 1987].)

87 Alvin Weinberg, "Science and Trans-science," *Minerva* 10 (1972): 209–22.

88 Philip Shabecoff, "Estimate of risk of dioxin is cut in cancer study," *New York Times*, 9 December 1987, A1.

89 Mark Rushevsky, *Making Cancer Policy* (Albany: State University of New York Press, 1986.)

90 Personal communication.

91 Glenn Bohn, "Salmon Safe, consumers told," *Vancouver Sun*, 6 December 1988, A8.

92 Mary Lynn Young, "High dioxin found in mothers' breast milk," *Vancouver Sun*, 29 October 1990, B2.

93 *Chemical Regulation Reporter,* 25 September 1987, 1006.

94 U.S. Congress, *Dioxin Contamination of Food and Water,* Hearing before the Subcommittee on Health and the Environment of the Committee on Energy and Commerce, House of Representatives, No. 100–184, 8 December 1988, 179.

95 U.S. Environmental Protection Agency, "A Cancer Risk-Specific Dose," Appendix A.

96 Sheila Jasanoff, *Risk Management and Political Culture* (New York: Russell Sage Foundation, 1986); Ronald Brickman, Sheila Jasanoff, and Thomas Ilgen, *Controlling Chemicals: The Politics of Regulation in Europe and the United States* (Ithaca: Cornell University Press, 1985), 185–6.

97 Jasanoff, *Risk Management and Political Culture,* 30.

98 Brickman, Jasanoff, and Ilgen, *Controlling Chemicals,* 185–6.

99 In her more recent work, Jasanoff also has noted that FDA's regulatory style is more "European" than that of other U.S. agencies. See Sheila Jasanoff, *The Fifth Branch: Science Advisors as Policymakers* (Cambridge: Harvard University Press, 1990), 227.

100 EPA does not have authority to regulate TCDD concentrations in fish, and the agency thus is careful not to make recommendations directly.

However, it was necessary for it to make judgments about acceptable risks from consumption of contaminated fish in order to derive its criteria for ambient water quality. For a discussion of the differences between FDA and EPA standards for fish, see National Council of the Paper Industry for Air and Stream Improvement, "Dioxin: A Critical Review of its Distribution, Mechanism of Action, Impacts on Human Health, and the Setting of Acceptable Exposure Limits," Technical Bulletin 524, 273.

101 For instance, those who consume large quantities of fish caught downstream from pulp mills have higher than average exposure to dioxins, as do breast-feeding infants. See Environment Canada, Health and Welfare Canada, *Priority Substances List Report No. 1.*

102 In fact, one state that proposed a less stringent standard for TCDD to EPA did so on the advice of a scientist at another federal agency. See Keith Schneider, "Scientist Criticized for Dioxin Stand," *New York Times*, 27 July 1990, A9.

103 Personal interviews with government officials in Canada and the U.S.

104 The formaldehyde, saccharin, alachlor, and Alar cases are reviewed in chapters 6, 5, and 4 of this volume, respectively. Doern reports a similar pattern in U.S. and Canadian evaluations of amaranth. See G. Bruce Doern, *The Peripheral Nature of Science and Technology Controversy in Federal Policy Formation* (Ottawa: Science Council of Canada, 1981), 74–8.

CHAPTER FOUR

1 For a description of the environmental problems posed by pesticides, see J.F. Castrilli and Toby Vigod, *Pesticides in Canada: An Examination of Federal Law and Policy*, Study Paper, Protection of Life Series (Ottawa: Law Reform Commission of Canada, 1987), chapter 1.

2 The section on alachlor is based on George Hoberg, "Risk, Science, and Politics: Alachlor Regulation in Canada and the United States," *Canadian Journal of Political Science* 23 (1990): 257–77.

3 7 U.S.C., 136 ff. For an overview of the U.S. regulatory framework, see U.S. General Accounting Office, *Pesticides: EPA's Formidable Task to Assess and Regulate Their Risks*, RCED-86-125, (Washington, DC: GAO, 1986). FIFRA was amended in 1988 in an effort to accelerate the process of reviewing old chemicals. See Scott Ferguson and Ed Gray, "1988 FIFRA Amendments: A Major Step in Pesticide Regulation," *Environmental Law Reporter* 19 (February 1989): 10070–82.

4 Pest Control Products Act, 1968–69, c. 50, s. 1. For an overview of the Canadian regulatory framework, see Castrilli and Vigod, *Pesticides in Canada.*

5 A major review of Canadian pesticide regulation recommended that jurisdiction be transferred from Agriculture Canada to an independent regulatory agency, as happened in the U.S. in 1970. Jurisdiction over pesticide regulation originally resided in the U.S. Department of Agriculture, but was transferred to EPA when it was created in that year. See Pesticide Registration Review, *Recommendations for a Revised Federal Pest Management Regulatory System: Final Report* (Ottawa: Minister of Supply and Services, December 1990). However, the Cabinet has rejected this recommendation.

6 Alachlor Review Board, *The Report of the Alachlor Review Board* (Ottawa: 1987), 23. Environment Canada and the Department of Fisheries and Oceans also provide input into the process.

7 21 U.S.C. 302 ff.

8 PCP Regulations, s. 20.

9 PCP Regulations, secs. 23–5. The minister may decide whether or not to leave the action against the chemical in place during the proceedings.

10 7 United States Code Annotated (U.S.C.A.) s. 136d.

11 52 FR 49,481 (31 December 1987).

12 The defects in testing for alachlor were part of a larger scandal involving the Industrial Bio-Test Laboratories. See Keith Schneider, "Faking It," *Amicus Journal* 4 (Spring 1983): 14–26.

13 50 FR 1115 (9 January 1985).

14 52 FR 49,480 (31 December 1987).

15 Personal interviews.

16 PCP Regulations, secs. 23–5.

17 "Blue Ribbon Panel Seems Well-Equipped," *Globe and Mail,* 17 August 1986, A13.

18 *Monsanto Canada Inc v. the Minster of Agriculture,* Federal Court of Appeal, A-149-88, 6 December 1988.

19 An extensive analysis of the scientific debate on alachlor in Canada can be found in Conrad Brunk, Lawrence Haworth, and Brenda Lee, *Value Assumptions in Risk Assessment: A Case Study of the Alachlor Controversy* (Waterloo, Ont: Wilfred Laurier Press, 1991).

20 52 FR 49,483 (31 December 1987); Alachlor Review Board, *Report,* 51. According to the classification system developed by the International Agency for Research on Cancer (IARC), alachlor is "Class 2B," used when there is a substantial evidence of carcinogenicity from animal data but no evidence from human data.

21 This policy can be found in EPA's Carcinogenic Risk Assessment Guidelines (51 FR 33,992 [24 September 1986]).

22 In the case of alachlor, EPA derived a Q* of 0.08 $(mg/kg/day)^{-1}$ (52 FR 49,485 [31 December 1987]).

23 Exposure to alachlor can also occur through food and groundwater, but for reasons of space this analysis will focus only on applicator exposure.

24 Health and Welfare Canada did not take into account the fact that applicators are only exposed to alachlor a few days per year (approximately 15). It also assumed 100 percent dermal absorption, almost certainly an overestimate, and that applicators either did not use protective gloves or that they were completely ineffective (Alachlor Review Board, *Report*, 65–8).

25 These figures are derived from EPA's estimate of 0.018–1.8 mg/kg/year, divided by EPA's assumed 15 days of application per year by commercial applicators (52 FR 49,486 [31 December 1987]).

26 Alachlor Review Board, *Report*, 60.

27 Letter from A.J. Liston, Assistant Deputy Minister, Health Protection Branch, Health and Welfare Canada, to Dr J.B. Morrissey, Assistant Deputy Minister, Food Production and Inspection Branch, Agriculture Canada, 26 November 1987.

28 Ibid.

29 Castrilli and Vigod, *Pesticides in Canada*, 54–5. The agriculture minister's final decision demonstrates this: "It is the Minister's responsibility to judge the acceptability of the risks associated with alachlor use, based on the advice received regarding both the risks and the benefits (Agriculture Canada, Pesticides Directorate, Canadian Association of Pesticide Control Officials (CAPCO) Note 88-04 27 January 1988).

30 The Alachlor Review Board was highly critical of the ad hoc manner in which Agriculture Canada assessed benefits (Alachlor Review Board, *Report*, 45–7).

31 Agriculture Canada, Pesticides Directorate, CAPCO Note 88-04 27 January 1988, 3.

32 Alachlor Review Board, *Report*, 108.

33 52 FR 49,495 (31 December 1987).

34 National Research Council, *Regulating Pesticides in Food: The Delaney Paradox* (Washington, DC: National Academy Press, 1987), 54.

35 Agriculture Canada, Pesticides Directorate, CAPCO Note 88–04 27 January 1988.

36 52 FR 49,500 (31 December 1987).

37 Interview, EPA official.

38 Agriculture Canada undertook consultations in the fall of 1984, but environmentalists apparently were not included (Alachlor Review Board, *Report*, 44).

39 Interview, Toby Vigod, Canadian Environmental Law Association, April 1989.

40 52 FR 49,480 (31 December 1987).

41 Hoberg, "Risk, Science, and Politics," 274.
42 In the mid-1980s, apples accounted for 75 percent of the pesticide's use, another 12 percent was used on peanuts, the remainder on a variety of commodities. Approximately 825,000 pounds of daminozide are used each year, compared to 80 million pounds of alachlor.
43 George Hoberg, "Reaganism, Pluralism, and the Politics of Pesticide Regulation," *Policy Sciences* 23 (1990): 257–89.
44 Ibid.
45 49 FR 29,136 (3 January 1984).
46 EPA *Position Document 2/3/4 on Daminozide* (Washington, DC: EPA, 12 September 1985).
47 For an account of the Science Advisory Panel's review of daminozide, see Sheila Jasanoff, "EPA's Regulation of Daminozide: Unscrambling the Messages of Risk," *Science, Technology, and Human Values* 12 (1987):116–24; and Jasanoff, *The Fifth Branch; Science Advisors as Policymakers* (Cambridge, MA: Harvard University Press, 1990), 141–9.
48 In particular, the animal studies in question relied on historic rather than concurrent controls, used only a single dose level, and apparently exceeded the maximum tolerated dose (52 FR 1913 [16 January 1987]).
49 *Chemical Regulation Reporter,* 4 October 1985, 727.
50 One EPA official offered the following defense of the program's decision to cancel registration despite the uncertainty: "We can't be absolutely certain, but if it looks like a duck and it walks like a duck and it sounds like a duck, there's a good chance it's a duck" (*Pesticide and Toxic Chemical News,* 2 October 1985, 28).
51 51 FR 12,889 (9 January 1986).
52 "The regulatory history of this chemical," the letter continued, "suggests a pattern of either general incompetency in the EPA review process or a tremendous vulnerability to political and corporate pressure" (Letter from Jay Feldman and Diane Baxter to Lee Thomas, Administrator, EPA, 28 January 1986).
53 For a discussion of the EDB case, see Sheldon Krimsky and Alonzo Plough, *Environmental Hazards: Communicating Risks as a Social Process* (Dover, MA: Auburn House, 1988), chapter 2.
54 *Chemical Regulation Reporter,* 4 April 1986, 6; 11 July 1986, 480. See also "Polishing the Apple's Image," *New York Times,* 25 May 1986, F4.
55 *New York Times,* 26 July 1986, 10; "Safeway Eliminates Sale of Treated Apples," *Washington Post,* 17 July 1986, C5.
56 Interview, representative of the International Apple Institute.
57 54 FR 22,558 (24 May 1989).
58 Environmental Protection Agency, Press Release, 1 February 1989.
59 Natural Resources Defense Council, *Intolerable Risk: Pesticides in our Children's Food: Summary,* 27 February 1989, 1.

60 One estimate suggested processed apple products declined 20 percent by May 1989 from the previous year's levels ("EPA to Ban Use of Alar in 2 Weeks," *Globe and Mail,* Toronto, 12 May 1989, A8.

61 "Official Rebukes Schools Over Apple Bans," *New York Times,* 16 March 1989, B10.

62 *Chemical Regulation Reporter,* 9 June 1989, 349.

63 Philip Shabecoff, "Apple Chemical Being Removed in U.S. Market," *New York Times,* 3 June 1989, A1.

64 *Chemical Regulation Reporter,* 8 September 1989, 717.

65 Allan Gold, "Overseas Sales of Apple-Ripening Agent End," *New York Times,* 18 October 1989, A14.

66 Pesticides Directorate, Agriculture Canada, Memorandum to Program Managers, re: Registration Status of Daminozide (Alar) Plant Growth Regulator, 17 April 1986.

67 Chris Rose, "U.S. Considers Ban on Chemical that B.C. Growers Stopped Using," *Vancouver Sun,* 3 February 1989, B4.

68 Larry Pynn, "Apple Juice Cancer Risk Dismissed," *Vancouver Sun,* 2 March 1989, B12; George Hoberg, "Forbidden Fruit, *Globe and Mail,* Toronto, 16 March 1989, A7.

69 For the year 1989, there were more stories (21) in the *New York Times* alone than there were in all of the newspapers covered by the *Canadian News Index* (17).

70 This statement is accurate for the *public* debate surrounding Alar. EPA did offer substantial analysis of the product's benefits in its various regulatory support documents. See for example 54 FR 22,558 (25 May 1989).

71 *New York Times,* 10 March 1989, 9.

72 Philip Shabecoff, "U.S. Agencies, to Allay Fears, Proclaim Apples Safe to Eat," *New York Times,* 17 March 1989, A16.

73 Interview, agency official.

74 Shabecoff, "U.S. Agencies."

75 EPA, Press Release, 1 February 1989.

76 This figure is based on a cancer potency, or Q*, of 0.88 (milligrams/kilogram/day)$^{-1}$, and a mean exposure of 0.000051 mg/kg/day (54 FR 6392 [10 February 1989]). See also 54 FR 22558 (24 May 1989); and Office of Pesticide Programs, Office of Pesticides and Toxic Substances, United States Environmental Protection Agency, *Daminozide Special Review Technical Support Document – Preliminary Determination to Cancel the Food Uses of Daminozide* (Washington, DC: EPA, May 1989).

77 54 FR 6392 (10 February 1989).

78 Indeed, EPA's John Moore claimed NRDC's calculations were "flat wrong," even though he had signed off on a risk assessment using the same figure three years earlier. Shabecoff, "U.S. Agencies."

79 Letter from Health Protection Branch, Health and Welfare Canada, 1 March 1989.

80 Health Protection Branch, Health and Welfare Canada, *Issues: Alar (Daminozide)*, 7 March 1989. Pamphlet.

81 Letter from Toby Vigod, Canadian Environmental Law Association, et al., to the Honourable Donald Mazankowski, Minister of Agriculture, 30 March 1989.

82 Letter to Toby Vigod, Canadian Environmental Law Association, from D.C. Kirkpatrick, Director, Bureau of Chemical Safety, Health and Welfare Canada, 11 April 1989 (emphasis added).

83 Canada's estimate ranged from 0.00002 to 0.00008 mg/kg/day, whereas EPA's was 0.00048 (Letter from Kirkpatrick to Vigod).

84 "11 Apples Growers Sue CBS Program," *New York Times*, 29 November 1990, A22; Timothy Egan, "Apple Growers Bruised and Bitter After Alar Scare," *New York Times*, 9 July 1991, A1; Eliot Marshall, "A Is for Apple, Alar, and ... Alarmist?" *Science* 254 (1991):20–2.

85 Aldicarb is an acute toxin, and residue analyses reveals contamination of banana shipments that were as high as ten times the legal limit. Given the role of bananas in children's diets, expectations of an Alar-like crisis reaction were high (interview, agency official).

86 Eleanor Randolph, "Venture in Managing News Backfires: Environmental Group Wins Attention but Angers Officials, Journalists," *Washington Post*, 3 March 1989, A17.

87 See especially Michael Fumento, *Science Under Siege: Balancing Technology and the Environment* (New York: William Morrow, 1993), chapter 1.

88 See especially Joseph D. Rosen, "Much Ado About Alar," *Issues in Science and Technology* 7 (Fall 1990):85–90.

89 Marshall, "A is for Apple."

90 Memorandum from Henry Spencer and George Ghali, to Janet Auerbach, Chief, Special Review Branch, U.S. Environmental Protection Agency, 26 July 1991.

91 Marshall, "A is for Apple." According to one expert on risk assessment, "given the vitriolic criticism of the earlier study, the new industry-sponsored results are only surprising for how much crow the critics may have to eat" (Letter from Adam Finkel, *Science* 255 [7 February 1992]:664–5).

92 Marshall, "A is for Apple."

93 A Health and Welfare Canada official asserted, "If there is a problem demonstrated by the final studies, Canada can have it off the shelves much more quickly than the United States can" ("EPA to Ban Use").

CHAPTER FIVE

1 U.S. Food and Drug Administration, "Saccharin and its Salts: Proposed Rule Making," 42 *Federal Register* (15 April 1977):19,896–20,010, at 20,001.

2 R.S.C. 1985, C. F-27.

3 R.S.C. 1985, C. F-27, S. 30(1).

4 Ibid.

5 Office of Privatization and Regulatory Affairs, "Regulatory Reform Strategy" (Ottawa: Office of Privatization and Regulatory Affairs, n.d.).

6 21 U.S.C.S. 301.

7 Richard A. Merrill, "Saccharin: A Regulator's View," in Robert W. Crandall and Lester B. Lave, eds., *The Scientific Basis of Health and Safety Regulation* (Washington, DC: Brookings Institution, 1981), 165.

8 21 U.S.C.S. 348(c)(3)(A).

9 Merrill, "Saccharin: A Regular View," 165.

10 21 U.S.C.S. 348(g)(1).

11 Linda C. Cummings, "The Political Reality of Artificial Sweeteners," in Harvey M. Sapolsky, ed., *Consuming Fears* (New York: Basic Books, 1986), 117.

12 The cyclamate case is discussed in Cummings, "The Political Reality of Artificial Sweeteners."

13 Health and Welfare Canada, "Canadian Position on Saccharin," News Release, 9 March 1977; Food and Drugs Act Regulation E.01.001.

14 The sale of drugs containing saccharin as a non-medicinal ingredient was not to be permitted after 31 December 1978, and saccharin-containing cosmetics likely to be ingested, such as mouthwash and toothpaste, were to be prohibited as of 31 December 1979. As of 1 September 1977 the sale of saccharin as a single ingredient drug or in combination with cyclamates was to be limited to pharmacies.

15 Health and Welfare Canada, "Short-term Extension to Permitted Use of Saccharin," News Release, 19 April 1977.

16 Reginald W. Rhein, Jr and Larry Marion, *The Saccharin Controversy: A Guide for Consumers* (New York: Monarch Press, 1977), 9.

17 "The Great Saccharin Snafu," *Consumer Reports* 42 (1977): 410–14, at 412.

18 Food and Drug Administration, "Saccharin and Its Salts," 20,010.

19 L. Bradshaw, D.L. Arnold, D. Krewski, "Case Study No. 2: A Century of Saccharin," in I. Burton, C.D. Fowle, and R.S. McCullough, eds., *Living with Risk: Environmental Risk Management in Canada* (Toronto: Institute for Environmental Studies, 1982), 120.

20 Oliver E. Williamson, "Saccharin: An Economist's View," in Robert W. Crandall and Lester B. Lave, eds., *The Scientific Basis of Health and Safety Regulation* (Washington, DC: Brookings Institution, 1981).

21 Representative James Martin, as cited by Rhein and Marion, *The Saccharin Controversy*, 7.

22 Rhein and Marion, *The Saccharin Controversy*, 7.

23 Public Law 95-203.

24 National Research Council/National Academy of Sciences, *Saccharin: Technical Assessment of Risks and Benefits* (Washington, DC: National Academy of Sciences, 1978), ES-4, ES-10.

25 Government of Canada, "Food and Drug Regulations, amendment," and "Cosmetic Regulations, amendment," *Canada Gazette Part II*, 19 (November 1992), 4789–92.

26 Instead of publishing a draft regulation in the *Canada Gazette Part I*, Health and Welfare Canada did publish a notice of its intent *not* to publish the draft regulation. (See "Food and Drug Regulations, amendments," 4790.)

27 Government of Canada, "Food and Drug Regulations, Amendments," *Canada Gazette Part II* 19 (November 1992), 4789.

28 Food and Drug Administration, "Saccharin and its Salts," 19,998.

29 D.L. Arnold, C.A. Moodie, et al., "Long-term toxicity of ortho-toluene-sulforamide and sodium saccharin in the rat," *Toxicology and Applied Pharmacology* 52 (1980):113–52.

30 Cummings, "The Political Reality of Artificial Sweeteners," 132.

31 National Academy of Sciences/National Research Council, *Safety of Saccharin and Sodium Saccharin in the Human Diet* (Washington, DC: National Academy of Sciences, 1974).

32 Bradshaw, Arnold, et al., "Case Study No. 2," 119; National Academy of Sciences, *Saccharin*; U.S. Congress, Office of Technology Assessment, *Cancer Testing Technology and Saccharin* (Washington, DC: U.S. Congress, 1977).

33 National Academy of Sciences, *Saccharin*, ES-4.

34 Food and Drug Administration, "Saccharin and its Salts," 20001.

35 Ibid.

36 Health and Welfare Canada, "Canadian Position on Saccharin," 3.

37 Dr A.B. Morrison, in House of Commons, Standing Committee on Health, Welfare and Social Affairs, *Minutes of Proceedings and Evidence*, 24 March 1977, 34:32.

38 Ibid., 33.

39 Health and Welfare Canada, "Saccharin in Drugs and Cosmetics," Information Letter, 5 December 1991.

40 Bruce Halliday, in Parliament of Canada, House of Commons, *Debates*, 11 March 1977, 3891.

41 Bradshaw, Arnold, et al., "Case Study No. 2," 120.

42 Ibid., 120–1.

43 Monique Bégin, in House of Commons, *Debates*, 15 December 1977, 1896. See also Marc Lalonde, in House of Commons, *Debates*, 10 March 1977, 3836; and Standing Committee on Health, Welfare and Social Affairs, *Minutes of Proceedings and Evidence*, 17 March 1977, 32:23.

44 Morrison, in *Minutes of Proceedings and Evidence*, 24 March 1977, 34:31–2.

45 "The Great Saccharin Snafu," 410. Indeed, the media appears to have been a force of its own which had an impact on the outcome, but this element will not receive attention here. See Philip F. Lawler, *Sweet Talk: Media Coverage of Artificial Sweeteners* (Washington, DC: The Media Institute, 1986).

46 "The Great Saccharin Snafu," 411.

47 Merrill, "Saccharin: A Regulator's View," 160.

48 Rhein and Marion, *The Saccharin Controversy*, 5.

49 U.S. General Accounting Office, "Need to Resolve Questions on Saccharin," Food and Drug Administration, Department of Health, Education, and Welfare: Report of the Comptroller General of the United States (Washington, DC: GAO, 1976).

50 Merrill, "Saccharin: A Regulator's View," 155.

51 In 1972 the agency removed saccharin from a list of substances "generally recognized as safe" (known as the GRAS list), and adopted interim measures to discourage an increase in consumption pending the completion of further studies already underway (the FDA and WARF studies.) Food and Drug Administration, "Saccharin and its Salts," 37 FR 2437–8 (1 February 1972).

52 Ibid., 20,002.

53 Ibid., 20,001.

54 Ibid., 20,001.

55 Ibid., 20,002.

56 *Congressional Record – House*, 15 March 1977, 7697; 4 April 1977, 10,268.

57 Rep. Montgomergy, in *Congressional Record – House*, 4 April 1977, 10,278.

58 *Congressional Record – House*, 18 March 1977, 8104.

59 Rep. Tucker, in *Congressional Record – House*, 15 March 1977, 7646.

60 See for instance, James Martin, in *Congressional Record – House*, 15 March 1977, 7697; 30 March 1977, 9726; 4 April 1977, 10,271.

61 See, for instance, statements by Rep. Collins, in *Congressional Record – House*, 4 April 1977, 10,274; and Rep. Hammerschmidt, in *Congressional Record – House*, 4 April 1977, 10,271.

62 Statement by Rep. Montgomery, in *Congressional Record – House*, 4 April 1977, 10,278.

63 See, for instance, statements by Richard Ottinger, (*Congressional Record – House*, 23 March 1977, 8883; 29 March 1977, 9393; 30 March 1977, 9712), and Gaylord Nelson (*Congressional Record – Senate*, 29 June 1977, 21,450).

64 Richard Ottinger, in *Congressional Record – House*, 23 March 1977, 8883.

65 Simma Holt, in House of Commons, *Debates*, 28 April 1977, 5117.
66 Stan Darling, in Standing Committee on Health, Welfare and Social Affairs, *Minutes of Proceedings and Evidence*, 24 March 1977, 34:35.
67 Merrill, "Saccharin: A Regulator's View," 168.
68 Reprinted in "The Great Saccharin Snafu," 413.
69 Cummings, "The Political Reality of Artificial Sweeteners," 136.
70 Congressional Quarterly, *Congressional Quarterly Almanac, 1977* 23:497.
71 Bradshaw, Arnold, et al., "Case Study No. 2," 121.
72 *Berryland Canning Co. Ltd. v. The Queen, Dominion Law Reports* 44 (1974):568–83.
73 Paul McRae, in House of Commons, *Debates*, 28 April 1977, 5117–18.
74 See for examples R. Wilson, "Saccharin Ban a Bitter Pill For Marketers," *Marketing* 83 (6 February 1978):2; and R. Winter, "Saccharin – Bitter Problem For Pop Market", *Marketing*, 82 (28 March 1977):3.
75 Edgar Z. Friedenberg, *Deference to Authority: The Case of Canada* (White Plains, NY: M.E. Sharpe, 1980); Seymour Martin Lipset, *Continental Divide: The Values and Institutions of the United States and Canada* (New York: Routledge, 1990).
76 Health and Welfare Canada, "Canadian Position on Saccharin," 2.
77 Health and Welfare Canada, "Short-term Extension to Permitted Use of Saccharin," 19 April 1977, 3. News release.
78 Cited in Rhein and Marion, *The Saccharin Controversy*, 13.
79 Rhein and Marion *(The Saccharin Controversy*, 44) report that Senator Ted Kennedy and Representative Paul Rodgers fashioned the compromise bill to deflect calls for amendment of Delaney.
80 In early 1993 the administrator of the EPA newly appointed by the Clinton Administration indicated her intent to ask Congress to amend the Delaney Clause. See Keith Schneider, "EPA Plan Asks Congress to Relax Rule on Pesticides," *New York Times*, 2 February 1993, A1.
81 Harvey Sapolsky, "The Politics of Product Controversies," in Harvey Sapolsky, ed., *Consuming Fears* (New York: Monarch Press, 1977).
82 Cummings, "The Political Reality of Artificial Sweeteners," 134.

CHAPTER SIX

1 The Canadian Development Corporation held 40 percent interest in Innocan Investments Ltd, which acquired 100 percent of the voting shares of Rapco Foams in 1976. See D.S. Cohen, "Public and Private Law Dimensions of the UFFI Problem," Minutes of Proceedings and Evidence of House of Commons Committee on Health and Welfare, No. 42, 10 October 1982, A:49.
2 House Standing Committee on Health and Welfare, No. 48, "Fifth Report," 32; 47 FR 14365 (2 April 1982).

3 National Research Council Committee on Aldehydes, *Formaldehyde and Other Aldehydes* (Washington, DC: National Academy Press, 1981).

4 Lloyd Tatryn, *Formaldehyde on Trial: The Politics of Health in a Chemical Society* (Toronto: Lorimer, 1983), 7.

5 R.S.C. 1985, C. H-3, S. 6(1)(a).

6 Treasury Board Canada, "Socio-Economic Impact Analysis," chapter 490 of *Administrative Policy Manual*, December 1979.

7 John M. Evans, H.N. Janisch, D.J. Mullan, *Administrative Law*, 3rd ed. (Toronto: Emond Montgomery, 1989), 236.

8 Office of Privatization and Regulatory Affairs, "Regulatory Reform Strategy" (Ottawa: Office of Privatization and Regulatory Affairs, n.d.).

9 R.S.C. 1985, C. H-3, S. 9(1).

10 R.S.C. 1985, C. H-3, S. 9(5).

11 Prior to 1978 the CGSB was known as the Canadian Government Specifications Board.

12 CMHC was previously known as the Central Mortgage and Housing Corporation.

13 G. Walt, Standing Committee on Health and Welfare, No. 47, 28 October 1982, 34.

14 Richard A. Merrill, "CPSC Regulation of Cancer Risks in Consumer Products: 1972–1981," *University of Virginia Law Review* 67 (1981):1261–375, at 1370.

15 CPSC administers two pieces of legislation, the Consumer Product Safety Act and the Federal Hazardous Substances Act. Although there is considerable overlap between the two statutes, the commission has tended to rely on CPSA, largely because it authorizes a more informal rulemaking process. See Merrill, "CPSC Regulation."

16 15 U.S.C. s.2056(b).

17 15 U.S.C. s.2056(a), s.2058(f)(3)(F).

18 15 U.S.C. s.2057(2).

19 15 U.S.C. s.2058((f)(3)(E).

20 15 U.S.C.S. s.2058.

21 15 U.S.C. s.2060.

22 Personal communication, U.S. Department of Housing and Urban Development official, 4 December 1990.

23 Hazardous Products Board of Review, *Report on Urea Formaldehyde Foam Insulation* (Ottawa: Consumer and Corporate Affairs Canada, 1982). Cohen (Standing Committee, 13, 41) notes that much of the manufacturers' product research was subsidized by the federal government.

24 There were also seven members from provincial government departments, research institutes, and Crown corporations, and two from professional associations. See Standing Committee on Health and Welfare, No. 48, 14.

25 Tataryn, *Formaldehyde on Trial*, 27.
26 There were concerns with shrinkage and crumbling, both of which reduced the insulation's effectiveness, with growth of molds as a result of the high water content of the wet foam, and with structural damage to wood and metal building structures, also as a result of the high water content.
27 Alan Bowles, Standing Committee on Health and Welfare, No. 42, 5 October 1982, 108–9.
28 See, for instance, Cliff Shirtliffe, Standing Committee on Health and Welfare, No. 41, 4 October 1982, 24; Bowles, Standing Committee, No. 42, 128.
29 Cohen, Standing Committee, No. 42, 43.
30 Bowles, Standing Committee, No. 42, 137–8.
31 Ibid., 110.
32 Walter Raepple, Standing Committee on Health and Welfare, No. 42, 5 October 1982, 31.
33 Walt, Standing Committee, No. 47, 23 and 39–40.
34 George Brewer, Standing Committee on Health and Welfare, No. 42, 5 October 1982, 62.
35 Cliff Shirtliffe, Standing Committee, No. 41, 26.
36 The officer responsible for acceptance stated, "We had to accept urea formaldehyde. [CMHC] does not have a choice, because it is an insulation; it has a standard." See Brewer, Standing Committee, No. 42, 52.
37 Standing Committee on Health and Welfare, No. 48, 32.
38 Tataryn, *Formaldehyde on Trial*, 44.
39 Brewer, Standing Committee, No. 42, 69.
40 Dr L. Kerwin, Standing Committee on Health and Welfare, No. 41, 4 October 1982, 11.
41 Brewer had also confirmed that UFFI was being installed in ceilings and in brick structures, neither of which was authorized under the CMHC program.
42 Walt, Standing Committee, No. 47, 12.
43 The conditions for reinstatement were far from onerous. The industry was required to accurately advertise the product's R value and risk of shrinkage (a reiteration of earlier conditions), work toward national standards for application and contractor certification, and accept periodic product testing. (Walt, Standing Committee, No. 47, 13–14.)
44 Walt, Standing Committee, No. 47. See also Brewer, Standing Committee, No. 42, 47ff.
45 Walt, Standing Committee, No. 47, 16.
46 Tataryn, *Formaldehyde on Trial*, 38.

47 E. Somers, "Formaldehyde and Indoor Air Quality – The Health Issues," in Corpus Information Services (CIS), *Formaldehyde: The Facts* (Toronto: Corpus Information Services, 1982).

48 Jim Travers, "Govt. issues warning about foam insulation," *Ottawa Citizen*, 4 August 1978, 9.

49 Clark Lowry, "Assistance Program for UFFI Homeowners," in CIS, *Formaldehyde: The Facts* (Toronto: Corpus Information Services, 1982), 3. The absence of consumer complaints before 1979 does not necessarily indicate that there was no problem. Some residents of UFFI-insulated homes may have been experiencing symptoms that they did not associate with the product until after seeing the CBC program.

50 See letter from Dr G.S. Wiberg to Alan Bowles, 2 November 1979, reprinted in Standing Committee on Health and Welfare, No. 46, A:1.

51 A.B. Morrison, in Standing Committee on Health and Welfare, No. 45, 7 October 1982, 5.

52 Standing Committee on Health and Welfare, No. 48, 12.

53 Tataryn, *Formaldehyde on Trial*, 61.

54 Standing Committee on Health and Welfare, No. 48, 12.

55 James Jefferson, "Ban on foam insulation proclaimed by Ottawa," *Globe and Mail*, 18 December 1980, A2.

56 James Rusk, "Used in federal program, urea insulation material banned," *Globe and Mail*, 24 April 1981, 9.

57 Lowry, "Assistance Program for UFFI Homeowners," 4.

58 Hazardous Product Board of Review, *Report*, Ottawa, 5 October 1982, 121.

59 Cohen, "Public and Private Law," 49.

60 Tataryn, *Formaldehyde on Trial*, 84.

61 Claude Masse, "La compensation des victimes de désastres collectifs au Québec," *Windsor Yearbook of Access to Justice* 9 (1989):3–29.

62 Masse, "La compensation des victimes de désastres collectifs."

63 André Picard, "Homeowners with urea-foam insulation lose civil suit for damages," *Globe and Mail*, 14 December 1991, A1.

64 The U.S. history of UFFI has been reviewed previously by Nicholas A. Ashford, C. William Ryan, Charles C. Caldart, "A Hard Look at Federal Regulation of Formaldehyde: A Departure from Reasoned Decisionmaking," *Harvard Environmental Law Review* 7 (1983):297–370; Sanford L. Weiner, "Banning Formaldehyde Insulation: Risk Assessment and Symbolic Politics," in Harvey M. Sapolsky, ed., *Consuming Fears: The Politics of Product Risks* (New York: Basic Books, 1986); and John D. Graham, Laura C. Green, Marc J. Roberts, *In Search of Safety: Chemicals and Cancer Risk* (Cambridge: Harvard University Press, 1988).

65 U.S. Department of Housing and Urban Development, "Use of Materials Bulletin 74" (Washington, DC: Department of Housing and Urban Development, 13 October 1977).

66 The tax credit was available for energy conservation expenditures made after 20 April 1977. See Patricia Ann Metzer, *Federal Income Taxation of Individuals*, 4th ed. (Philadelphia: American Law Institute, 1984), 478.

67 47 FR 14,367 (2 April 1982).

68 Edward M. Fox, "Urea Formaldehyde Foam Insulation: Defusing a Time Bomb," *American Journal of Law and Medicine* 11 (1985): 81–104.

69 47 FR 14,393 (2 April 1982).

70 47 FR 14,369 (2 April 1982). As required under the Toxic Substances Control Act, the industry concurrently informed the Environmental Protection Agency of the research findings.

71 Merrill, "CPSC Regulation."

72 Graham, Green, and Roberts, *In Search of Safety*, 17.

73 Merrill, "CPSC Regulation."

74 Ashford, Ryan, and Caldart, "A Hard Look at Federal Regulation of Formaldehyde."

75 "Report of the Federal Panel on Formaldehyde," *Environmental Health Perspectives* 43 (1982):139–68, at 165.

76 National Research Council, Committee on Toxicology, *Formaldehyde: An Assessment of its Health Effects* (Washington, DC: National Academy of Sciences, March 1980), vi.

77 45 FR 39,434 (10 June 1980).

78 46 FR 11,188 (5 February 1981). Subsequent notices were published in October (46 FR 49,140 [16 October 1981]) and November (46 FR 56,762 [18 November 1981]), extending the deadline for submissions and seeking public comments on additional information.

79 47 FR 14,365 (2 April 1982).

80 Marjorie Sun, "Formaldehyde Ban is Overturned," *Science* 220 (1983):699.

81 The decision also disagreed with CPSC's reasoning for use of the Consumer Product Safety Act rather than the Federal Hazardous Substances Act. Gulf South Insulation v. CPSC, 701 *Federal Reporter*, 2nd Series, 1137 (Fifth Cir. 1983).

82 U.S. Consumer Product Safety Commission, *1983 Annual Report*.

83 Although a thorough review of all U.S. UFFI litigation has not been undertaken, one Department of Energy official who was aware of approximately 150 UFFI-related cases could not recall the federal government's ever being sued for damages. However one UFFI manufacturer did attempt, without success, to seek damages from CPSC for damaging the product's reputation with the shortlived ban.

84 "Report of the Federal Panel on Formaldehyde," 159.

85 NRC Committee on Aldehydes, *Formaldehyde and Other Aldehydes*, 7.

86 Health and Welfare Canada, "Final Report of the Department of National Health and Welfare Expert Advisory Committee on Urea-Formaldehyde Foam Insulation," April 1981, 4–5. Mimeo.

87 Different scientific interpretations of the CIIT findings are discussed in laypersons' terms by Graham, Green, and Roberts (*In Search of Safety,* chapter 3).

88 Ibid., 40.

89 47 FR 14,371 (2 April 1982).

90 Graham, Green, and Roberts, *In Search of Safety,* chapter 3.

91 47 FR 14,373 (2 April 1982).

92 CPSC uncovered only 2200 complaints of acute effects associated with UFFI by August 1981, although the product had been installed in half a million homes (47 FR 14,382 [2 April 1982]). That figure does not include any future cancer cases that could result if formaldehyde is, in fact, a human carcinogen. Nor does it include any consumers experiencing UFFI-related symptoms who did not associate them with the insulation.

93 Regulatory action may, however, have contributed to devaluation of UFFI homes to the extent that banning the product created an exaggerated public perception of the risks.

94 Health and Welfare Canada, "Final Report of the Expert Committee," 5.

95 Graham, Green, and Roberts, *In Search of Safety,* 152.

96 Health and Welfare Canada, "Final Report of the Expert Committee," 6.

97 Hazardous Products Board of Review, *Report,* 45–51.

98 Ibid., 87–8.

99 Sheila Jasanoff, *Risk Management and Political Culture* (New York: Russell Sage Foundation, 1986), 52.

100 One was the director of toxicology for the Celanese Corporation in New York, while the other was president of the Chemical Industry Institute of Toxicology in North Carolina. The committee also included two Canadian academics and the Vancouver public health officer. See Health and Welfare Canada, "Final Report of the Expert Advisory Committee," 20.

101 Health and Welfare Canada, "Final Report of the Expert Committee," 5, 16.

102 Tataryn, *Formaldehyde on Trial,* 64.

103 Health and Welfare Canada, "Final Report of the Expert Committee," 1.

104 G. Vardi, Board of Review on UFFI, 21 September 1981, 140–1.

105 *Globe and Mail,* 24 April 1981, 9; Morrison, 8.

106 47 FR 14,365 (2 April 1982).

107 *Gulf South Insulation v. U.S. CPSC,* 1146.

108 Ashford, Ryan, and Caldart, "A Hard Look at Federal Regulation of Formaldehyde"; Devra Lee Davis, "The 'Shotgun Wedding' of Science

and Law: Risk Assessment and Judicial Review," *Columbia Journal of Environmental Law* 10 (1985):67–109, at 85; Kenneth S. Abraham, Richard A. Merrill, "Scientific Uncertainty in the Courts," *Issues in Science and Technology* (Winter 1986):93–107, at 99.

109 Nevertheless, CPSC estimated a loss of 800 jobs among contractors who would be forced out of business by a UFFI ban. 47 FR 14,395 (2 April 1982).

110 47 FR 14,400 (2 April 1982).

111 47 FR 14,395 (2 April 1982).

112 Weiner, "Banning Formaldehyde Insulation."

113 See Tataryn, *Formaldehyde on Trial*, chapter 3.

114 47 FR 14,369 (2 April 1982).

115 Weiner ("Banning Formaldehyde Foam," 171), notes that by 1980, all the foam installers in the U.S. were represented by a single poorly equipped Washington lobbyist.

116 Graham, Green, and Roberts, *In Search of Safety*, 48.

117 Weiner, "Banning Formaldehyde Insulation," 172–3.

118 David Vogel, *National Styles of Regulation: Environmental Policy in Great Britain and the United States* (Ithaca: Cornell University Press, 1986).

119 For a discussion of changes in the regulatory regime, see Richard B. Stewart, "The Reformation of American Administrative Law," *Harvard Law Review* 88 (1975):1667–813.

120 One can suggest several possible reasons for this difference. First, because UFFI ultimately was not banned in the U.S., any problems with the product remained a private matter to be settled between consumers and manufacturers or contractors. Second, tax concessions were offered for a wide variety of energy conservation measures, of which UFFI was only one. In contrast most Canadian CHIP subsidies were used to install UFFI. Thus there was less a sense of selective promotion of a particular product. Third, U.S. homeowners may have been less inclined to blame the government for their losses because tax credits are a less visible form of subsidy than a cash payment. Finally, while there was no single scapegoat in the U.S., it is easier to attribute blame in a parliamentary system of "responsible government." (See Kent Weaver, "The Politics of Blame Avoidance," *Journal of Public Policy* 6 [1986]:371–98.)

CHAPTER SEVEN

1 The other types of asbestos are crocidolite, amosite, anthophyllite, tremolite, and actinolite.

2 The Royal Commission on Matters of Health and Safety Arising from the Use of Asbestos in Ontario, *Report* (Toronto: Queen's Printer, 1984).

3 There have been a number of scholarly studies of OSHA regulation in the U.S. See especially John Mendelhoff, *The Dilemma of Toxic Substance Regulation* (Cambridge, MA: MIT Press, 1988); Charles Noble, *Liberalism at Work* (Philadelphia: Temple University Press, 1986); David McCaffrey, *OSHA and the Politics of Health Regulation* (New York: Plenum Press, 1982).

4 Caroline Digby and Craig Riddell, "Occupational Health and Safety in Canada," in Craig Riddell, ed., *Canadian Labour Relations* (Toronto: University of Toronto Press, 1986); Richard Brown, "Canadian Occupational Health and Safety Legislation," *Osgoode Hall Law Review* 20 (1982):90–118; G. Bruce Doern, Michael Prince, and Garth McNaughton, *Living with Contradictions: Health and Safety Regulation in Ontario*, prepared for the Royal Commission on Matters of Health and Safety Arising from the Use of Asbestos in Ontario, February 1982; Law Reform Commission of Canada, *Workplace Pollution*, Working Paper 53 (Ottawa: Law Reform Commission of Canada, 1986).

5 Carolyn Tuohy, "Regulation and Scientific Complexity," *Osgoode Hall Law Journal* 20 (1982):562–609, at 598.

6 R.S.O. 1978, c. O-1, as amended.

7 John R. Wilson, *Regulation of Occupational Exposure to Toxic Substances in Ontario: The Designated Substances Program*, Masters Thesis, Department of Chemical Engineering and Applied Chemistry, University of Toronto, 1985.

8 R.S.Q., c. S-2.1; as amended.

9 Carolyn Tuohy, "Institutions and Interests in the Occupational Health Arena: The Case of Quebec," in William Coleman and Grace Skogstad, eds., *Policy Communities and Public Policy in Canada: A Structural Approach* (Toronto: Copp Clark Pitman, 1990).

10 29 United States Code (U.S.C.) sec. 655(b)(5).

11 *Industrial Union Department v. American Petroleum Institute*, 448 U.S. 607 (1980).

12 *American Textile Manufacturers' Institute v. Donovan*, 452 U.S. 490 (1981).

13 15 U.S.C. s. 2601 ff. For an analysis of the history and design of TSCA, see David Doniger, *The Law and Policy of Toxic Substance Control* (Baltimore: Johns Hopkins University Press, 1978).

14 See Cynthia Ruggerio, "Referral of Toxic Chemical Regulation under the Toxic Substances Control Act: EPA's Adminstrative Dumping Ground," *Boston College Environmental Affairs Law Review* 17 (1989):75–122.

15 15 U.S.C. secs. 2641–54.

16 The evolution of scientific knowledge on the health effects of asbestos is documented by Charlotte Twight, "Regulation of Asbestos: The Microanalytics of Government Failure," *Policy Studies Review* 10

(1991):9–39. See also Charlotte Twight, "From Credit Claiming to Avoiding Blame: The Evolution of Congressional Strategy for Asbestos Management," *Journal of Public Policy* 11 (1991):153–96.

17 Brodeur's articles were published as *Expendable Americans* (New York: Viking, 1973).

18 *Asbestos Information Association v. OSHA*, 727 F.2d 415 (Fifth Cir., 1984). The asbestos case up to this point is analyzed in Mendlehoff, *The Dilemma of Toxic Substance Regulation.*

19 *Building and Construction Trades Department v. Brock*, 838 F.2d 1258 (DC Cir. 1988).

20 55 FR 29,712 (12 July 1990).

21 44 FR 60,061 (17 October 1979).

22 U.S. Congress, House Committee on Energy and Commerce, Subcommittee on Oversight and Investigations, *EPA's Asbestos Regulations: Report on a Case Study on OMB Interference in Agency Rulemaking*, Committee Print, 99th Cong., 1st Sess., October 1985.

23 54 FR 29,460 (12 July 1989).

24 *Corrosion Proof Fittings et al v. EPA*, 947 F.2d 1201 (Fifth Cir., 1991).

25 Interview, EPA official.

26 15 U.S.C. secs. 2641–54. The asbestos in schools issue is discussed by Twight, "From Claiming Credit to Avoiding Blame."

27 See for instance Joseph Hooper, "The Asbestos Mess," *New York Times Magazine*, 25 November 1990, 38–41, 48, 53.

28 Richard Stone, "No Meeting of the Minds on Asbestos," *Science* 254 (15 November 1991):928–31.

29 Lloyd Tataryn, *Dying for a Living* (Ottawa: Deneau and Greenberg, 1979), chapter 2; G. Bruce Doern, *Regulatory Processes and Jurisdictional Issues in the Regulation of Hazardous Products in Canada*, Science Council of Canada Background Study No. 41, October 1977, 108; and G. Bruce Doern, "The Political Economy of Regulating Occupational Health: The Ham and Beaudry Reports," *Canadian Public Administration* 20 (1977):1–35.

30 The Quebec government agreed to establish the commission in exchange for workers striking at Thetford Mines dropping demands for more stringent health regulations as a part of their contract settlement. See Doern, *Regulatory Process*, 108.

31 Dennis Trudeau, "Safer mines may hurt PQ asbestos plans," *Montreal Star*, 31 March 1978, A8.

32 Doern, *Regulatory Processes*, 109. This 5 f/cc standards was to be adopted in 1978.

33 Jeanne Kirk Laux and Maureen Appel Molot, *State Capitalism: Public Enterprise in Canada* (Ithaca: Cornell University Press, 1988), 114–21.

34 Royal Commission on Asbestos, *Report.*

35 Charlotte Montgomery, "Ontario to Regulate Asbestos Before Commission Issues Study," *Globe and Mail,* 10 July 1981, 5.

36 *Canadian Employment Safety & Health Guide,* #21, 30 August 1982. Occupational Health and Safety Division, Ontario Ministry of Labour, *The Report on the Designation of Asbestos in Ontario* (Toronto: Ontario Ministry of Labour, January 1982).

37 Royal Commission on Asbestos, *Report,* 10–11.

38 *Ontario Gazette,* 4 July 1987, 3180–210.

39 O. Reg. 654/85. Officially, the 1985 regulations exempted all activities other than asbestos mining and manufacturing, very little of which occurs in Ontario, from the 1982 exposure limits. However, the intent of imposing requirements for safety practices was to ensure that levels of exposure comparable to the 1982 limits were met in non-industrial workplaces, where controlled monitoring of exposure can be very difficult. (Personal communication, Ontario government official.) Thus it is reasonable to continue to use the 1982 exposure limits as a benchmark for comparison to US regulations.

40 Interview, government official. See also Vic Pakalnis, Director, Industrial Health and Safety Branch, Ontario Ministry of Labour, *Asbestos in Schools: Public Policy Implications,* report to Ontario Public Schools Board Association, 8 June 1990.

41 *Quebec Gazette* 122(5):339–41.

42 *Montreal Gazette,* 6 March 1986, 3(C).

43 ILO, *International Labour Conference, 72nd Session: Record of Proceedings,* (Geneva: ILO, 1987).

44 *Chemical Regulation Reporter,* 16 May 1986, 176.

45 Marcel Masse, Minister of Mines, Press Conference on Asbestos, 12 Septembre 1989, 113.

46 51 FR 22,612 (20 June 1986). Two years later, OSHA amended the rule to add a short-term exposure limit of 1 f/cc over a half-hour period (53 FR 35,610 [14 September 1988]).

47 The figures cited are eight-hour time-weighted averages. In addition Ontario has established maximum permissible levels of 1.0 f/cc for crocidolite, 2.5 f/cc for amosite, and 5.0 f/cc for all others (*Occupational Health and Safety Act,* Regulation Respecting Asbestos [O. Reg. 570/82, s. 4]).

48 Until January 1990 Quebec standards were significantly weaker – roughly 5 f/cc.

49 These limits can be found in the Regulation Respecting Industrial and Commercial Establishments, the Regulation Respecting the Quality of the Work Environment, and the Regulation Respecting the Salubrity and Safety of Workmen in Mines and Quarries. Maximum limits for

each type are established at 5 for all but crocidolite and amosite which are set at 1 f/cc respectively. *Quebec Gazette*, 122(5):339–341.

50 For instance, between 90 and 95 percent of asbestos used commercially in Ontario is chrysotile. See Ontario Ministry of Labour, Occupational Health and Safety Division, *The Report on the Designation of Asbestos in Ontario* (Toronto: Ministry of Labour, January 1982), 2.3.

51 52 FR 41,846 (30 October 1987).

52 EPA has been sued by the Service Employees International Union for failing to issue regulations on asbestos in buildings. A district court required EPA to render a decision on the issue by 1 July 1991, but the agency since has been granted an extension (*Chemical Regulation Reporter*, 28 June 1991, 390).

53 Asbestos in Construction Projects and in Building and Repair Operations (O. Reg. 654/85).

54 Vic Pakalnis, *Asbestos in Schools*.

55 54 FR 29,460 (12 July 1989).

56 54 FR 29,464 (12 July 1989).

57 Regulation Respecting the Quality of Work Environment, s. 5, *Quebec Gazette*, 122(5):336–9.

58 The Royal Commission on Asbestos, in *Report*; National Research Council, *Asbestiform Fibers: Nonoccupational Health Risks*, (Washington, DC: National Academy Press, 1984).

59 51 FR 22,612 (20 June 1986).

60 Royal Commission on Asbestos, *Report*, chapter 5; B.T. Mossman, J. Bignon, et al., "Asbestos: Scientific Developments and Implications for Public Policy," *Science* 247 (19 January 1990):294–301.

61 Hooper, "The Asbestos Mess," 48.

62 See also National Research Council, *Asbestiform Fibers*, 132–3.

63 54 FR 29,470 (12 July 1989). OSHA draws similar conclusions: "Epidemiological and animal evidence, taken together, fail to establish a definitive risk differential for the various types of asbestos fiber. Accordingly, OSHA has ... recognized that all types of asbestos fiber have the same fibrogenic and carcinogenic potential" (51 FR 22,628 [20 June 1986]).

64 54 FR 29,483 (12 July 1989).

65 *Corrosion Proof Fittings et al. v. EPA*, 1221.

66 51 FR 22,644 (20 June 1986).

67 54 FR 29,477 (12 July 1989).

68 54 FR 29,479 (12 July 1989).

69 54 FR 29,485 (12 July 1989).

70 51 FR 22,666, 22,669 (20 June 1986).

71 The cost-effectivess of the proposals range from $0.9 mllion per life saved in ship repair to $12.2 million per life saved in secondary manufacturing (51 FR 22,666–9 [20 June 1986]).

72 51 FR 22,681 (20 June 1986).
73 *Building and Construction Trades Department, AFL-CIO v. Brock*, 838 F.2d 1258 (DC Cir. 1988).
74 55 FR 29712 (20 July 1990).
75 54 FR 29,484–7 (12 July 1989).
76 54 FR 29,487 (12 July 1989).
77 *Corrosion Proof Fittings et al v. EPA*, 1223.
78 Royal Commission on Asbestos, *Report.*
79 Occupational Health and Safety Division, Ministry of Labour, *The Report on the Designation of Asbestos in Ontario* (Toronto: Ontario Ministry of Labour, January 1982), 4.9, 5.3.
80 Royal Commission on Asbestos, *Report*, 8.
81 The Royal Commission on Asbestos *Report* also related these differences to variations in the type of industrial process because the amount of respirable fibres released is largely a function of the industrial process involved.
82 Ibid., 408.
83 In particular, most of the laboratory studies are based on injection rather than inhalation of asbestos fibres, which fails to account for the fact that certain types of fibres are more easily respirable than others (Ibid., 268–9).
84 For instance, the Royal Commission on Asbestos *Report* stated: "It is extremely unlikely that such differences are the result of errors of methodology in the studies or chance variations in lung cancer mortality" (411).
85 Ibid., 359. See also Health and Welfare Canada, Health Protection Branch, "Asbestos," *Issues*, 11 September 1989.
86 Royal Commission on Asbestos, *Report*, 411.
87 51 FR 22,644 (20 June 1986).
88 Royal Commission on Asbestos, *Report*, 583.
89 Ibid., 666.
90 52 FR 41,826 (30 October 1987).
91 Royal Commission on Asbestos, *Report*, 439.
92 The commission considers adopting the U.S.-style feasibility approach and explicitly rejects it (ibid., 423).
93 Ibid., 425.
94 Ibid., 11.
95 Ibid., 14. Because risks from asbestos in the ambient air are even smaller, they are also considered acceptable.
96 Ministry of Labour, *Report on the Designation of Asbestos*, 5.4 (emphasis not in original).
97 Ibid., G.31.
98 *Canadian Employment Safety and Health Guide*, #68, 4 July 1986, 2.

99 Sheila McGovern, "Imports Cut Spells Doom for Town of Asbestos," *Montreal Gazette*, 25 January 1986, A4.

100 Jennifer Robinson, "Quebec Mines Minister on Mission to Support Claim Asbestos is Safe," *Montreal Gazette*, 5 July 1986, A7.

101 "Deterring eco-zealotry," *Globe and Mail*, 24 October 1991, A18.

102 See for instance *Public Citizen Health Research Group et al v. Auchter et al.*, 702 F.2d 1150 (DC Cir. 1983).

103 *Industrial Union Department, AFL-CIO v. Hodgson*, 499 F.2d 467 (DC Cir. 1974).

104 *Asbestos Information Association/North America v. OSHA*, 727 F.2d 415 (Fifth Cir. 1984).

105 *Building and Construction Trades Dept., AFL-CIO v. Brock*, 838 F.2d 1258 (DC Cir. 1988).

106 One exception to the characteristically adversarial U.S. process was EPA's rule on asbestos in schools, which was developed through the innovative procedure of "regulatory negotiation" (52 FR 41,826 [30 October 1987]). While this more informal, cooperative style has also been used in other cases, the more legalistic process continues to dominate U.S. environmental, health and safety regulations. In fact the use of negotiation did not stop EPA from being sued on the schools rule (*Safe Building Alliance v. EPA*, 846 F.2d 79 [DC Cir. 1988]). For a discussion of regulatory negotiation, see David Pritzker and Deborah Dalton, eds., *Negotiated Rulemaking Sourcebook* (Washington, DC: Administrative Conference of the United States, 1990).

107 *Chemical Regulation Reporter*, 14 September 1983, 604.

108 *Corrosion Proof Fittings et al v. EPA*.

109 R. Shep Melnick, "The Politics of Partnership," *Public Administration Review* 45 (1985):653–60.

110 See for instance Richard Harris and Sidney Milkis, *The Politics of Regulatory Change* (New York: Oxford University Press, 1989), chapter 4.

111 U.S. Congress, House Committee on Energy and Commerce, Subcommittee on Oversight and Investigations, *EPA's Asbestos Regulations: Report on a Case Study on OMB Interference in Agency Rulemaking*, Committee Print 99-V, 99th Cong, 1st sess., October 1985.

112 Christopher H. Foreman, Jr, "Legislators, Regulators, and the OMB: The Congressional Challenge to Presidential Regulatory Relief," in James Thurber, ed., *Divided Democracy: Cooperation and Conflict Between the President and Congress* (Washington, DC: CQ Press, 1991).

113 Tuohy, "Regulation and Scientific Complexity."

114 Of course the Royal Commission on Asbestos, by undertaking extensive hearings and consultation with a wide variety of groups, also provided a forum for interest representation.

115 John R. Wilson, "Development of Designated Substances Regulations by the Ontario Ministry of Labour" (Toronto: Ontario Ministry of Labour, 1988).

116 Between 27 March and 21 April 1980, there are at least nine significant references to asbestos in the *Ontario Hansard.*

117 The role of media exposure and NDP pressure in the decision to establish the Royal Commission is described by G. Bruce Doern, *The Politics of Risk,* prepared for the Royal Commission on Matters of Health and Safety Arising from the Use of Asbestos in Ontario, January 1982, chapter 2.

118 *Ontario Hansard,* 18 June 1982, 2838.

119 Regulation Repecting Control of Exposure to Biological and Chemical Agents (O. Reg. 654/86).

120 Ontario Ministry of Labour, Occupational Health and Safety Division, *The First Report of the Steering Committee on Hazardous Substances in the Workplace, December 1, 1987 to March 31, 1990.* (Toronto: Ontario Ministry of Labour, 1990).

121 For an overview of how the European model functions, see Joseph L. Badaracco, Jr, *Loading the Dice* (Boston: Harvard Business School Press, 1985).

122 Tuohy, "The Occupational Health Arena," 241.

123 Ibid., 258.

124 Ronald Brickman, Sheila Jasanoff, and Thomas Ilgen, *Controlling Chemicals* (Ithaca: Cornell University Press, 1985).

125 Ministry of Labour, *Report on the Designation of Asbestos,* 5.4.

126 Digby and Riddell, "Occupational Health and Safety."

CHAPTER EIGHT

1 For a recent review of the evidence, see Committee on the Biological Effects of Ionizing Radiation, National Research Council, *Health Risks of Radon and Other Internally Deposited Alpha-Emitters* (Washington, DC: National Academy Press, 1988). See also Douglas G. Brookins, *The Indoor Radon Problem* (New York: Columbia University Press, 1990).

2 The approach of other countries appears to be far more similar to that of Canada, with the U.S. the outlier. See Leonard A. Cole, "Political Institutions, Culture, and Science Policy: Radon Policies in the United States, Sweden, and Finland," prepared for delivery at the 1992 Annual Meeting of the American Political Science Association, Chicago, 3–6 September 1992.

3 Sheldon Krimsky and Alonzo Plough, *Environmental Hazards: Communicating Risks as a Social Process* (Dover, MA: Auburn House Publishing, 1988), 133.

4 Allan Mazur, "Putting Radon on the Public's Risk Agenda," *Science, Technology, and Human Values* 12 (1987):86.

5 Mazur, "Putting Radon on the Public's Risk Agenda," 92.

6 U.S. Environmental Protection Agency, "Health Risks Due to Radon in Structures: A Strategy and Management Plan for Assessment and Mitigation," September 1985.

7 U.S. Environmental Protection Agency, *A Citizen's Guide To Radon,* OPA-86-004 (Washington, DC: EPA, August 1986).

8 Krimsky and Plough, *Environmental Hazards,* 140–1.

9 U.S. Environmental Protection Agency, *Radon Reduction Methods: A Homeowner's Guide,* OPA-86-005 (Washington, DC: EPA, August 1986). Its public information efforts were further supported by a special radon issue of the agency's public interest periodical, *The EPA Journal,* published in August 1986.

10 *New York Times,* 5 August 1987, A 14.

11 Philip Shabecoff, "Major Radon Peril is Declared by U.S. in Call for Tests," *New York Times,* 13 September 1988, A 1.

12 *U.S. Code Congressional and Administrative News,* 1988, 3618–19.

13 Indoor Radon Abatement, Public Law 100-551, 28 October 1988 (102 stat. 2755). The new law was passed as an amendment to the Toxic Substances Control Act.

14 The agency estimated that 10 percent of all American homes have radon levels higher that the 4 pCi/l action level, with some areas having considerably higher levels. For instance, 70 percent of the homes tested in the state of Iowa had levels higher than the action levels (*Environment Reporter,* 27 October 1989, 1127–8).

15 Philip Abelson, "Radon Today: The Role of Flimflam in Public Policy," *Regulation: CATO Review of Business and Government* (Fall 1991):95–100; Ben Bolch and Harold Lyons, "A Multibillion-dollar Radon Scare," *Public Interest* 99 (Spring 1990):61–7.

16 U.S. Environmental Protection Agency, U.S. Department of Health and Human Services, U.S. Public Health Service, *A Citizen's Guide to Radon (Second Edition): The Guide to Protecting Yourself and Your Family from Radon,* 402-K92-001, (Washington, DC: U.S. Government Printing Office, May 1992).

17 U.S. Environmental Protection Agency, Air and Radiation, *Technical Support Document for the 1992 Citizen's Guide to Radon,* EPA 400-R-92-011 (Washington, DC: EPA, May 1992), 6-1.

18 Keith Schneider, "U.S. Urges Radon Curbs in New Houses," *New York Times,* 7 April 1993, A8.

19 The results of the survey are presented in R.G. McGregor, P. Vasudev, et al., "Background Concentrations of Radon and Radon Daughters in Canadian Homes," *Health Physics* 39 (1980):285–9.

20 "Invisible Menace," *Maclean's* 97 (29 October 1984):16. This story was only one paragraph long.

21 "Radioactive Gas Kills Hundreds a Year," *Montreal Gazette,* 9 January 1987, B1; Christine McLaren, "Radon Gas in Homes a Silent Killer," *Toronto Globe and Mail,* 19 May 1987, A1; "Measuring Danger: Survey for Radioactive Gas in Houses Reveal Highest Levels in Saskatchewan," 20 May 1987, A13; "Ottawa Says Cost of Cleanup Outweighs Risk of Lung Cancer," 21 May 1987, A12.

22 The media in Canada paid less attention to the issue than their American counterparts. Over the period January 1986 to August 1989, the *Canadian Periodicals Index, Canadian Business Index,* and the *Canadian Newspaper Index* reveals a total of 69 stories on radon. In contrast, over the same period, the *New York Times* alone printed 120 stories on the subject.

23 McLaren, "Radon Gas in Homes," A8.

24 Roger Eaton, "Radon: Is it Really Dangerous? Technical and Social Aspects," *Emergency Preparedness Digest* (1988):12–17.

25 Health and Welfare Canada, *Radon: You and Your Family – A Personal Perspective* (Ottawa: Minister of Supply and Services, 1989).

26 "Radon Tests on Houses Rejected," *Toronto Globe and Mail,* 14 September 1988, A11; Nora Underwood, "Dangerous Grounds: Confronting the Threat Posed by Radon Gas," *Maclean's* 101 (4 October 1988), 48.

27 Government of Manitoba, *Radon: An Interim Guide for Manitoba Homeowners* (Winnipeg: Government of Manitoba, September 1989).

28 Saskatchewan, Mines and Pollution Branch, *Radon Surveys in Saskatchewan* (Prince Albert: Saskatchewan Environment, March 1985).

29 Saskatchewan Environment and Public Safety, *Radon in Saskatchewan Homes* (Regina: Saskatchewan Environment and Public Safety, n.d.).

30 Krewski, Miller, et al., "Managing Environmental Radon Risks: A Canadian Perspective," in L. Friej, ed., *Management of Risk from Genotoxic Substances in the Environment* (Stockholm: Swedish National Chemicals Inspectorate, 1989); National Research Council, *Health Risks of Radon.*

31 EPA, "Health Risks Due to Radon in Structures"; Naomi Harley, "Comparing Radon Daughter Dosimetric and Risk Models," in R.B. Gammage and S.V. Kaye, *Indoor Air and Human Health* (Chelsea, MI: Lewis Publishers, 1985), 74–5; William Nazaroff and Kevin Teichman, "Indoor Radon: Exploring Federal Policy for Controlling Human Exposures," *Environmental Science and Technology* 24 (1990):77.

32 U.S. Environmental Protection Agency, *Technical Support Document for the 1992 Citizen's Guide to Radon,* 2–35.

33 U.S. Environmental Protection Agency, *Unfinished Business: A Comparative Assessment of Environmental Problems* (Washington, DC: EPA, February 1987).

34 EPA, *Technical Support Document*, 6–11.
35 E.G. Letourneau, V. Mao, et al, "Lung Cancer Mortality and Indoor Radon Concentrations in 18 Canadian Cities," Proceedings of Sixteenth Midyear Topical Symposium "Epidemiology Applied to Health Physics," Health Physics Society, 10–14 January 1983, Albuquerque, New Mexico, 470–83.
36 Krewski, Miller, et al., "Managing Environmental Radon Risks."
37 E.G. Letourneau, D. Krewski, J. Choi, M.J. Goddard, R.G. McGregor, J.M. Zielinski, and J. Du, "A Case-Control Study of Residential Radon and Lung Cancer in Winnipeg, Manitoba," *American Journal of Epidemiology* (forthcoming).
38 Goran Pershagen, Gustav Akerblom, et al., "Residential Radon Exposure and Lung Cancer in Sweden," *The New England Journal of Medicine* 330 (20 January 1994):159–64. For a brief commentary comparing the Canadian and Swedish studies, see Richard Stone, "New Radon Study: No Smoking Gun," *Science* 263 (28 January 1994):465.
39 Personal interview, Roger Eaton, 27 June 1989.
40 Health and Welfare Canada, *Radon: You and Your Family – A Personal Perspective* (Ottawa: Minister of Supply and Services, 1989), 5.
41 Roger Eaton, "The Guidelines for Radon in Canada – An Extended Interpretation," presented at the 5th International Conference on Indoor Air Quality and Climate: Indoor Air '90, Toronto, Canada, 29 July–3 August 1990, vol. 5, 283–5.
42 EPA, *Technical Support Document for the 1992 Citizen's Guide to Radon*, 2-19, 2-25.
43 Eaton, "The Guidelines for Radon in Canada"; and Krewski, Miller, et al., "Managing Environmental Radon Risks," 251.
44 Roger Eaton, "Radon: Is it Really Dangerous?"
45 According to Health and Welfare Canada officials, the estimate was based on the following "ICRP50" report, without proper citation: International Commission on Radiological Protection 50, *Lung Cancer Risk from Indoor Exposures to Radon Daughters* (Oxford: Pergamon Press, 1987).
46 Health and Welfare Canada, *Radon: You and Your Family – A Personal Perspective* (Ottawa: Minister of Supply and Services, 1989), 5. Neither the Manitoba nor Saskatchewan pamphlet provides any quantitative risk estimates or comparative risk figures.
47 EPA, *Technical Support Document*, 5–15.
48 E.G. Letourneau, "Limitation of Exposure to Natural Radioactivity in Canada," *The Science of the Total Environment* 45 (1985):647–56.
49 EPA, *Technical Support Document*, 4–7.
50 E.B. Letourneau, D. Krewski, J.M Zielinski, and R.G. McGregor, "Cost-Effectiveness of Radon Mitigation in Canada," *Radiation Protection Dosimetry* 45 (1993):593–8.

51 In response to comments from reviewers an earlier, more dramatic conclusion was softened to the current version. The earlier version claimed, with no discussion, that "the total costs of these radon mitigation strategies far exceeds their likely public health benefit particularly when viewed in competition with other programs that could be implemented to improve public health in Canada." (E.B. Letourneau, D. Krewski, J.M Zielinski, and R.G. McGregor, "Cost-Effectiveness of Radon Mitigation in Canada," Fifth International Symposium on the Natural Radiation Environment, Salzburg, Austria, 22–28 September 1991, 6).

52 McLaren, "Radon Gas in Homes a Silent Killer."

53 Personal interview, Roger Eaton, 27 June 1989.

54 U.S. Congress, House Committee on Energy and Commerce, Subcommittee on Health and the Environment, *Radon Exposure: Human Health Threat*, Hearings, 100th Cong., 1st sess, 5 November 1987.

55 Personal interview, 26 July 1989.

56 For an analysis of the linkage between environmental group strategies and anti-business ideologies, see Mary Douglas and Aaron Wildavsky, *Risk and Culture* (Berkeley: University of California Press, 1982).

57 Personal interview.

58 Mazur, "Putting Radon on the Public's Risk Agenda."

59 House of Commons, *Debates*, 14 September 1988, 19229.

60 Personal interviews.

61 Chauncey Starr, "Social Benefit versus Technological Risk," *Science* 165 (1969):1232–8.

CHAPTER NINE

1 George Hoberg, "Comparing Canadian Performance in Environmental Policy," in Robert Boardman, ed., *Canadian Environmental Policy: Ecosystems, Politics, and Process* (Toronto: Oxford University Press, 1992); George Hoberg, "Sleeping with an Elephant: The American Influence on Canadian Environmental Regulation," *Journal of Public Policy* 11 (1991):107–32.

2 See for instance, David M. O'Brien, *What Process is Due? Courts and Science Policy Disputes* (New York: Russell Sage Foundation, 1987), 146–9; Peter Nemetz, W.T. Stanbury, and Fred Thompson, "Social Regulation in Canada," *Policy Studies Journal* 14 (1986):590–603, at 597.

3 Ronald Brickman, Sheila Jasanoff, and Thomas Ilgen, *Controlling Chemicals* (Ithaca: Cornell University Press, 1985); Sheila Jasanoff, *Risk Management and Political Culture* (New York: Russell Sage Foundation, 1986).

4 The one exception was FDA's reliance on the safety factor approach when it established a recommended tolerance for dioxins in fish. However the

agency later reverted to an approach consistent with the no-threshold assumption.

5 Liora Salter, *Mandated Science* (Boston: Kluwer Academic Publishers, 1988), chapter 7.

6 Jasanoff, *Risk Management and Political Culture*, 33. Despite this danger of rigidity, it is important to note that the u.s. epa did successfully revise its cancer policy guidelines to accommodate new scientific information in 1986 (Sheila Jasanoff, *The Fifth Branch: Science Advisors as Policymakers* [Cambridge, MA: Harvard University Press, 1990], chapter 9).

7 However, it is relevant to distinguish between information that improves the precision of risk estimates and that which improves the accuracy. As Finkel has argued, "While new science cannot increase uncertainty, it assuredly can reveal (in hindsight) that we knew less about the situation than we thought." ("Is Risk Assessment Really Too Conservative?: Revising the Revisionists," *Columbia Journal of Environmental Law* 14 (1989):427–67, at 457). Thus regulators will sometimes need to revise their risk estimates upward in response to advances in science.

8 An extensive survey of risk assessment practices of Health and Welfare Canada revealed inconsistencies in the Canadian approach. While the department offered the lack of evidence of genotoxicity as a rationale for the safety factor approach, it occasionally reverted to non-threshold models for substances believed to act via non-genotoxic mechanisms. R. Stephen McColl, *Biological Safety Factors in Toxicological Risk Assessment*, A report produced for the Environmental Health Directorate, Health Protection Branch, Health and Welfare Canada (Ottawa: Minister of Supply and Services Canada, 1990), 27.

9 Confidential interview.

10 The same outcome occurred when Canada banned cyclamates, a food additive. The court upheld the government's ban even though it failed to produce any substantial scientific rationale for the decision. *Berryland Canning Co. Ltd. v. The Queen*, 44 D.L.R. (3d) Federal Court, Trial Division, 1974.

11 Sharon Sutherland, "The Public Service and Policy Development," in Michael Atkinson, ed., *Governing Canada: State Institutions and Public Policy* (Toronto: HBJ-Holt, 1993), 103. See also, C.E.S. Franks, *Parliament of Canada* (Toronto: Toronto University Press, 1987), chapter 8; Magnus Gunther and Conrad Winn, *House of Commons Reform* (Ottawa: Parliamentary Internship Program, 1991).

12 While this tradeoff has been the theme of scholarly studies for years, it was most recently explicitly posed by Sheila Jasanoff in *The Fifth Branch*.

13 Letter from John Moore, Acting Administrator, epa, to International Apple Institute, 1 February 1989, 3.

14 R. Kent Weaver and Bert Rockman, eds., *Do Institutions Matter? Government Capability in the United States and Abroad* (Washington, DC: Brookings Institution, 1993); Michael Atkinson, ed., *Governing Canada: State Institutions and Public Policy,* (Toronto: HBJ-Holt, 1993), especially 22–3.
15 George Hoberg, "Risk, Science, and Politics: Regulating Alachlor in Canada and the United States," *Canadian Journal of Political Science* 23 (1990):257–77.
16 Sheila Jasanoff, "Norms for Evaluating Regulatory Science," *Risk Analysis* 9 (1989): 271–73, at 273.
17 Letter from Thomas Jefferson to William Charles Jarvis, 28 September 1820, reprinted in *The Writings of Thomas Jefferson*, vol. 15 (Washington, DC: The Thomas Jefferson Memorial Association, 1903), 278. We first saw this quote in David Bazelon, "Risk and Responsibility," *Science* 205 (1979):277–80, at 278.

Index